Hedge Funds

Hedge Funds

Myths and Limits

François-Serge Lhabitant

JOHN WILEY & SONS, LTD

Other Wiley Editorial Offices

John Wiley & Sons, Inc., 605 Third Avenue,
New York, NY 10158-0012, USA

WILEY-VCH GmbH, Pappelallee 3,
D-69469 Weinheim, Germany

John Wiley & Sons Australia Ltd, 33 Park Road, Milton,
Queensland 4064, Australia

John Wiley & Sons (Asia) Pte Ltd, 2 Clementi Loop #02-01,
Jin Xing Distripark, Singapore 129809

John Wiley & Sons (Canada) Ltd, 22 Worcester Road,
Rexdale, Ontario M9W 1L1, Canada

Library of Congress Cataloging-in-Publication Data

A Library of Congress record has been applied for

British Library Cataloguing in Publication Data

A catalogue record for this book is available from the British Library

ISBN 0-470-84477-9

Typeset in 10/12pt Times by Laserwords Private Limited, Chennai, India
Printed and bound in Great Britain by TJ International Ltd, Padstow, Cornwall
This book is printed on acid-free paper responsibly manufactured from sustainable forestation, for
which at least two trees are planted for each one used for paper production.

Contents

Preface

Writing this book was a great learning experience, and it is a pleasure to thank those who provided valuable suggestions and insights along the way. I would like to thank in particular Rajna Gibson and Denis Mirlesse, whose knowledge of derivatives and insight into the alternative asset management industry enabled me to understand the complex world of hedge funds, among numerous other things.

I am grateful to a variety of individuals who read draft copies of chapters and whose comments were extremely valuable. In particular, I would like to thank Vishal Bohra, Shelley Collum, Didier Cossin, Karim Ibrahim, Harry Kat, Cristina Parlogea, Patrick Rey and Nils Tuchschmid for their suggestions and comments on earlier versions of the manuscript, as well as for fruitful discussions on the topic of hedge funds. I would also like to thank my colleagues at Union Bancaire Privée, at Thunderbird, the American Graduate School of International Management, and at HEC University of Lausanne for their help and advice.

I am grateful to the publishers, John Wiley & Sons, in particular Sally Smith and Benjamin Earl, who allowed me to pursue this undertaking. I should also mention that writing this book would not have been possible without the invaluable editorial assistance of Michelle Learned and Ian Hamilton. Their willingness to accept innumerable changes and their commitment was key to the quality of the final work.

Last but by no means least, my thanks go to my family for their support. This book was written in time that was literally stolen from them. Of course, I remain solely responsible for any errors, omissions and ambiguities.

It is now time for you to begin your work—to begin work reading—and I hope that you will also find some pleasure in it.

François-Serge Lhabitant
francois@lhabitant.net

1

Introduction

Institutional and private investors alike have always been fascinated by the world of "alternative investments." However, finding a universally accepted definition of what constitutes an alternative investment is devilishly difficult. The scope of the term has widened significantly over the years and now encompasses a broad series of assets and investment strategies. All definitions share two common characteristics: (a) alternative investments still have to gain complete acceptance from the financial community, and (b) alternative investments are regarded as profitable by some marginal investors, many of whom are wealthy individuals willing to take greater risks in order to obtain higher returns.

What is considered "traditional" and what is labeled "alternative" varies from one organization to another and has also evolved over time. For instance, domestic stocks and actively managed bonds were considered to be alternative investments in the 1960s, and were primarily the domain of high net worth individuals. A similar perception existed for international stocks in the 1970s and for real estate and emerging market equities in the 1980s. Today these asset classes are included in the core of most investment portfolios. The new alternative investments are private equity, venture capital, commodities, precious metals, art, forestry, and last but not least, hedge funds.

Hedge funds constitute one of the fastest-growing sectors of asset management. They experienced tremendous growth throughout the 1990s. In the space of a few years, the hedge fund universe has grown from a small number of firms led by legendary managers (George Soros, Julian Robertson, and others) to a large market with thousands of players. Originally exclusively serving the needs of very high net worth individuals, the cloistered and mysterious kingdom of hedge funds has progressively opened its doors to private and institutional investors seeking diversification alternatives, lower risks, higher returns, or any combination of these. They have become, and are likely to remain, an important element of modern financial markets.

Numerous observers even speculate that the hedge fund realm has entered a critical consolidation and institutionalization phase paralleling the mutual fund consolidation in the 1980s. Most investment banks and traditional asset management houses have announced the launch of in-house hedge funds, and commercial banks are also setting up funds of hedge funds. Traditional portfolio managers, often assisted by keen seed investors, leave their employers to start their own hedge funds. An increasing number of institutional and private investors have started investing in hedge funds on a significant scale. They are seeking higher risk-adjusted returns, greater portfolio diversification and more protection from risks associated with the end of an aging bull market. And the growth is expected to continue as more individuals than ever are becoming eligible to invest.

Nevertheless, considerable confusion and misconceptions still exist concerning hedge funds, what they are, what they are not, how they operate and what they can really add to traditional portfolios. At one extreme, exempt from regulation and shrouded in secrecy, hedge funds are often perceived as excessively leveraged high-risk high-return vehicles, managed by sophisticated traders and designed only for the elite. Not only do they offer the prospect of huge financial returns, they also appear to have the ability to undermine central banks and national currencies, and even destabilize international capital markets. This widespread myth was propagated over the past two decades by press reports of spectacular gains and losses achieved by large, but nonrepresentative players such as the Quantum Fund, the Tiger Fund and Long Term Capital Management. At the other extreme, commission-rewarded professional investment advisers claim that hedge funds are capable of offering high absolute returns without incurring additional and unnecessary risks, as well as low correlation with traditional investment performance. This qualifies them as ideal complements to traditional portfolios.

The reality is of course far more complex. Hedge funds can no longer be seen as a homogeneous asset class. There are now between 4000 and 6000 hedge funds active in several asset classes, sectors and/or regions. Strangely, in a world saturated with statistics, nobody knows exactly how many funds there are. They utilize a variety of trading and investment strategies. Within the same investment category, managers differ in the leverage they use and the hedging policies they employ. What is needed, therefore, is a common framework to understand and analyze hedge funds rather than a series of unverifiable claims.

Numerous articles and books have been written on hedge funds, so why a new one? In order to answer this question, let us first see what this book does not attempt to do. First of all, this book does not attempt to promote hedge funds as a promising asset class. Most investment banks and professional investment advisers have produced excellent brochures that fulfill this task and describe the advantages of hedge funds over other types of asset. Wishful thinking and the desire for a free lunch make the consumer/investor very susceptible to this sales pitch. However, one should remember that Wall Street is not an independent source of academic research. Rather it is a manufacturer with a huge vested interest in supporting its products.

Neither does this book attempt to depict hedge funds as being inherently risky, dangerous or overleveraged. Since the debacle of the hedge fund Long Term Capital Management, it is now common knowledge that the simultaneous use of leverage, concentration of positions, and volatile or illiquid markets can produce a toxic cocktail of risks. Like any other investment, hedge funds involve risks, and this should be understood before taking the plunge.

Rather, this book attempts to dispel several misconceptions and shed new light on the kingdom of hedge funds. It provides an integrated, up-to-date and comprehensive blend of theoretical and practical analysis of the market, strategies and empirical evidence supporting today's ever more complex, diverse and growing world of hedge funds. It aims to give readers the fundamental concepts, detailed knowledge, self-confidence and necessary quantitative and qualitative material to fully understand hedge funds, their strategies, and their potential positive and negative contributions to investment portfolios.

This book is meant to stimulate thought and debate and should always be taken that way. It raises a large number of questions, but certainly does not claim to have all the answers. Some may argue that it is easier to point out the fallacies in others' arguments than to figure out the answers. Still, when fallacies rule the land, somebody has to point at the naked emperor.

One of the merits of this book is that it is self-contained. It does not require any previous knowledge of the field, and can be read and understood by anyone. It is intended to be an introduction and at the same time a reference book for any serious finance student or investment professional. For that reason, the level of mathematical and financial knowledge assumed is kept as modest as possible. This results in some passages being lengthier than expected, but I have preferred to bore a few advanced readers slightly rather than to lose many on the way.

This particular intention explains the book's structure. I have divided the material into three parts. The first part is essentially descriptive and covers the historical and structural aspects of hedge funds and their environment. The major characteristics of hedge funds versus traditional funds are carefully examined, as well as the legal framework in the US and in several other countries. I believe this information is necessary to understand hedge fund activities and the secrecy that has surrounded them for more than fifty years now.

The second part of the book focuses on the various strategies followed by hedge funds. Each strategy is described in detail, and several examples and practical cases of real transactions are provided as illustrations. I also describe the various hedge fund indices that are available, as well as the major specificity of hedge funds regarding the calculation of their net asset value.

The third part deals with more advanced aspects, principally the matter of investing in hedge funds. Asset allocation and the hedge fund selection process are investigated and illustrated by numerous examples. It examines new investment vehicles such as funds of hedge funds and capital-protected notes linked to hedge funds. Finally, a chapter on advanced topics surveys the most recent developments concerning academic research in the domain of hedge funds.

Last but not least, the appendix contains an overview of statistical concepts, with particular emphasis on those commonly used in the hedge fund industry. It may be useful when reading the chapters, and it may serve as a guide to understanding and analyzing performance reports. A bibliography is also provided.

All chapters are designed to inform and to challenge. Examples and case studies are used extensively to illustrate the concepts. There is a lot to be learned here. Of course, this book is not a substitute for professional and independent advice. But in the world of hedge funds, independence is both essential and, unfortunately, elusive.

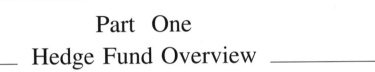

Part One
Hedge Fund Overview

2
The basics revisited

An analysis of more than fifty years of hedge fund history reveals distinct cycles, which we review below. We then focus on hedge funds as they are today and describe their major characteristics.

FROM ALFRED W. JONES TO LTCM

The creation of the first hedge fund is generally credited to Alfred Winslow Jones, a truly remarkable individual. Born in Melbourne, Australia, Alfred Winslow Jones lived in the United States from the age of four. After graduating from Harvard in 1923, he toured the world while working on steamers, later serving as a diplomat in Germany, and as a journalist during the Spanish Civil War. In 1941 he returned to the United States, obtained a doctorate in sociology from Columbia University and started reporting for *Fortune* magazine. His thesis, *Life, Liberty and Property*, is a reference text in sociology.

Jones's involvement with finance started in 1949, when he started reviewing the practices of the asset management industry and wrote a remarkable article about technical methods of market analysis, trends in investing and market forecasting (Jones 1949). Convinced that he was capable of implementing a better investment model than anything available, he raised $100 000 (including $40 000 of his own capital) and started an equity fund. It was originally structured as a general partnership to avoid the restrictive Securities and Exchange Commission (SEC) regulation and allow for maximum latitude and flexibility in portfolio construction. Thus, the first hedge fund was born.

Relatively few people grasped the beauty and simplicity of Alfred Jones's investment model, which relied on two assumptions. First, Jones was convinced that he had superior stock selection ability; in other words, he was to be able to identify stocks that would rise more than the market, as well as stocks that would rise less than the market. Second, Jones believed that he had no market timing skills; that is, he was unable to predict market directions. Therefore, his strategy consisted in combining long positions in undervalued stocks and short positions in overvalued stocks. This allowed him to yield a small net profit in all markets, capitalizing on his stock-picking abilities while simultaneously reducing overall risk through lesser net market exposure. To magnify his portfolio's returns, Jones added leverage; that is, he used the proceeds from his short sales to finance the purchase of additional long positions.

Short sales and leverage had been known for several years, but were traditionally used to take advantage of investment opportunities by assuming more risk. Jones's innovation was therefore to merge these two speculative tools into a conservative investing approach. To attract investors, Jones also decided to charge performance-linked fees (20% of realized profits) but no asset-based management fee. The fund's expenses were paid 20% by the general partner and 80% by the limited partners, except for salaries, which were paid entirely by the general partner. Finally, acknowledging that it was unreasonable for him to receive incentive fees for risking solely his partners' capital, Jones invested all $40 000 of his personal wealth.

Jones's model performed remarkably well and managed to beat the market for several years. He operated in almost complete secrecy with very few changes to the original approach. Years before the official birth of modern portfolio theory, he started developing and using what he called "velocity," a measure of the speed at which a stock's price would change in relation to changes in the market. Although informally defined, velocity was the ancestor of beta. In today's terms, one would simply say that Jones was trying to isolate and double his alpha (one on the short side, one on the long side) while keeping a small beta (low net sensitivity to the market). Surprisingly, Jones also rapidly became uncomfortable with his own ability to pick stocks. He therefore converted his general partnership into a limited partnership in 1952 and hired Dick Radcliffe in 1954 to supplement his stock-picking choices, and autonomously run a portion of the fund. Later he hired other portfolio managers and gave them tremendous autonomy, ending up creating what was probably the first multimanager fund.

Although investment funds became the darlings of Wall Street in the 1960s, Jones kept operating in almost complete secrecy. However, he finally came under the spotlight in 1966, after a newspaper article (Loomis 1966) detailed how his after-fees track record had outperformed the most successful mutual funds over five years (Fidelity Trend Fund by 44%) and over ten years (Dreyfus Fund by 87%). Interest in hedge funds and their investment approach suddenly sprang up.

There are no reliable data on the number of hedge funds that were created in the ensuing period. Nevertheless, a 1968 SEC survey found that out of 215 investment partnerships, 140 were probably hedge funds, the majority having been formed in that year. Not surprisingly, Jones's partnership was probably the major hedge fund manager incubator. Several of its managers left it to set up their own hedge funds, including Carl Jones (no relation) in 1964, who set up City Associates, and Dick Radcliffe himself, who in 1965 established Fairfield Partners. Many of the future industry leaders also started their funds independently during this period, including Warren Buffett's Omaha-based Buffett Partners, Walter Schloss's WJS Partners, Leveraged Capital Holdings—the first fund of hedge funds—and George Soros's Quantum Fund.

However, given the strong bull market of the 1960s (Figure 2.1), hedging with short sales came to be considered as time-consuming and ended up reducing performance. Simply leveraging long positions and ignoring the short side often yielded much better results. Most of the new hedge funds started doing this, thus departing from the original Jones model. As the industry says, they were "swimming naked," and the sudden bear market of the early 1970s caught them by surprise (Figure 2.2). From 1969 through 1974, the broad market, measured by the Value Line Composite index, declined by more than 70%. Many hedge funds suffered heavy losses and subsequent withdrawals. Several hedge fund managers went out of business, whittling down the amount of assets under management. Only a few hedge fund managers survived the bursting of the bubble. Most of them returned and operated in relative obscurity for several years, following their path in relatively rising markets (Figure 2.3). As an illustration, in 1984, when Sandra Manske formed the Tremont Partners agency to track hedge fund performance, she was able to identify only 68 funds in activity. Most were limited partnerships with high minimum investment requirements, access thus being restricted to an exclusive club of high net worth individuals. An interesting sidelight is that, in 1982, at age 82, Jones amended

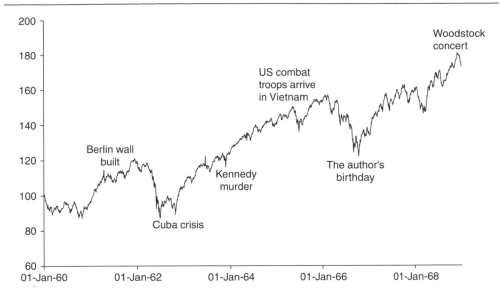

Figure 2.1   Evolution of the US stock market in the 1960s (S&P 500). The index has been scaled to a basis equal to 100 on January 1, 1960

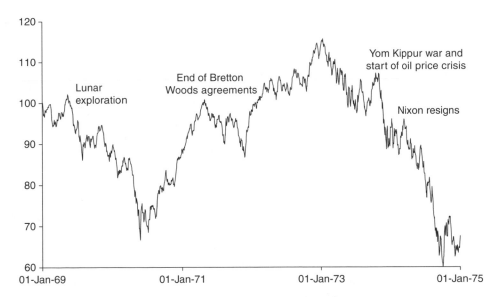

Figure 2.2   Evolution of the US stock market in the period 1969–1974 (S&P 500). The index has been scaled to a basis equal to 100 on January 1, 1969

his partnership agreement, formally becoming a fund of funds investing in a diversified selection of external managers.

The popularity of hedge funds was revived in 1986 by an article in *Institutional Investor* (Rohrer 1986), which described the impressive performance of Julian Robertson's Tiger Fund. The Tiger Fund had offered investors a compound annual return of 43% during its

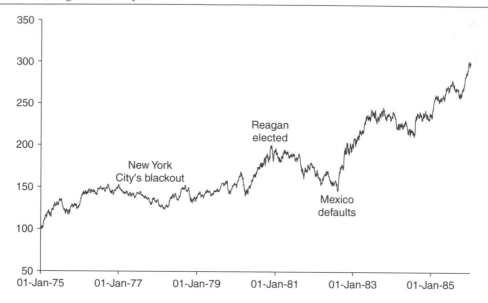

Figure 2.3   Evolution of the US stock market in the period 1975–1985 (S&P 500). The index has been scaled to a basis equal to 100 on January 1, 1975

first six years of existence, net of expenses and incentive fees. By way of comparison, a large diversified index such as the Standard and Poor's 500 (S&P 500) compounded at only 18.7% for the same period.

Julian Robertson's investment approach relied on taking aggressive and purely market-directional bets with no particular hedging policy, a significant move from Jones's original concept. Despite the inherent risks, his approach rapidly became popular and numerous hedge funds started applying it, particularly in the domain of currencies and interest rates. Alfred Winslow Jones died in 1989, right in the middle of the golden age of the so-called global-macro funds. Some of these emerged as major players in financial markets and even attracted widespread media attention, because they took very large and aggressive positions making huge profits, particularly during market crises (Figure 2.4). As an illustration, George Soros's Quantum Fund notched up a billion dollars gain in 1992 when the British pound exited from the European Monetary System. Whether or not Soros and his fund were entirely responsible for the pound's collapse is still an unanswered question, but the size of his gains gave rise to concern that hedge funds could contribute to financial instability and imbalance the efficient operation of markets. This line of thought actually gained momentum in 1997, when several hedge funds were blamed for triggering the Asian currency crisis and press reports vilified hedge fund managers as wild-eyed speculators operating outside government regulations, bound only by the laws and rules of the markets in which they operated.

However, we should recall that several hedge funds also suffered heavy losses as a result of unusual market events. For example, David Askin's three hedge funds (Granite Partners, Granite Corp., and Quartz Hedge) lost $420 million in 1994 when the Federal Reserve unexpectedly raised interest rates. Victor Niederhoffer bankrupted his three hedge funds (Global Systems, Friends, and Diversified) by selling short S&P 500 put options prior to the October 1997 plunge of the index (Figure 2.5). The High Risk Opportunity

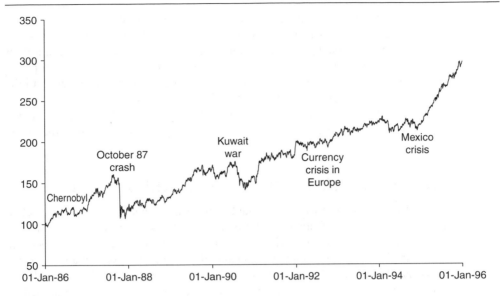

Figure 2.4 Evolution of the US stock market in the period 1986–1996 (S&P 500). The index has been scaled to a basis equal to 100 on January 1, 1986

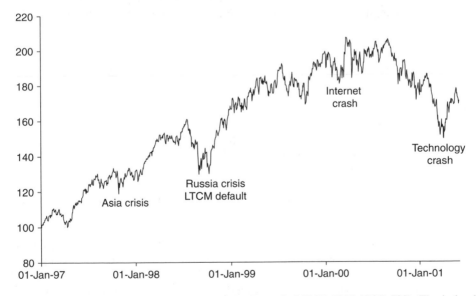

Figure 2.5 Evolution of the US stock market in the period 1997–2001 (S&P 500). The index has been scaled to a basis equal to 100 on January 1, 1997

Hub Fund managed by III Offshore Investors as well as three funds managed by Dana McGinnis (Partner's Focus, Global, and Russian Value) filed for bankruptcy in 1998 after Russia had devalued the ruble and defaulted on ruble-denominated debt. The III Offshore Investors fund lost more than $350 million and McGinnis's funds lost roughly $200 million. Even George Soros's Quantum Fund posted losses of $2 billion after the

Russian crisis. But the major event in hedge fund history was the collapse of Long Term Capital Management. This hedge fund was founded by Robert Merton and Myron Scholes (both received the Nobel prize for economics in 1997), John Meriwether, a former legendary trader at Salomon Brothers, and David Mullen, a former vice-chairman of the Federal Reserve. Its excessive leverage and the size of its positions almost resulted in the collapse of global capital markets and forced the Federal Reserve to negotiate a bailout in which 12 banks and financial institutions put up $3.625 billion. Nevertheless, as we will see later, this series of successes and disasters is rather unrepresentative of the hedge fund industry as a whole.

CHARACTERISTICS OF THE NEW HEDGE FUNDS

What would Alfred Winslow Jones say today? His original hedge fund model relied on isolating investment skills from market trends by placing a portion of a portfolio within a hedged structure, fully justifying the term "hedge fund." However, since the 1950s, financial institutions and markets have changed dramatically. New financial instruments such as listed and over-the-counter derivatives have appeared and improved efficiency by allocating risk to those most willing to accept it. Technological innovation, and in particular the spread of information technology, has revolutionized investing. Smart portfolio managers now widely use rigorous asset pricing models, optimizers and other quantitative tools to help them in their day-to-day business. As might be expected, this changing environment has significantly affected the hedge fund universe (Figure 2.6).

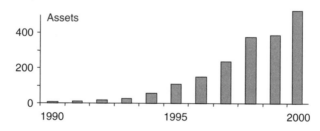

Figure 2.6   Assets managed by the hedge fund industry: assets are expressed in billions of dollars

Over the last decade, the growth of hedge funds accelerated dramatically, both in terms of assets under management and number of funds. Although precise figures are difficult to obtain, recent industry reports estimate that there are now between 4000 and 6000 hedge funds worldwide, managing a total wealth of $400–600 billion (Figure 2.7). This is compared to a figure of about 600 hedge funds worldwide in 1990, with less than $20 billion of assets. And the implied annual growth rate of 25% should continue to apply in the future according to KPMG Peat Marwick and RR Capital Management Corp.

Although growth rates are increasing, the success in attracting investors is not evenly spread, and statistics such as the average hedge fund size ($87 million) or the median

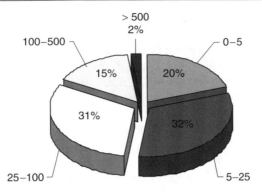

Figure 2.7 Breakdown of hedge funds by size: assets are expressed in millions of dollars

size ($22 million) hide a wide disparity between the various actors. At one end of the spectrum, about 20% of hedge funds are small niche players with less than $5 million under management. At the other end of the spectrum, 15% of hedge funds manage $100–500 million, while only 2% manage more than $500 million. The vast majority of the funds are therefore in the range $5–25 million (32%) or the range $25–100 million (31%). As already observed by Peltz (1996), about 15% of the hedge funds control over 80% of the total assets under management. These funds tend to be better organized, have longer track records, rely on multiple managers and decision-makers, and rely on improved risk management systems. Not surprisingly, they are the ones often cited in the media, but they are not necessarily representative of the industry.

Another interesting aspect is the changing geographic distribution of hedge funds. For many years, the presence of the largest, most liquid stock market in the world combined with the greatest pool of investment talent resulted in the United States dominating the hedge fund scene in terms of assets managed, number of hedge funds, and sources of invested capital. But as the US markets matured, Europe started to emerge as a valuable alternative and gradually became the new focus area for hedge fund management companies. Although US managers still control almost three-quarters of the global assets of the hedge fund industry, Europe and Asia are now at the leading edge of the hedge fund industry's growth and appear to be avid in their quest for hedge funds. In particular, 1999 and 2000 saw substantial amounts of capital move into European single-manager hedge funds, both new and existing. Also, an increased number of US hedge funds have set up European offices as well as completed alliances, acquisitions, or distribution agreements.

Despite a great deal of media attention, the term "hedge fund" still has no precise legal definition. Even worse, several contradictory definitions exist (Box 2.1) based on legal structures, investment strategies, superior returns, risk taking or hedging, etc. Clearly, disagreement over a uniform definition of hedge funds reflects the exponential growth in the number of products in existence. The industry has expanded to include indiscriminately pooled investment funds with strategies departing from long positions in bonds, equities or money markets, or a mix of these. This leads to a misleading situation, where the term "hedge fund" no longer refers to a systematic hedging attitude.

Box 2.1 DEFINITIONS OF A HEDGE FUND

- A risky investment pool, generally open only to well-heeled investors, that seeks very high returns by taking very great risks. (Money Central Investor)
- A hedge fund is a private investment portfolio, usually structured as a limited partnership, open to accredited investors, charging an incentive based fee, and managed by a general partner with every financial tool imaginable at his disposal. (Sierra Capital Planning Inc.)
- An aggressively managed portfolio taking positions on speculative opportunities. (Investopedia.com)
- A multitude of skill-based investment strategies with a broad range of risk and return objectives. A common element is the use of investment and risk management skills to seek positive returns regardless of market direction. (Goldman Sachs & Co.)
- A loosely regulated private pooled investment vehicle that can invest in both cash and derivative markets on a leveraged basis for the benefits of its investors. (Thomas Schneeweis, University of Massachusetts)

Fortunately, most new hedge funds still share a series of common characteristics that distinguish them easily from more conventional investment funds. Let us now review some of them, while keeping in mind that these are just positive indicators of hedge fund activities rather than absolute signals.

Hedge funds are actively managed

Managers of hedge funds seek to add value through active management and skill-based strategies. They reject traditional investment paradigms, such as the efficient market hypothesis or modern portfolio theory. The efficient market hypothesis states that, at any given time, security prices fully reflect all publicly available information. Modern portfolio theory believes in perfect markets and results in the systematic passive indexing of portfolios. Hedge fund managers believe that markets do not price all assets correctly. Therefore, they set up specific strategies to exploit these inefficiencies. They attempt to build a competitive advantage by having faster information collection, cheaper access to markets, better analysis of investment opportunities, and superior trade or portfolio structuring.

Hedge funds are securitized trading floors

From a functional perspective, hedge funds are also very similar to the trading floors of investment banks. Indeed, several of the hedge fund strategies find their roots in investment banking activities, and the fund managers themselves often have a trading or investment banker background. The emergence of new technologies simply gave talented individuals and investment banking gurus (genuine or fake) the opportunity to start doing for their own account what they had been doing for several years within large institutions.

In addition, following the Asian crisis of 1998, several investment banks became a lot more nervous about proprietary trading, that is, taking risky positions on their own books. Consequently, they farmed out a lot of their proprietary trading activities to hedge funds, and a lot of proprietary traders started creating their own hedge fund. Therefore, shrinkage in proprietary trading activities coincides neatly with a welter of hedge fund launches.

Hedge funds have flexible investment policies

To provide greater possibilities of outstanding returns, hedge fund managers are given broad discretion over the investment styles, asset classes and investment techniques they can use. In particular, they can combine both long and short positions, concentrate investments rather than diversify, sometimes with some risk (Box 2.2), borrow and leverage their portfolios, invest in illiquid assets, trade derivatives and hold unlisted securities. This is clearly a double-edged sword: it subjects the fund to greater "manager risk" but also gives the fund greater discretion to outperform. It is, however, important to understand that a hedge fund does not necessarily employ all of the permitted tools or pursue simultaneously all of the available trading strategies. They merely have them at their disposal, if necessary.

Box 2.2 eNOTE.COM AND THE DANGERS OF CONCENTRATED POSITIONS

The dangers of concentrated positions, illiquid stocks and price manipulation are perfectly illustrated by the eNote case. eNote.com Inc. is a small Vermont firm that develops a television-based internet mail appliance for consumers and businesses that do not need or want to use personal computers. In May 2001 the Securities and Exchange Corporation sued Burton G. Friedlander for having misrepresented the performance of his hedge fund, Friedlander International Inc. According to the SEC, Friedlander's hedge fund bought 5 million shares of eNote preferred shares and 2 million warrants for eNote common stock in April 1999. It rapidly became eNote's biggest shareholders and kept increasing his position. In December 2000 it owned warrants for 11.7 million eNote shares, and eNote represented 40% of its portfolio.

Then Friedlander's fund started inflating the net asset value of his fund by buying large volumes of eNote shares at prices over their market value. Meanwhile Friedlander kept soliciting new shareholders for his hedge fund, while simultaneously redeeming his personal shares at artificially inflated prices. The figure shows the evolution of eNotes share price.

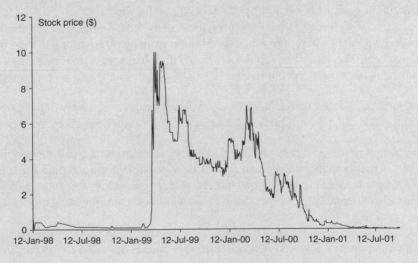

Hedge funds use unusual legal structures

Hedge funds come in a variety of legal forms. However, to avoid the numerous regulations that apply to financial intermediaries and/or to minimize their tax bills, hedge funds use legal structures that are unusual in the asset management world. These are often limited partnerships or limited liability companies when targeting US investors, and offshore investment companies established in tax-favorable jurisdictions when operating outside the United States.

Hedge funds have limited liquidity

Traditional investment funds offer daily subscription and redemption. Investors perceive this daily liquidity as an advantage, because they can enter or exit a fund whenever they wish. However, they often forget that increased liquidity has hidden costs:

- The fund needs to maintain a small cash pool as a liquidity buffer. Whether between the fund and the investor, or purely within the fund, most operations will actually impact this cash pool. For example, an investor purchasing shares in the fund will pay for them using cash that will go into the pool. An investor redeeming his shares in the fund will receive cash from the pool. And selling an asset in the fund will also generate cash for the pool, while purchasing an asset will require cash from the pool. Since the return on cash is usually lower than the expected return on other investments, the existence of the cash pool tends to lower the overall performance of the fund.
- The fund's shareholders are penalized with respect to newcomers or early withdrawers. When subscribing, new shareholders start participating in the fund's existing assets as soon as they receive their shares, while in reality their cash contribution is still not yet invested. Moreover, their cash contribution will result in transaction costs (when the fund will invest) to be shared between all shareholders. Similarly, when redeeming their shares, old shareholders are paid on the basis of the market value of the fund's assets, while in reality some of these assets will be sold to ensure the repayment, generating transaction costs to be shared by the remaining shareholders.
- Managers lose focus. Fund managers must also face the hassle of anticipating and dealing with daily subscription and redemption from investors trying to time the markets themselves. They progressively become cash flow managers rather than asset managers, and focus on shorter-term horizons.

The solution chosen by hedge funds to solve these problems is simply to limit the subscription and redemption possibilities and to insist upon a minimum investment period:

- The *terms of subscription* specify the dates when investors can enter into a hedge fund. Subscribing to a closed-end fund is only possible during its initial issuing period, while open-end funds offer new subscription windows on a regular basis (typically quarterly or monthly). Except during these windows, entering into an open-end fund is not possible.
- An initial *lockup period* is mandatory. It is the minimum time an investor is required to keep his money invested in a hedge fund before being allowed to redeem his shares according to the terms of redemption. The usual lockup period is one year, but longer periods are not uncommon, particularly in well-reputed funds. For instance, relying

on its aura, the famous hedge fund Long Term Capital Management used to require a three-year lockup from its investors, before it collapsed in 1998.

- The *terms of redemption* specify on what dates and under which conditions investors can redeem their shares. The current market standard seems to be at the end of each quarter, but longer redemption periods are not unusual, particularly in funds investing in rather illiquid markets or securities. However, many funds also have provisions to extend the terms of redemption if necessary, and some charge decreasing penalty fees to dissuade early redemption, or limit the number of shares that can be redeemed on any given redemption date. Moreover, it is often required that investors give *advance notice* of their wish to redeem (typically 30–90 days before actual redemption).

Although somewhat limiting from an investor's viewpoint, these restrictions should have a positive impact on a hedge fund's performance. They benefit all of the partners by controlling cash flow transactions, allowing managers to focus on investing instead of redeeming assets of investors trying to time the markets themselves. With these guidelines, managers can also focus on relatively long-term horizons, hold illiquid positions (emerging markets, distressed or unlisted securities, etc.) and reduce cash holdings.

Hedge funds charge performance fees and target absolute returns

While traditional fund managers charge solely a management fee, hedge fund managers impose both a management fee and an incentive fee. *Management fees* are usually expressed as a percentage of assets under management and are charged annually or quarterly. They range from 1% to 3% per year and are essentially intended to meet operating expenses. *Incentive fees* aim at encouraging managers to achieve maximum returns. They typically range from 15% to 25% of the annual realized performance and enable hedge funds to attract the high-end talent necessary to run them (Box 2.3).

Box 2.3   JEFF VINIK AND JULIAN ROBERTSON

Two interesting cases of the potential side effects of performance fees are the legendary hedge fund managers Jeffrey Vinik and Julian Roberston.

After four years running Vinik Asset Management, Jeffrey Vinik announced in October 2000 that he was quitting the industry to spend more time with his family. In these four years the assets of his fund had soared from $800 million to $4.2 billion, for a gross return of 645.8%. This red-hot track record on Wall Street had allowed Jeffrey Vinik, Mike Gordon and Mark Hostetter, the three partners in the fund, to collect about $1.7 billion of performance fees.

More recently Julian Robertson, one of the most successful stock pickers on Wall Street for more than two decades, announced that he was closing his Tiger Management LLC hedge fund group. In 18 months the assets under management had dwindled by $16 billion to $6 billion. The firm did not generate enough cash to pay its employees, essentially because it was unable to collect fees. Given the −4% performance in 1998, −19% in 1999 and −13% at the beginning of 2000, Robertson would have needed to earn 48% before resuming fees to his clients.

To avoid agency problems and excessive risk taking, many funds include a *high water mark* clause in their offering memorandum. This clause states that a minimum rate of return must be achieved and any previous losses recouped by new profits before the incentive fee is to be paid. This explains why several hedge funds pursue an *absolute return target*, meaning that their goal is to be profitable regardless of the stock or bond market environment. This differs significantly from traditional investment vehicles, which do compare their performance relative to standard market benchmarks.

Note that several hedge funds also include a proportional adjustment clause in their bylaws. This clause states that if the fund manager loses money and some investors consequently withdraw their assets, the fund manager is allowed to reduce proportionally the amount of loss he has to recover by the percentage of the assets that were removed. As an illustration, a fund manager who lost $20 out of $100 would have to recover the same $20 before charging performance fees. But if investors withdraw $40 out of the remaining $80 (i.e. 50% of the remaining assets), the carry forward loss would be reduced to $10 (i.e. 50% of the loss).

However, incentive fees and high water marks might have adverse gambling effects on managers' behavior. For instance, a manager who has achieved a good performance at the beginning of a given year may be tempted to lock in and secure his incentive fee by avoiding any risk taking until the fee is paid. Conversely, a manager with a high water mark who has recorded a relatively poor performance has nothing to lose and may take on much more risk in an attempt to recover or eventually close his fund to start a new one (Brown *et al.* 1999b). Fortunately, reputation costs will mitigate these effects (Fung and Hsieh 1997b).

Hedge fund managers are partners, not employees

A hedge fund manager generally shares both upside and downside risks with investors because he has a significant personal stake in his fund. Combined with the incentive fee, his stake is supposed to closely align the hedge fund manager's interests with those of his or her investors, and encourage managers to seek to achieve substantial total returns while prudently controlling risks.

However, contrary to common belief, personal wealth commitment is not necessarily a good indicator of motivation and can even produce undesirable side effects. At the beginning of his career, for example, the fund manager has little to lose. He may be tempted to increase risk, knowing that in case of disaster, he can go back to a traditional asset manager and recover quickly. At the other extreme, a successful fund manager at the end of his career will have so large a commitment in the fund that he will refrain from taking risks, even though these are well remunerated.

Hedge funds have limited transparency

The issue of transparency is a controversial one in the hedge fund community. First of all, let us recall that *transparency* is derived from the Latin words *trans* and *parere* 'to show one self'. In the world of fund managers, this can be understood as the ability to see what is behind the net asset value.

Hedge funds have traditionally been characterized by a lack of transparency, which can easily be explained by two factors. First, the particular legal structure and/or offshore registration of hedge funds (see hereafter) precludes them from publicly disclosing performance information, detailed asset allocations or earnings. Second, revealing specific positions about individual holdings or strategies could be precarious, both for the fund and for its investors. For instance, a fund beginning to accumulate shares to achieve a strategic position in a company would not want to publicly announce what it was doing until it had finished accumulating the position. Nor would a fund short in an illiquid market disclose its holdings, fearing a short-squeeze.

Therefore, hedge funds consider transparency as a double-edged sword. They prefer to remain rather discreet and sometimes opaque, at least when compared to mutual funds. This has contributed to perpetuating the mystery and uneasiness surrounding the hedge fund industry. However, the situation is gradually changing. Investors constantly request more information, and a minimum level of transparency for effective due diligence is now usually provided.

Hedge fund strategies are not scalable

Unlike the case of traditional investment management, size is not a factor of success in the hedge fund industry. The reason is that hedge fund strategies crucially depend on manager skills and available investment opportunities, two factors that are not scalable. Therefore, hedge funds have a limited ability to absorb large sums of assets, and several managers prefer to close their funds to new subscriptions once they have reached a target size. The recent demise of Julian Robertson's Tiger Fund, the liquidation of Jeff Vinik's fund, and the capitulation of George Soros's Quantum Fund are anecdotal evidence that smaller is usually better.

Hedge funds target specific investors

While mutual funds typically target retail investors, hedge funds focus rather on high net worth private individuals and institutional investors (Table 2.1 and Figure 2.8). Here are some of the reasons:

- The legal limits on number of partners if the fund is structured as a limited partnership. These limits imply a large minimum capital investment per investor, frequently between $100 000 and $1 000 000, to ensure that the fund has a sufficient amount of capital to operate properly.
- The relative complexity of hedge fund strategies and the lack of understanding of such strategies among smaller investors.
- Other regulatory reasons requiring that only sophisticated investors may gain access to hedge funds.

High net worth, private individuals are the first investors in hedge funds, both historically and from an asset-based perspective. The term "high" usually encompasses individuals with more than $5 million in net worth, as well as family offices and trust departments of private banks. Ready to commit themselves for the long run, willing to bear high risks in exchange for high return prospects and having a sufficient level of net worth to invest sizable amounts directly in a fund as partners, high net worth private individuals are ideal targets for hedge funds. Their numbers have soared in recent years thanks to the sudden creation of new wealth in successful initial public offerings, creation and sales of

Table 2.1   Categories of hedge fund investor

	Investable assets	Major distribution channels
Ultra high net worth individuals	More than $50 million	Private banks, trust companies, family offices, financial advisers
High net worth individuals	$5–50 million	Private banks, trust companies, brokerage firms, attorneys, financial advisers
Affluent investors	$1–5 million	Commercial banks, mutual fund companies, brokerage firms, attorneys, insurers, financial advisers

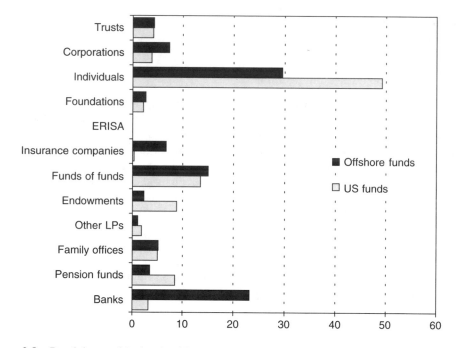

Figure 2.8   Breakdown of hedge fund investors in percentage terms
Reprinted, with permission, from HFR (1999)

businesses, mergers and acquisitions activities, and the expansion of stock option plans as incentive compensation.

Affluent private individuals are also becoming increasingly interested in hedge funds, particularly because of the introduction of lower minimum fund requirements by hedge funds and the existence of capital-guaranteed products. This "affluent" group comprises individuals with net worth ranging between $1 million and $5 million.

THE FUTURE

The major source of future growth for hedge funds is the category of institutional investors; this includes pension and benefit plans, endowments and foundations, insurance companies, banks and corporations. Entangled in their bureaucratic investment decision-making process while restricted by their strict fiduciary responsibilities and the "prudent man" rule, institutional investors only recently started focusing on hedge funds. Initially, only the most adventurous institutions began allocating small amounts of capital to hedge funds, with the goal of diversifying their sources of returns and reducing portfolio risk. The wake-up call came with the decision of the California Public Employees Retirement System (Calpers) to commit $11 billion dollars in alternative investments, including one billion in hedge funds. Since then, the flow of funds from pension funds, endowments and foundations into alternative investments has never ceased. US institutions are clearly well ahead in this process, but European institutions are also increasingly attracted to hedge funds. This constitutes a radical departure from their traditional approach, which was heavily centered on bonds and light on anything remotely associated with risk.

According to a Goldman Sachs and Frank Russell survey, alternative investments now represent over 7% of institutional assets, and institutional investors control about 25% of the total hedge funds' assets (Goldman Sachs & Co. and Frank Russell Capital 1997). Optimistic forecasts talk of a doubling of the institutional market share by 2005 (Rao and Szilagyi 1998). According to a Watson Wyatt/Indocam (2001a, 2001b) survey, pension funds in Switzerland, Denmark, Netherlands, UK and Sweden have the strongest appetite for hedge funds, while Belgian, French and Portuguese institutional investors are less predisposed to alternative investments. However, several issues are still open, such as the lack of transparency; the lack of regulation and risk control; and the high level of fees. The answers to these and the increasing use of consultants for alternative investment manager selection will undoubtedly determine the shape of the hedge fund industry in the coming years.

3
Legal environment and structures

Financial regulation essentially pursues three objectives:

- Protecting investors from abuse and default through licensing/registration, minimum disclosure requirements and increased transparency
- Reducing systemic risks while ensuring soundness and integrity of the financial system by imposing capital adequacy and margin requirements
- Ensuring market price stability through position limits/trade practice restrictions

Every advanced country regulates its traditional financial institutions such as banks, investment funds, brokerage houses and insurance companies in this regard. Very few have explicit regulations on hedge funds.

Nevertheless, hedge funds are not completely unregulated. It is true that hedge funds generally have broad investment policy statements that can encompass a wide variety of asset classes, with no strict limits on leverage, shorting, and the use of derivatives. This ability to operate with maximum flexibility is crucial for the funds to implement their strategies efficiently. Therefore hedge funds search for exemptions from the registration or licensing requirements generally applicable to investment companies and tend to structure themselves in order to avoid direct regulation oversight. But hedge funds are indirectly regulated, since they operate in regulated financial markets, utilize the infrastructure of regulated financial centers and deal with regulated financial institutions (e.g. brokers and banks) to implement their investment strategies.

In the wake of the rescue of Long Term Capital Management (LTCM), several politicians started calling for some form of direct regulation of hedge funds. After careful examination, most international financial authorities and regulators seem to have concluded that attempts to directly regulate hedge fund activities would not achieve the desired aims. The reasons are twofold. First, the blurring of lines between institutions with different primary regulators and supervisors (e.g. banks, asset management firms and mutual funds) may result in similar activities being treated inconsistently. This would create incentives for regulatory arbitrage and thwart the intent of regulation. Second, opinions are more in favor of requiring greater transparency about the size and risk of hedge fund portfolios since most of the desired effects could probably be obtained by relying on disclosure rather than regulation.[1]

This chapter provides a snapshot of the major regulatory environments as well as the solutions adopted by the industry, both within the US (onshore funds) and outside of the US (offshore funds). Regulatory environments and industry solutions are intrinsically interdependent and necessary to understand the business landscape. Indeed, as we will see, most of the complexities of hedge fund structures result from the need to benefit from regulatory exemptions and/or to cater to the needs of specific taxable or nontaxable investors.

INSIDE THE US AND ITS ONSHORE FUNDS

The US economy is essentially founded upon market discipline. Government intervention is viewed as a remedy for the failure of market forces to properly address certain disruptions. Therefore, impetus for federal securities legislation was a direct consequence of the great stock market crash of 1929 and the ensuing depression. Three sets of federal regulators oversee financial institutions dealing with the public. The Securities and Exchange Commission (SEC) is concerned with public issues or trades of securities. The Commodity Futures Trading Commission (CFTC) monitors futures and commodities. The Federal Reserve, the Office of the Comptroller of the Currency and the Office of Thrift Supervision are in charge of banks. Hedge funds operating in the US are essentially concerned with the SEC and, to a lesser extent, with the CFTC.

Securities and Exchange Commission

The Securities and Exchange Commission (SEC) is a quasi-judicial government agency that was set up in the aftermath of the 1929 crash. Its primary mission is to protect investors, maintain the integrity of the securities markets, and guarantee equal access to certain basic facts about an investment to all investors. The SEC derives its regulatory powers from a series of acts; here are some of them:

- The Securities Act 1933 regulates the issue of securities to the public, as well as the necessary information disclosure.
- The Securities Exchange Act 1934 regulates brokerage firms, transfer agents and clearing agencies as well as the nation's securities self-regulatory organizations, including stock exchanges.
- The Investment Company Act 1940 regulates the organization of companies that engage primarily in investing and trading in securities, and whose own securities are offered to the investing public.
- The Investment Advisers Act 1940, amended in 1996, regulates firms or individual practitioners remunerated for advising others about securities investments.

All these acts impose mandatory guidelines that are necessary for monitoring and limiting risks for traditional financial intermediaries, but raise major issues and are often incompatible with hedge fund operations and policies (Table 3.1). Fortunately, there are well-established routes for obtaining exemptions from registration under US securities laws.

Securities Act

For a fund targeting non-US investors, Regulation S provides a safe harbor from the registration requirements of the Securities Act. Regulation S exemptions were originally applicable if both the offer and the sale of securities physically occurred outside the United States. After a series of abuses,[2] the regulation was amended in 1998. Exemption is now subject to a number of conditions that vary depending upon the type of issuer and security involved.

For a fund issuing securities in the US, exemption from the Securities Act 1933 can be granted under Regulation D, also called the private placement exemption. All the following conditions must be fulfilled: (a) all but 35 holders of the fund's securities must be accredited investors; (b) the securities must be privately placed; and (c) the securities

Table 3.1 Impact of SEC and federal securities laws on US-registered hedge funds

	Typical target	Most stringent requirements
Securities Act 1933	Security issuers	Compliance with SEC filing and registration requirements for securities Compulsory transparency, such as providing to the public regular and accurate information about management, holdings, fees and expenses
Securities Exchange Act 1934	Brokers	Maintenance of detailed records of trades to avoid conflicts of interest in executing customer orders as well as trading on own account Costly reporting requirements
Investment Advisers Act 1940	Investment advisers	Registration and conformity to statutory standards designed to protect investors Restriction on fees structures (particularly on incentive fees) Limits on potential investor's minimum wealth and/or investment portfolio value
Investment Company Act 1940	Mutual funds	Registration as an investment company Restrictions on leverage Restrictions on fees Investment diversification rules Mandatory disclosure Required distributions to equity owners each year Requirement of a majority of disinterested directors on board of directors

sold to US investors must be acquired for investment purposes only and not for immediate resale or distribution.

Rule 501(a) of Regulation D defines an accredited investor as an individual who has a net worth of $1 million or more, or had an annual income of $200 000 or more in each of the most two recent years—or $300 000 jointly with a spouse—and a reasonable expectation of reaching the same income level in the current year. Prospective purchasers are responsible for providing truthful and accurate answers to the inquiries in an investor questionnaire. In particular, they are required to state that they are accredited investors, but issuers can use good faith in determining whether a potential subscriber can effectively be considered as accredited. They do not need to verify through financial statements or other means the accuracy of the financial data supplied, unless they have reason to believe it is inaccurate. Note that implicit in the purely arbitrary definition of an accredited investor is the presumption that nonaccredited (read nonwealthy) investors are not sophisticated (read smart) enough to make certain types of investment decisions which are not overseen by the government.

Benefiting from the private placement exemption implies that any general solicitation, seminar or meeting whose attendees have been invited by a general solicitation, as well as any general advertising or public circulation of marketing material[3] are strictly prohibited within the United States. A key criterion to analyze whether this rule was effectively respected in a particular case is the proof of a substantive preexisting relationship between the investor and the general partner or any person acting on the general partner's behalf.

Offers must be personally directed to the investor, and the fund manager should be aware of the financial status and sophistication of the investor.

Note that a private offering does not mean an undocumented one. Hedge funds are introduced to potential investors through an offering memorandum (also known as an offering circular). This confidential document presents a general overview of the fund and should contain the key elements needed to make an investment decision. These include the investment objectives, fees and expenses, risk factors, method of allocating profits and losses, minimum investment, withdrawal policy, and tax status, as well as the biographies and additional information about the key investment-making individuals. In addition, the Securities Act states that if (at most 35) nonaccredited investors participate in a hedge fund, the latter must provide them with additional disclosure information (audited financial statements, including an audited balance sheet, statement of cash flows, and an income statement). In practice, most hedge funds only accept accredited investors.

Securities Exchange Act

To avoid the costly reporting procedures of the Securities Exchange Act 1934, hedge funds need to trade solely on their own account, and therefore avoid executing trades directly for clients. The fund's adviser as well as any of the fund's employees must not receive any commission when selling securities to US investors, since this would qualify them as broker-dealers, therefore requiring registration.

Investment Company Act

Exemption from the Investment Company Act 1940 is granted to a hedge fund if one of the following conditions is fulfilled: the fund has less than one hundred US beneficial owners (Section 3(c)(1)); the fund's partners, who may be of unlimited number, are all qualified purchasers[4] (Section 3(c)(7)). Note that counting to one hundred is not as straightforward as it might seem. In particular, if an entity comprising several investors has control over 10% or more of the outstanding voting securities of the fund, the fund must "look through" the investing entity and count each of its investors.

Obviously, hedge fund managers could attempt to circumvent the limitation on the number of investors by simply opening as many US funds as needed. But under the current rules, if a manager runs more than one hedge fund, investment strategies should not even be similar. Otherwise, regulatory agencies would consider the funds as being essentially the same fund and require the manager to register.

Investment Advisers Act

Hedge fund managers have mixed reactions to the Investment Advisers Act 1940. Some managers feel it is easier to get investors to invest in the hedge fund if they register as investment advisers. In particular, certain institutional investors will only place funds with registered investment advisers. But registration also conveys its limits. In particular, if the manager charges an incentive fee, access to the fund should be limited to individuals who either (i) have a net worth over $1 500 000, (ii) have more than $750 000 under management with the adviser, (iii) are qualified purchasers, as described by the Investment Company Act, or (iv) are "knowledgeable employees" of the investment manager.

To enjoy exemption from the registration requirements of the Investment Advisers Act 1940, a hedge fund manager or general partner must manage less than $25 million in assets or must have fewer than 15 clients in any 12-month period. A hedge fund is deemed, under certain circumstances, to be considered as being one single client. Once exempted, the fund manager cannot hold itself out as an investment adviser to the general public, nor can he serve as an investment adviser to a registered investment company.

Blue-sky laws and new developments

In addition to the federal laws discussed above, each state has its own statutes and regulations that supplement the federal laws and govern the offer and sale of securities into or from such states or to residents of such states. These laws are nicknamed "blue-sky laws" after the preamble to an early Wisconsin law designed to prevent companies from selling pieces of the blue sky to unsuspecting investors. In theory, compliance with a state's blue-sky laws needs to be determined before any offer is made into or from the state or to a resident of such state. Fortunately, in 1956, a Uniform Securities Act was adopted in about 40 states to bring some consistency to state securities regulation, and to integrate that system as far as possible with the federal securities laws.

National Securities Markets Improvement Act

On October 11, 1996 President Clinton signed the National Securities Markets Improvement Act, which has been modestly described by its sponsors as the "first major overhaul of securities law in sixty years." It provides a number of crucial amendments to the above acts:

- It impacts a fund's ability to sell interests to more than 99 investors by adding a new Section 3(c)(7) to the Investment Company Act, which excludes from the definition of "investment company" any issuer whose securities are privately offered and owned solely by qualified purchasers. It also allows Section 3(c)(1) funds to convert into Section 3(c)(7) funds and be covered by the expanded exemptions, provided that existing beneficial owners are given an opportunity to redeem.
- It includes a "grandfather" clause, which enables nonqualified beneficial owners of Section 3(c)(1) funds that convert to Section 3(c)(7) funds to continue to participate in the fund and even increase their investments.
- It preempts the blue-sky registration for federally registered investment advisers offering and selling fund interests to "qualified purchasers."
- It simplifies the "look-through" provisions. Previously, if certain types of entities such as endowments and foundations owned more than 10% of the fund's assets, the look-through rule would count them as multiple investors. Under the new law, they are counted as one single investor.
- It changes the requirements to comply with state blue-sky laws regarding registration as an investment adviser.
- It enhances a registered adviser's ability to charge performance-based fees.

By removing some arbitrary and burdensome limits and recognizing that some investors did not need these protections, the National Securities Markets Improvement Act has significantly reshaped the landscape of the hedge fund industry. In particular, it has effectively increased the number of hedge funds and investors that would be exempt from government regulation.

Finally, we should also mention the restrictions regarding the Employee Retirement Income Security Act 1974 (ERISA). If 25% or more of a hedge fund's aggregate assets consist of ERISA assets or other employee benefit plans, the hedge fund must comply with the various restrictions and prohibitions of ERISA. In practice, most hedge funds simply keep investments from ERISA plans below the 25% limit.

Commodity Futures Trading Commission

The Commodity Futures Trading Commission (CFTC) is a federal regulatory body established by the Commodity Exchange Act in 1974. It has exclusive jurisdiction over all US commodity futures trading, futures exchanges, futures commission merchants and their agents, floor brokers, floor traders, commodity trading advisers, commodity pool operators, leverage transaction merchants and associated persons of any of the foregoing. It also supervises a self-regulatory organization called the National Futures Association (NFA).

Although there are some notable exceptions, any hedge fund trading US commodity futures or options on futures, or soliciting US funds to engage in the purchase and sale of commodity interests will be considered as a commodity pool (CP). The fund manager himself will be considered as a commodity pool operator (CPO) and therefore subject to registration with the CFTC. Similarly, any hedge fund manager advising directly or through publications on US commodity futures or options on futures will be considered as a commodity trading adviser (CTA) and must register with the CFTC.

Registration with the CFTC implies compliance with a series of core principles. These are essentially centered on disclosure, ethics training, accounting, reporting and record keeping, and are particularly problematic for hedge funds. As an illustration, let us consider the offering document requirements. The CFTC mandates that all prospective investors receive an offering document before a commodity pool may accept subscriptions. This document needs to comply with CFTC requirements and must be approved by the NFA. Among other things, it should contain a series of information such as:

- The various types of securities that will be traded and the investment policies that will be followed by the commodity pool, including any material restriction
- A detail of all the expenses of the commodity pool, including an expense ratio that includes all trading commissions
- A tabular presentation of the hypothetical amount of income the commodity pool would have to generate over 12 months in order to offset all expenses allocable or chargeable to the investor and enable the investor to recoup its initial investment upon withdrawal

This type of information is usually not found in offering memorandums for hedge funds that do not trade commodity interests. In addition to the offering document, a commodity pool should also provide all its investors with a quarterly account statement, and provide all its investors and the CFTC with annual audited statements within 90 days of the end of the fund's fiscal year. All performance presentations should be in accordance with CFTC rules. This implies calculating performance net of all fees, expenses and performance allocations, and disclosing statistics such as monthly returns, the largest monthly drawdown and the worst "peak to valley" drawdown for the most recent five full years[5] as well as the year to date. Any use of simulated data should be clearly disclosed and accompanied with meaningful disclaimers.

The situation is even worse for a commodity pool investing in other commodity pools, particularly when they start to concentrate their investments. Regulators refer to a commodity pool holding more than 10% of the assets of another commodity pool as a "major investee pool." In such a case the owning pool operator should report information on all its major investee pools, such as their past returns, volatility, leverage, the strategies they utilized, as well as a five-year business background of their managers. Any significant change in the asset allocation (such as a commodity pool going below or above this 10% threshold) should also be immediately disclosed and amended in a new offering document. The commodity pool operator should also report performance of its major investee pools in accordance with the above CFTC principles.

Most of the disclosure requirements concern positions on US commodity futures and options exchanges, but not positions in the over-the-counter (OTC) derivatives market. This was particularly striking with the debacle of Long Term Capital Management, which was registered as a commodity pool operator and reported all its positions on US futures exchanges daily to the CFTC. But neither the CFTC nor the US futures exchanges had information on its positions on the OTC derivative markets where most of the risks were concentrated.

Nevertheless, it is natural that most fund operators and advisers prefer to avoid the complexity of compliance with CFTC registration and rules, as well as the burden of undergoing periodic examinations by NFA examiners. In theory, there are a few exemptions available. Here are the major ones:

- The fund has less than $200 000 in capital and fewer than 15 participants.
- The fund access is restricted to family members.
- The general partner manages only one fund, does not receive any compensation for that, and is not subject to CFTC registration by virtue of its other activities.
- The fund is already regulated by another US domestic federal agency. This is the case for registered investment companies, regulated insurance companies, banks, trust companies and other ERISA fiduciaries.
- The fund avoids any transactions in US regulated commodities futures and options and use surrogate instruments, such as OTC instruments or equity index options (which are not regulated by the CFTC).
- The fund limits its security offers to "qualified eligible persons" (QEPs). The QEP rule is much more complex than the accredited investor rule applicable to a Regulation D private placement, particularly for nonnatural persons and funds of funds. As a brief summary, we will say that qualified eligible persons include

    - registered commodities and securities professionals
    - those considered as accredited investors under the 1933 act who also have an investment portfolio of at least $2 000 000 or $200 000 on deposit as commodities margin
    - attorneys, accountants, auditors and other financial service providers similarly engaged whose activities and degree of sophistication would merit their being treated as qualified eligible participants
    - non-US persons

- The fund is primarily engaged in security transactions. It infrequently uses futures and options on futures, and limits the amount of margins and premiums invested in commodity futures to 10% of the current fair market value of its assets

While significant profits can be made in trading commodities futures and options, these should be weighed against the additional operating expenses, compliance duties and legal risks inherent to these transactions. Given that even a small investment in futures or commodity options could result in significant administrative compliance obligations, most hedge fund managers tend to prefer avoiding commodity markets, or limiting their commodity investments to 10% of the then current fair market value of their fund.

Structures for US-domiciled hedge funds

Hedge funds targeting US investors typically look for business structures that combine the following attributes:

- *Exemption from SEC registration*: to enjoy investment flexibility, nondisclosure of assets and use of leverage, derivatives, etc.
- *Pass-through taxation*: to avoid double taxation, the fund itself should not pay taxes; its income, gains, losses and deductions should all "pass through" to investors who will take them directly on their own tax bills.
- *Limited liability*: investors should not be personally liable for the fund's losses in excess of what they have invested; this is particularly important if the fund is going to use leveraging or derivatives.

Historically, hedge funds for US investors were formed as limited partnerships. However, now that most states have passed legislation approving the limited liability company as an entity that provides liability protection to investors, hedge funds are progressively adopting this new structure. It is beyond the scope of this book to look in depth at the benefits and disadvantages of the two forms of organization. Hereafter we simply review their major characteristics.

Limited partnerships (LPs)

A limited partnership is a legal entity governed by a partnership agreement that includes at least one general partner and one or more limited partners. It is usually formed for a limited time period (e.g. 25 years).

The general partner is usually the individual or the entity that started the fund. He is responsible for managing the entity and handles all of the trading activity and day-to-day operations. Originally he had to maintain at least a 1% interest in the partnership, even after receiving contributions from limited partners, but this rule was repealed with the Tax Relief Act of 1997. Several states also impose minimum qualifications. For instance, in Texas, general partners need to have taken a general securities law exam (usually Series 7) and the exam on state law (usually the Series 65 exam). However, since the general partner still has unlimited personal liability for the partnership's debts, it is common to see a separate corporation (another limited partnership or a limited liability corporation) acting as a general partner to further reduce the unlimited liability risk.[6]

Limited partners are usually passive investors, who only invest their capital in the partnership and therefore enjoy limited liability; they are responsible for losses only to the extent of their investment. To avoid forfeiting this limited liability advantage, they cannot take part in the daily operation or management of the business. They must all be treated equally,[7] and cannot transfer their shares without the general partner's approval.

This limited partnership structure allows easy commingling and pooling of assets and can accommodate a wide variety of incentive arrangements and profit allocations. In addition, it benefits from the flow-through treatment for tax purposes by the Internal Revenue Service, since dividends distributed to all partners are declared in the partners' personal income tax returns. Some states such as Delaware, Nevada and Wyoming, have clearly welcomed limited partnerships, offering low annual taxes and filing fees, and therefore attract a sizable part of the hedge fund industry.[8]

Limited liability companies (LLCs)

Limited liability companies (LLCs) are a more recent form of legal entity. Owners are called "members" and may directly manage the LLC or may delegate the management. Ownership and voting rights can be divided in very unconventional ways, and members can be virtually any entity, including individuals (residents or foreigners), corporations, other LLCs, trusts, pension plans, etc.

LLCs combine the limited liability advantage of a corporation (all of the members of an LLC are protected from personal liability, similarly to limited partners in the limited partnership) with the tax status of a sole proprietor or partnership (pass-through taxation). On the downside, there are currently three major drawbacks to LLCs. First, most investors are still unfamiliar with them and do not understand or are not comfortable with their status as a "member" of an LLC as opposed to a "partner" in a partnership. Second, an increasing number of states are imposing taxes and annual filing fees on LLCs that make them considerably more costly than limited partnerships. Third, all states do not have identical LLC laws; consequently, an LLC may not be qualified in another state. This may result in a corporate look-through, thereby making individual members liable for LLC debts. Accordingly, limited partnerships remain the entity of choice for hedge funds.

Other structures

The other forms of business available in the US are generally not suitable for hedge funds. The sole proprietorship only allows for one owner who is personally liable for the company, thus placing his or her entire personal wealth at risk. The general partnership implies that each partner is, jointly and severally, personally liable for the debts and taxes of the partnership. And corporations are not very efficient from the tax viewpoint, since they result in double taxation—the corporation is taxed on its own profits, then any profits paid out in the form of dividends are taxed again as dividend income at the individual shareholder's tax rate. Therefore, most US hedge funds are structured as limited partnerships or, to a lesser extent, as limited liability companies.

OUTSIDE THE US AND OFFSHORE FUNDS

While a large number of funds operate within the United States, notwithstanding structural and offering constraints, there also exist a large number of investment advisers who wish to market their funds to non-US investors. Conversely, there exist foreign investors who seek to profit from the US securities markets but are leery of possibly subjecting the resulting income and assets to US income and estate taxes. To cater for all of these, the answer lies in establishing funds offshore, that is, anywhere outside the US.[9]

The choice of a particular place of incorporation is far more complex than one might think. The short list of favored countries usually includes Bermuda, Cayman Islands, Curacao, British Virgin Islands and Bahamas for funds investing in North and South America; and Luxembourg, Ireland (Dublin), Gibraltar, Isle of Man and Liechtenstein for funds targeting Europe, while Mauritius and Singapore are the favorite offshore centers for Far East investing. Several requirements will usually dictate the final answer:

- The tax-free or tax-favorable nature of the jurisdiction (profits, capital gains, distributions, withholding taxes, deferring of incentive fees, etc.).
- The public image of the country, since this will directly affect the fund. In particular, the Financial Action Task Force of the Organization for Economic Cooperation and Development (OECD) identifying a series of "noncooperative" jurisdictions with respect to fighting money laundering. Hedge funds are increasingly concerned with their image and tend to avoid countries mentioned on this list.
- The availability of competent local service providers, such as banks, lawyers, accountants, administrators and staff.
- The available types of investment vehicle.
- The operating costs. Some countries (e.g. Cayman Islands) have developed a comprehensive scheme for the organization and administration of investment funds. This provides additional security to potential investors, but increases the costs of establishing and maintaining a fund there.
- The convenience of the location in terms of travel time, time zone difference, language, etc. In particular, the time difference with European offshore jurisdictions can create important administrative difficulties for US managers.
- The local regulations regarding confidentiality and secrecy, money laundering, restrictions on investment policy, etc.
- The targeted investments.
- The targeted investors and their countries' regulations.

However, most offshore funds only maintain their custody and administration in the offshore country, while the manager will direct operations from elsewhere, e.g. the United States or Europe.

By far the most popular vehicles for establishing offshore funds are limited liability companies (also known as international business companies), limited partnerships, and unit trusts. The first two are similar to their US equivalents. In unit trusts, investors or unit holders are the beneficiaries under the trust and, pursuant to general trust principles, the trust can at any time be brought to an end by collective vote of all the unit holders. Unit trusts often offer advantages to investors in particular jurisdictions since the units will be treated differently from shares for regulatory or tax purposes.

In order to understand the choice of a particular jurisdiction, let us now examine the situation in a few European countries. We have chosen Switzerland, Germany, Italy and France, four countries where hedge funds are at very different stages of their life cycle. We will also briefly discuss the case of Ireland, an untypical offshore location within Europe.

Switzerland

The regulatory framework governing Swiss investment funds depends on their chosen organizational structure. Investment companies are regulated by a specific section of the Swiss Code of Obligations, while multiple investors' contracts and investment funds are subject to the Law on Investment Funds and are regulated and audited by the Swiss Federal Banking Commission.

There was initially a strong tendency to structure hedge funds and multiple investors' contracts as investment companies, mostly to avoid the stricter rules of the Law on Investment Funds. This gave rise to entities such as Creinvest AG (Bank Julius Baer), Castle Alternative Investment AG (LGT), Altin AG (Banque Syz & Co.), and Alpine Select AG (Citibank). The Swiss stock exchange reacted in 1997 by enacting additional rules for the listing and necessary disclosure of investment companies[10] and later created a special segment for the trading of their shares, closing the regulatory gap.

The Law on Investment Funds as amended in 1994 distinguishes three types of funds: real estate funds, securities funds and so-called other funds; the other funds may be with or without special risks. Hedge funds are considered by the Federal Banking Commission to be "other funds with special risks," because of the few restrictions they place on their investment strategies and the sort of financial instruments they can use. The distribution of their shares in Switzerland is subject to (i) meeting the requirements of the law for such funds and (ii) successfully passing the Federal Banking Commission's extensive due diligence process.

The due diligence is aimed at verifying that the fund managers, as well as their representatives and agents (i.e. administrators, custodians, trustees and auditors), have sufficient know-how, training and experience in dealing with hedge funds, as well as a suitable internal organization to control the particular risks attached to hedge funds. In addition, the legal basis of the management contracts and the content of the prospectus are also carefully examined. In particular, the prospectus has to explicitly disclose and explain the particular risks faced by investors. A "warning clause" has to specify the fund's name and declare that (a) the particular hedge fund is a fund with special risks and may thus (b) be engaged in alternative investment strategies; (c) use alternative investment instruments and (d) has, if applicable, an alternative structure (e.g. fund of funds, feeder fund). In addition, the warning clause has to explicitly mention that (e) the investor might face the possibility of incurring considerable losses.

Once authorized by the Federal Banking Commission, hedge funds can freely advertise in Switzerland. They are not required to impose minimum investment requirements or a maximum number of investors. They face only a few investment restrictions, such as no investments in closed-ended funds that are not listed on an exchange or on a regulated market, and no investments in managed accounts. However, the funds have no limitations with respect to markets, products, asset classes, concentration of positions, leverage, etc., as long as this is declared in the fund's prospectus.

Although the law was amended in 1994, it was only in 1997 that the general public had access to hedge fund investments for the first time, when the Federal Banking Commission first approved two domestic and three foreign hedge funds for public sale and marketing in Switzerland. These were AHL Alpha plc, AHL Diversified plc, Leu Prima Global Fund, Sinclair Global Macro Fund, and Von Graffenried Olympia Multi-Manager Arbitrage Fund. The market has since boomed, and Switzerland has become the leading European center for hedge funds on the demand and supply sides. Private banks in particular have been key actors investing in hedge funds and introducing hedge funds in their clients' recommended asset allocations.

What is the situation of nonauthorized offshore funds? The Swiss authorities have adopted a more pragmatic attitude than their US counterparts. As a rule of thumb, nonregistered securities (including hedge funds) may be sold to investors as long as the purchase request emanates solely from the investor. Public demand is therefore authorized, but the problem lies on the supply side—any solicitation, regardless of its form, which is targeted at persons other than a very narrowly defined group[11] is deemed to be public solicitation and therefore requires the registration of the offering fund according to Swiss law.

Germany

Germany is one of the European latecomers to alternative investments. Indeed, until recently, virtually no alternative investments were offered to German investors, essentially for regulatory and tax reasons.

On the demand side, most private pension funds and insurance companies are subject to the German Insurance Supervisory Act. The act prohibits investments in funds that do not fulfill minimum liquidity and risk diversification requirements. Most hedge funds are therefore regarded as noneligible investments for German institutional investors.

On the supply side, starting a hedge fund onshore in Germany is extremely difficult. Two investment vehicles are theoretically available: the German investment fund and the German corporation. However, by law, the German investment fund may invest only in listed securities, cannot take short positions, and should not use leverage, three requirements that are often incompatible with hedge fund activities. The German corporation allows for more flexibility in terms of investments, but profits are taxed at the corporate level and later at the investor level, which makes it highly inefficient.

The situation of offshore (non-German) hedge funds is hardly enviable. First, their promotion among German investors is restricted to private placements. The promoter should generally have an existing investment advisory relationship with each prospective investor, and presentations should be made on a one-to-one basis. Second, offshore funds are subject to the German Foreign Investment Act, which distinguishes three fund categories:

- *White funds* are listed on a German stock exchange or have a license for public offering. They enjoy the same taxation status as the German funds, but their activities are strictly regulated so that, in practice, their status is only applicable to a few nonleveraged long/short equity funds and certain low-risk event-driven strategies.
- *Grey funds* are not listed on a German stock exchange and instead of a license for public offering, they have mandated a [a mandated] German tax representative. They are taxable on all their income (for both institutional and private investors).
- *Black funds* encompass all the other offshore hedge funds and they are heavily penalized: 90% of the annual net asset value variation (when positive) or 10% of the net asset value at the year end (if higher) is deemed to be a taxable capital gain.

This particular unattractive regulatory and tax framework explains the scarcity of alternative products offered in Germany. Until 1998 the only exception were managed futures funds, which can be set up and distributed more easily. Several successful products were launched at this time, such as the Global Futures Funds of ED&F Man. Offering a capital guarantee at maturity, these funds were sold mainly to private investors through direct marketing and raised €400 million, establishing ED& F Man as one of the largest commodity trading advisers worldwide. But most of the other issues did not raise much investor interest.

The situation started changing in 1998. Following the equity market crash, the quest for diversification suddenly became a hot topic among German investors, naturally arousing interest in alternative investments. To exploit this opportunity, several intermediaries turned to financial engineering and came back with a perfect solution to bypass the regulation and make hedge funds palatable for retail and institutional investors—structured products, and more particularly, index-linked bonds. Index-linked bonds are tax-free for a private investor after a one-year period and can be sold to institutional investors if the principal is guaranteed.

As might be expected, this resulted in an explosion of zero-coupon notes whose repayment was linked to the performance of a portfolio of hedge funds but was at least equal to the principal. The Landesbank Baden-Württemberg started with a conservative guaranteed hedge fund product in early 1999, shortly followed by Commerzbank with its Comas series, and Vereins und Westbank with its Prince product.

But the major surprise came in September 2000, when Deutsche Bank announced that its new product, Xavex HedgeSelect Certificate, had attracted around €1.8 billion in four weeks from retail and institutional investors, essentially in Germany, Switzerland and Benelux (Box 3.1). Since then most German banks have launched their own alternative investment products, attracting an increasing numbers of investors.

Box 3.1   THE XAVEX HEDGESELECT CERTIFICATES

Deutsche Bank AG issued the Xavex HedgeSelect Certificate on September 29, 2000. This new member of the Xavex product family was structured as an eight-year index certificate. It aimed at providing investors full participation in the upside and downside performance of the HedgeSelect index. That is, a performance objective of 12–15% annual growth with neither a maximum nor a minimum redemption amount, and a risk as close as possible to the risk level of bonds (as represented by the J.P. Morgan Global Government Bond index). Actively managed by Deutsche Asset Management on a continuous basis according to a "judgment with quantitative discipline" approach, the HedgeSelect index reflects the performance of a diversified portfolio of 15–50 hedge funds, plus a cash balance.

With respect to other products available in Germany, the HedgeSelect certificate had several innovative features. First, the minimum investment was small (€10 000 with €1000 increments), allowing all types of investor to subscribe. Second, the certificates were denominated in euros and the US dollar exchange rate risk was hedged by rolling over one-month currency forwards. Third, the certificates enjoyed a favorable tax treatment in Germany. For instance, capital gains were tax-free for private investors if the certificate was held more than one year.

To enhance liquidity, Deutsche Bank offered a two-tiered market-making feature. On the one hand, the certificates were listed on the Frankfurt Stock Exchange, allowing immediate trading with a bid/ask spread expected to be about 5% around the estimated net asset value. On the other hand, investors could redeem their shares at the official net asset value at the end of each month, but this implied in practice at least 85 days between the exit notice and the cash settlement. Consider for instance an investor willing to redeem his shares at the end of March. He would need to give an early notice at least 35 business days (i.e. 7 weeks) before the end of March—around the beginning of February. The settlement amount would be based on the official value of the index at the end of March. This official index value is calculated and released by Morgan Grenfell & Co. usually 45 days after the end of the corresponding month; that is, the end-March value is only known around May 15. Finally, the corresponding payment would occur 5 days later.

In terms of fees, the certificates charged an origination fee of 2% (included in the offered price) plus a flat fee of 0.27% every month, but no performance fee. In exchange, Deutsche Asset Management guaranteed that the hedge funds included in the portfolio would not charge entry or exit fees.

Italy

Italy is another latecomer with respect to alternative investments. Indeed, the continual changes in government[12] and the resulting regulatory changes helped developing and maintaining uncertainty among sophisticated investors. The result was money flowing out of the country, particularly to Lugano (Switzerland), a more favorable Italian-speaking place for alternative investments. And in January 1999 the first Italian bank to launch a hedge fund, Milan-based UniCredito Italiano, chose to set up its operations in Ireland. This is not surprising when considering, for instance, that Italian residents were allowed to buy offshore hedge funds but were taxed on their gains at their marginal tax rate (in excess of 45%), whereas Switzerland has no taxes on capital gains and strong banking secrecy.

Conscious of the problem, the Bank of Italy established in 1999 a new legal framework allowing hedge funds to be set up onshore. According to this new law, any group willing to establish onshore hedge funds in Italy needs (a) to be authorized by the Bank of Italy; (b) to set up a special investment management entity (*societá di gestione del risparmio*); and (c) to request approval of each individual hedge fund, on a case-by-case basis.

Two types of fund are available, the *fondi di reservati* for professional investors and the *fondi di speculativi*. Both enjoy broad investment discretion,[13] but may only be distributed through private placements, with at most one hundred Italian investors, each with a minimum investment of €1 million. Last but not least, the approved hedge funds are subject to a 12.5% withholding tax, as ordinary mutual funds.

The Italian alternative investment industry has since grown, but at a much slower pace than some had expected. Several firms (Kairos Partners, Ersel Asset Management or Banca Intermobiliare di Investimenti e Gestione) have been authorized to start Italy-based funds of hedge funds, but only Kairos Partners has effectively launched a series of four funds. Despite its temporary monopoly, the amount of capital committed by Italian investors was still very low, with $86 million raised in the four funds. The major reason is probably that the market is not mature enough. Most potential investors are still in the process of moving from domestic bonds and equities to international investments, and are not yet familiar with hedge funds. Several pension funds do not much use the services of consultants and still pay more attention to fees than to performance. In addition, all potential hedge fund managers complain about the lack of effective prime brokerage services on the peninsula, as well as the legal difficulties when using a long position as a collateral against a borrowed stock.[14] In this context, the creation of a true Italian hedge fund (rather than a fund of funds) would still be a nightmare.

Nevertheless, since Italian investors have a keen appetite for performance coupled with a strong aversion to risk, there is an ongoing debate about the benefits that these products could bring to private and institutional portfolios, as well as numerous signals that the market share of hedge funds should increase significantly in the coming years. There are three reasons. First, the size of pension fund markets is still ridiculously small compared to the size of the mutual funds, which are mostly controlled and distributed by banks and their asset management subsidiaries. However, the law allowing the creation of complementary pension funds came into force in 1999. These new actors are mainly investing in bonds and equities, but should increase their allocation to hedge funds in the future. Second, although it is not yet possible to register foreign hedge funds or funds of funds, there might be an opening for these products in the near future through the emergence of capital-guaranteed notes, as was the case in Germany. Third, the Milan Stock Exchange is considering changes designed to ease share trading. These include (i) allowing trades of just one share at a time, and (ii) allowing shareholders of companies traded on the Nuovo Mercato (the local version of the Nasdaq) to lend part of their stock, even if they are bound by an agreement not to sell their holding.

France

France is currently in a unique situation within Europe. Simply stated, French investors, government and regulators greatly lack an equity culture. This is the result of several years of fiscal privileges granted to life insurance products as well as pay-as-you-go state-funded pension schemes. Both diverted the attention of French investors from long-term investing in equity markets, which is now too often associated with gambling at casinos.

Following the same line of thought, onshore hedge funds are legally banned in France. This is easy to understand once one knows that using leverage and making profits through speculation are perceived as almost criminal activities in France. The result has simply been a massive brain drain toward more accommodating countries. All hedge funds set up by French companies were simply registered in and managed from offshore locations.[15]

Unfortunately, the perception of French authorities was that offshore investing was synonymous with tax evasion. They riposted immediately by imposing prior authorization by both the Ministry of Finance and the Commission des Opérations de Bourse for any act of solicitation from a collective investment scheme constituted outside the European Economic Area. Of course, advertising, mailing a prospectus or an offering memorandum, meeting with or calling potential investors as well as organizing presentations were considered as an act of solicitation. The same rule applies when marketing to banks. Predictably, the approval has never been granted in practice. In addition, any document used to inform French clients was required to be in the French language, creating an important barrier to entry for foreign groups.

However, since individual freedom cannot be totally constrained in a democracy, shares in such offshore funds can still be sold to any individual who applies on a wholly unsolicited basis. Not surprisingly, disappointed by the stock market's poor performance and worried by the almost bankrupt status of state-funded pension schemes, investors are more and more interested in alternative products, and banks that had shunned hedge funds after a string of failures are lining up offerings, hypocritically waiting for "unsolicited requests." So far, the demands have primarily originated from institutional investors, but euro convergence and the rising interest that individual investors are showing in customized and structured products could provide strong conditions for growth in the forthcoming years.

Ireland

Over the last ten years, Ireland has emerged with the approval of the European Union (EU) as a leading European jurisdiction for the registration of offshore investment funds, including hedge funds. It has now an investor base that represents many times the size of the domestic investor base. We will therefore look at Ireland in a different way; that is, as a potential regulated jurisdiction to register a hedge fund.

Ireland's financial sector is based principally in the International Financial Services Center (IFSC) in Dublin's central Custom House Docks area. The principal regulator for fund-related activities is the Central Bank of Ireland, which is responsible for the authorization of new funds and the ongoing supervision of the investment fund industry. The original legislation that is relevant to hedge funds can be found in sections 126 and 127 of the Finance Act 1995.

The Irish legislation allows for a wide range of fund structures. Broadly speaking, these can be categorized as undertakings for collective investment in transferable securities (UCITS) and non-UCITS. UCITS funds are extremely popular with traditional asset managers. They can be constituted as unit trusts, variable capital or fixed capital companies. Once authorized, they may sell their units or shares in any EU member state without the need for further domestic authorization. However, they are not allowed to sell short, use leverage or concentrate their investments, which makes them not suitable for hedge fund activities.

Non-UCITS funds can be constituted as unit trusts, variable capital or fixed capital companies as well as limited partnerships. Depending on the targeted investors, they should be divided into four subcategories:

- Retail schemes have no minimum subscription requirements, but are extremely regulated in terms of investments.
- Qualifying investor schemes have a minimum subscription requirement of €250 000 per investor and can only be marketed to "qualified investors." Qualified investors are defined as natural persons with a minimum net worth requirement of €1 250 000, entities owning or investing on a discretionary basis at least €25 000 000, or the beneficial owners of which are qualifying investors in their own right. Qualified investors must self-certify that they meet these minimum criteria and that they are aware of the risks involved in the proposed investment. The qualifying investor fund structure is an ideal one for hedge funds because there are no investment restrictions and no limits on leverage.
- Professional investor schemes have a minimum subscription requirement of €125 000 per investor or its equivalent in another currency. They face some investment restrictions, such as a maximum 2:1 leverage and a maximum of 20% of their assets invested in unlisted securities or a single issuer.

- Collective investor schemes were introduced by the Finance Act 1995 and are specifically designed for "collective investors" (life assurance companies, pension funds, etc.). They are tax-exempt, cannot be sold publicly, and if they are set up as an investment company, can be nondesignated, meaning that there are no minimum subscription requirements and no investment or borrowing restrictions.

The Central Bank of Ireland's requirements for hedge funds domiciled in Ireland are contained in a series of non-UCITS notices. They cover issues such as the information to be provided in the prospectus, the appointment of a trustee or custodian, and the minimum requirements for prime brokers (including a minimum credit rating of A1/P1, and a regulated broker status granted by a recognized regulatory authority).

Another interesting characteristic of Ireland is the Irish Stock Exchange. Created in 1989 as part of the development of the funds industry in the IFSC, it allows for the listing of Irish and non-Irish funds. It is therefore widely regarded as a leading location for listing offshore investment funds and hedge funds. Such a listing usually does not provide a large secondary liquidity in the fund's securities, but it may help to meet specific investors' regulatory and technical requirements (e.g. pension funds that can invest only in listed products).

Other European countries

In the rest of Europe most regulators are still lagging behind their US counterparts. Hedge funds are usually not recognized as specific investment structures, and their registration as domestic investment funds is not possible. The marketing and distribution of offshore funds is often prohibited, particularly when targeting the general public. However, it is still possible for investors who know precisely what they want to invest in offshore funds, as well as to conduct private placements. And there is no law to prevent private investors from requesting information from companies managing hedge funds.

THE GLOBAL VILLAGE

The development of the internet has attracted the attention of asset managers as a convenient, efficient and economical means of marketing, selling and providing information on products and services to a global audience. The high accessibility and low cost have created a tendency to use this new media in a more informal way to conduct securities-related business. This is clearly fraught with risk for the unwary. Since the information posted locally may be accessed instantly and globally, it is often necessary to comply with both local and foreign regulators' requirements.

As an illustration, let us consider the situation in the United States. In its release number 33.7233 (October 6, 1995), the Securities and Exchange Commission stated its position very clearly:

> The Commission appreciates the promise of electronic distribution of information in enhancing investors' ability to access, research, and analyze information, and in the provision of information by issuers and others. The Commission believes that, given the numerous benefits of electronic distribution of information and the fact that in many respects it may be more useful to investors than paper, its use should not be disfavored. Given the numerous benefits of electronic media, the Commission encourages further technological research, development and application. The Commission

believes that the use of electronic media should be at least an equal alternative to the use of paper-based media. Accordingly, issuer or third party information that can be delivered in paper under the federal securities laws may be delivered in electronic format.

What was good news for most of the money management industry heralded the demise of hedge funds on the internet.

A website is accessible to millions of people, a significant number of whom could be potential investors. And this is strengthened by the existence of search engines and hyperlinks from other sites. As a side effect of allowing internet distribution of information, a homepage describing a fund or indicating that it is offering its securities could be construed as conducting a general solicitation. The fund would then be considered as engaging in a public offering, which would disqualify it from the private placement exemption and require the registration of its securities with the SEC, which would in turn require the fund to register as an investment company under the 1940 act. Consequently, hedge funds need to be extremely cautious when using the internet.

Later on, in 1998, the SEC issued an instructive report entitled *Use of internet websites to offer securities, solicit securities transaction or advertise investment opportunities offshore*. It clearly presents its opinion as to the general application of US securities laws to the internet activities of offshore funds, issuers and other market participants. It also establishes a clear distinction between the active electronic targeting of US investors and the passive use of the internet to disseminate information to selected authorized investors. Three cases need to be distinguished.

Domestic offerings

In the case of domestic offerings, hedge funds must be privately placed and cannot engage in public solicitation, including on the internet. In particular, the SEC determined that spamming (i.e. sending out mass emails), providing offering materials for a hedge fund on a website or offering links to this material constituted a general advertisement or solicitation. Internet usage is therefore limited to providing fund-specific information to qualified investors. In order to fulfill this requirement, most hedge funds have implemented password-protected sites, whose access is only granted after the operator of the site has confirmed that the investor is properly qualified. Most funds also request a 30-day waiting period between granting access to their website and accepting an investment from a given investor.

Offshore offerings

In the case of offshore offerings, the corresponding hedge funds are off limits to most US investors. Nevertheless, the SEC is also aware that the global nature of the internet means that the websites of offshore funds are still accessible to US investors, and has issued a policy statement on the matter.[16] This set of guidelines states that offshore funds must "implement measures that are reasonably designed" to guard against sales to US investors through electronic media. Such measures must include, but are not limited to, prominent meaningful disclaimers indicating the non-US nature of the offering,[17] and obtaining proofs of non-US residency: checking mailing address, telephone number, or area code before sale; refusing checks drawn on US banks; and so on.

Concurrent funds

Funds concurrently conducting a security offering offshore and a private placement in the US must take reasonable steps (meaningful disclaimers, passwords, etc.) and exercise extra care to safeguard against a US investor accessing documents originally targeted at offshore investors. In addition, the hedge fund should not allow a US person accessing the offshore website to participate in the US private placement, even if otherwise an accredited investor.

Third-party providers

An interesting situation is that of a hedge fund posting information about itself on the internet through a database operated by a third-party information provider. The SEC addressed this situation in two no-action letters sent in 1997 and 1998 to Lamp Technologies. This company was primarily engaged in the business of data processing, software development, and the creation and maintenance of internet websites. It had the intention of offering non-US registered hedge funds the possibility of posting descriptive and performance-related information on a common website. All these funds would be paying Lamp Technologies a fixed fee for the posting service, independent of the number of sales and/or performance of the manager. Before starting operations, Lamp Technologies requested the SEC opinion.

In its letters, the SEC confirmed that internet posting of hedge funds' private information on a third-party website was allowed. This would not be considered as a general solicitation nor would it constitute a public offering of securities if certain procedures were followed: (a) any fund information on the site was password protected; (b) potential subscribers to the site were prescreened to determine if they would qualify to invest; (c) the screening questionnaire and any invitation to complete the questionnaire were generic and did not mention any particular fund; and (d) subscribers would be required to wait during a cooling-off period of 30 days after receiving their password before investing in any fund listed on the site (other than those for which the subscriber was being solicited or in which the subscriber had invested or was actively considering investing).

Finally, persons trading commodities, but who are not registered with the CFTC as commodity pool operators or commodity trading advisers, may only use websites containing contact information. The posting of other material (e.g. performance data, biographies) will be considered as solicitation, therefore necessitating the establishment of specific disclosure documents in accordance with the CFTC rules.

As the internet transcends national boundaries, there is increased scrutiny and enforcement by foreign jurisdictions, so that hedge funds should also be cautious when posting information that may be accessible to foreign investors. For instance, in Germany, an offshore site written in the German language and providing information about a hedge fund is considered by the regulatory authority (BAKred) as a public offer to German citizens, and therefore the fund should be regulated and taxed by the German authorities. A similar regulation exists in the UK concerning websites accessible to British investors. In the UK, the Financial Services Authority issued a guidance release in February 1998. This release clearly states the need to include disclaimers and warnings on a website indicating that the site is addressed only to persons who can lawfully receive investment services, an approach similar to that of the SEC.

NOTES

1. A group within the hedge fund community—Caxton Corporation, Kingdon Capital Management LLC, Moore Capital Management, Inc., Soros Fund Management LLC and Tudor Investment Corporation—has recently made a proposal for self-regulation and circulated a set of risk management guidelines in a sponsored report (Various 2000).

2. For instance, the GFL Ultra Fund, a British Virgin Islands corporation, engaged in the following strategy for more than a year. It purchased securities issued overseas at significant discounts from the US market price pursuant to Regulation S and hedged these purchases through short sales in the US. After the 40-day Regulation S restricted period, the fund unwound its short positions by covering them with the Regulation S shares. Clearly, this was an abuse of Regulation S to offer securities in the US before the end of a restricted period.

3. The SEC has taken the view that the term "marketing material" encompasses any letter or written communication addressed to more than one person and containing any analysis, report, graph, chart, testimonial, formula or advisory service that could be used to determine when to buy or sell securities, or which securities to buy or sell. This naturally includes offering memorandums.

4. There are four categories of qualified purchasers, also referred to as "super-accredited" investors: individuals (including holders of joint or community property) owning "investments" of at least $5 million; family-owned businesses owning not less than $5 million in "investments"; trusts not formed for the specific purpose of acquiring the securities offered, whose trustees or equivalent decision makers and whose settlers or other asset contributors are all qualified purchasers; any person (acting for his own account or for other qualified purchasers) who has discretion over $25 million in investments.

5. If a fund has less than three years of existence, its partner should then disclose the performance of any other pool he operated during the corresponding five-year period, if any.

6. If some of the unexpected liabilities arise because of a securities law violation, the general partner can be held personally liable, regardless of the intermediary legal structures.

7. This equal-treatment clause sometimes has unexpected consequences. For instance, a general partner investing in his own fund is considered as a limited partner, and must abide by all the terms and conditions of the other limited partners, including paying a pro rata portion of the fund's management fees to himself, with all the corresponding tax consequences.

8. In addition, Delaware does not request a minimum capital; it accepts non-US citizens as shareholders, maintains confidentiality on the owners' names, and does not charge any corporate income tax if the business is done out of Delaware.

9. The term "offshore" refers to the situation with respect to the US. An offshore fund with respect to a given country will be considered as an onshore fund in its country of incorporation.

10. For more information, refer to the Swiss stock exchange's Règlement Complémentaire de Cotation des Sociétés d'Investissement.

11. An important amendment to law is the Institutional Investors' Exemption, which allows nonregistered foreign investment and hedge funds to be offered and sold in

Switzerland to institutional investors with a professional treasury, such as banks, insurance companies and pension funds.

12. Berlusconi's is the 59th government that Italy has had since World War II.

13. Note that the *fondi di reservati* cannot implement long/short strategies because of the prudent investment rules for institutional investors, but they can invest in units of other hedge funds.

14. Due to an incompatibility between Italy's Civil Code and Common Law and English law in general, the right of the prime broker to hold guarantees in hedge fund busts is not clearly established. Clarification would require a change in the Civil Code, implying a lengthy parliamentary process.

15. In particular, London and Geneva were the favorite destinations of French hedge fund managers willing to enjoy lower tax rates and more flexibility.

16. See *Statement of the commission regarding use of internet web sites to offer securities, solicit securities transactions, or advertise investment services offshore* (Releases 33.7516, 34-39779, IA-1710, IC-23071 of March 23, 1998).

17. This standard disclaimer is not considered meaningful: The offer is not being made in any jurisdiction in which the offer would or could be illegal.

4
Operational and organizational structures

OPERATIONAL STRUCTURES

Hedge funds are usually not operated in-house by their own employees. They are just investment vehicles owned by investors and sponsors (or limited and general partners) and rely on external service providers to conduct the fund's day-to-day business, including managing the fund's portfolio and providing administrative services. In return, these service providers receive a specified fee from the fund pursuant to various agreements.

This outsourcing of operations often surprises traditional asset managers, who are used to in-house integration, but it has proved to result in better quality of service and cost-effectiveness. For instance, the 1999 Global Investor/Latchly Management survey of UK investment management firms evidenced the poor support of in-house back office for core operational functions, even in the larger firms. Most hedge funds have recognized these benefits and, before starting operations, they establish relationships with all the necessary industry service providers (Figure 4.1). The various roles of each of these players are described below.

The sponsor and the investors

The sponsor is the creator of the fund and he will typically hold a number of founder shares in the fund; these voting shares control management of the fund, apart from a limited number of major decisions, but they are usually not entitled to any distribution or share in the equity. All of the remaining equity belongs to the investors (including the sponsor), typically in the form of nonvoting preferred redeemable shares. In a limited partnership, the sponsor will be the general partner, and the investors the limited partners.

The sponsor/general manager usually receives an allocation of income from the fund based on performance (typically 20% of realized and unrealized appreciation of the fund each year over a high water mark).

The manager or management company

The investment manager is often structured as a management company that belongs to or is affiliated to the fund sponsor. It employs the sponsors' personnel, is responsible for office overhead, and is usually established in a major onshore financial center, such as London or New York. Its primary responsibility consists of determining the investment strategy of the fund, making the investment decisions according to the stated objectives, and taking all operational decisions for the fund. It covers its operating expenses by an asset-based fee. The fee is usually in the range of 1–3% per year of net fund assets, calculated and paid on a regular basis, plus an incentive or participation fee. This fee is

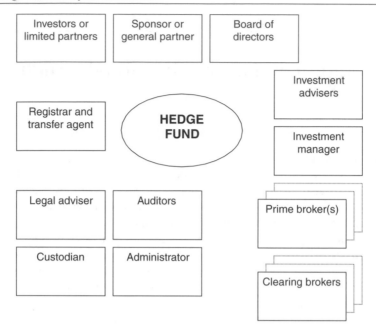

Figure 4.1   The typical hedge fund network

usually based on any increase in the net asset value, and may range from 6% to 50% of the profit or gain.

In the case of offshore funds, a single entity often acts as both a sponsor and a manager. If a sponsor jointly operates an offshore fund and a US limited partnership, the sponsor typically receives its asset-based management fee and its performance-based fee for the offshore fund in a single entity, which is usually the same entity that serves as the management company, and it receives the fixed management fee from the domestic fund.

The investment adviser

The role of the investment adviser is simply to give professional advice on the fund's investments in a way that is consistent with the fund's investment objectives and policies, as described in the prospectus. The investment adviser may be a part of the same overall organization as the hedge fund he serves, or he may be unrelated to it. His reward is usually a fixed fee.

The board of directors

The board of directors is responsible for monitoring the overall operations of the fund. It supervises the manager and other principal agents. It also oversees matters where the interests of the fund and its shareholders differ from the interests of its investment adviser or management company. In practice the board of directors often delegates the responsibility for the day-to-day asset allocation of the fund and the supervision of the manager's activities to an executive committee.

At least in theory, the board of directors should review and approve investment advisers' contracts and fees, the selection of independent auditors and attorneys, and the appointment of the fund's transfer agent, custodian, etc., and veto any management proposal that is not in the shareholders' interests. This seldom happens in practice since most of the time the board of directors is not independent of the investment adviser and the fund's other service providers.

The fund administrator

Several local regulations explicitly require hedge funds—not hedge fund managers—to appoint an independent administrator. His primary task is to ensure accurate calculation of the net asset value at regular time intervals called break periods. Break periods will typically end with redemption and subscription dates, departures or admittance of new partners, etc. Any action that affects the partnership's capital is likely to result in a break period and in the administrative costs of valuing the entire portfolio. Note that reducing the number of break periods to reduce administrative costs is not really effective, since a valuation must obviously be done each time a contribution or redemption is made.

This is straightforward in the case of securities where market quotations are readily available, but complications arise when there is no market price, when some securities are restricted, or when some underlying assets are illiquid and irregularly traded. In these cases the administrator must establish guidelines and determine a "fair value" for these securities. Except in very exceptional, fully disclosed and auditor-approved circumstances, the administrator should never rely on fund managers' valuations.

In addition to net asset value calculations, most administrators also perform several administrative services, including accounting and bookkeeping, payment of fund expenses, including the calculation of fees, preparation and mailing of reports to existing shareholders, help with tax assessment, basic legal support and investor relations. In the US, hedge fund administrators also ensure blue-sky laws compliance, prepare and file tax returns (including the realized and nonrealized capital gains), and report to the SEC.

Finally, the administrator can supply data, but should not participate in the risk management function. The reason is that this latter task is judgmental, and therefore, should be performed by another independent party. Nevertheless, in time of crisis, the administrator should be proactive in the interests of shareholders.

Depending on the complexity of the fund and the number of tasks performed, the administrator's fees may be as little as a few thousand dollars a year or as much as 0.5% to 0.65% of the net asset value per year.

The custodian

The custodian's primary responsibilities include safekeeping of the fund's assets, clearing and settling all trades (i.e. confirming transactions with counterparties, providing payment when securities are bought, and receiving payment when securities are sold) and monitoring corporate actions such as dividend payments and proxy-related information. Most of the time, the fund's assets consist of cash and securities that the custodian does not possess, but maintains on an accounting system through a central depository. The custodian is also responsible for providing periodic reports on the transactions within the account, and sometimes for verifying fund managers' compliance with the investment guidelines. The custodial fee can be a fixed fee or a percentage of net asset value, but when a broker acts as *de facto custodian*, it is usually charged on a transactional basis.

The legal adviser or lawyer

The legal adviser or lawyer assists the hedge fund with any tax code and/or legal matters, and ensures compliance with domestic investment regulations as well as with regulations of countries where the fund is distributed. He usually prepares the private placement memorandum, draft and reviews the documentation, the partnership/subscription agreement, and all necessary questionnaires (e.g. access-accredited investors, qualified purchasers and hot issues). He is also involved in any listing process and addresses tax issues.

The auditors

Most funds provide nonaudited monthly or quarterly statements to their shareholders, but the annual statement is audited, since most third parties will not agree to work with a never-audited entity. The auditors' role is to ensure that the hedge fund is in compliance with accounting practices and any applicable laws, and to verify the annual financial statement, if any.

The registrar and transfer agent

The registrar and transfer agent keeps and updates a register of shareholders of the hedge fund. He also processes and takes necessary actions for subscriptions and withdrawals of shares in the fund, as well as for the payment of any dividends and distributions. When a fund has no dedicated registrar and transfer agent, the administrator usually handles this role.

The distributors

Some hedge funds handle their distribution internally, that is, without a separate distributor. Their investors purchase shares in the fund directly from the fund or its registrar and transfer agent. However, in most cases, shares are distributed through a sales force, which may be affiliated to the fund or independent (e.g. employees of independent broker-dealer firms, financial planners, bank representatives and insurance agents). This sales force will contact potential clients directly (in jurisdictions where this is legally possible) or assist clients willing to invest in the fund on an "unsolicited basis."

In both cases, investors pay for the marketing and distribution of fund shares through a front-end load charge that usually varies between 2% and 5% of the amount invested and is deducted from the net proceeds. Note that dealing directly with the registrar and transfer agent does not necessarily reduce this fee. In some cases it may even increase the fee, since some banks refund a portion of their distribution commission to their clients when subscribing to third-party hedge funds.

The executing or clearing brokers

Unless a hedge fund has direct access to the market, it needs to place its orders with a broker. Most hedge funds prefer to use the services of several executing/clearing brokers, who compile the best bids and offers, execute trades, and provide full reconciliation as well as limited administrative services. Depending on the hedge fund, best execution encompasses a number of factors, starting with the price and cost of the execution, the opportunity for price improvement, or the speed and likelihood of execution. Spreading around the commission also allows funds to deal with more brokers, therefore participating in more initial public offerings and new issues.

The prime brokers

The role of prime brokers goes beyond just replacing the hedge fund's back office. Rather, they should be seen as full service providers across the core functions of execution and operations. Here are some examples:

- *Clearing the trades*: prime brokers clear trades executed with their own broker-dealer, or if desired by the fund, trades executed with other brokers. In the latter case, both the hedge fund and its executing brokers will report the trade to the prime broker, who will settle the trade and report to the custodian if the details match, or resolve the case with the fund and the executing broker in the case of a mismatch.
- *Acting as global custodian*: a key item of information for a hedge fund is the consolidated reporting of trades, positions and performance. It is therefore common to see prime brokers acting as custodian for hedge funds.
- *Margin financing*: most hedge funds employ leverage to gain greater exposure to their chosen investment strategy, and the prime brokers are usually able to provide the service in a transparent manner through revolving lines of credit, loans, or repurchase transactions.
- *Securities lending*: the ability of a hedge fund to take short positions is a key part of its trading strategy and it will be the securities lending desk at the prime broker that mainly facilitates this process. Prime brokers maintain a securities lending network comprising banks, large institutional holders and other broker-dealers. Although some pure custodians do offer limited securities lending and financing to hedge funds, this is on a very small scale compared to the operations of prime brokers operating out of broker-dealers.

To cover their exposure in the borrowing and securities lending obligations incurred by the hedge fund and ensure their rights of legal recourse in the event of the default of the fund, prime brokers usually request some collateral. This collateral may take the form of either a full transfer of some assets or a conventional mortgage or charge over the hedge fund's assets. In the particular case of a prime broker acting simultaneously as a custodian, there exists a potential conflict of interest if the fund defaults. Should the broker set the emphasis on holding the assets as collateral or rather as a safe custody function? This should be clarified initially.

A number of hedge funds combine a prime broker and several executing brokers. This gives them the best executions and access to specialists, as well as a centralized source of information and leverage.

The move to prime brokers is a paradigm shift that was both significant and beneficial for the hedge fund industry, but has significantly reduced the role of other parties, particularly the custodian and executing brokers. Using a prime broker results in a simplified operational procedure, better service, and lower costs. Without prime brokers, hedge funds would be unable to carry out their investment strategies efficiently, particularly in illiquid securities, or in over-the-counter and emerging markets.

Today the business of prime brokerage is concentrated in the hands of a few major investment banks (e.g. Morgan Stanley, Bear Stearns, Goldman Sachs, Merrill Lynch and Bank of America). They have natural competitive advantages because of their existing asset management, securities lending and custody activities, and are able to offer a complete "front to back" suite of technology products. These prime brokers were initially imposing strict criteria for being accepted as a prime brokerage client, such as minimum requirement of partnership capital or capital commitments, volume of transactions, size of debit balances, or volume of shorting transactions.

However, the increased competition among prime brokers has progressively switched the prime brokerage market from demand driven to supply driven. Prime brokers have attempted to lock hedge fund managers into exclusive relationships by offering value-added services (such as research, tax compliance reporting, online communication, trade date versus settlement date reconciliation, etc.). Nevertheless, the desire to reduce counterparty risk, to preserve some privacy on their proprietary trades and to clear and settle trades in multiple time zones has gradually persuaded the largest funds to use several prime brokers. This reduces the potential consequences of a major prime broker failure, but increases the complexity of the administrator's task, since he must ensure that he has all the feeds necessary to give a daily profit and loss or position statement. Otherwise, the consequences could be dramatic (Box 4.1)

Box 4.1   MICHAEL BERGER'S MANHATTAN FUND AND DAVID MOBLEY'S MARICOPA FAMILY

In 1996 Michael Berger, a 29-year-old Austrian, started a hedge fund called the Manhattan Investment Fund Ltd. Following a strategy based on the overvaluation of the market, specifically the internet sector, Berger engaged in short selling. He immediately started to sustain losses but kept reporting large positive gains to his investors. This allowed him to raise over $350 million over a period of three years, while most short sellers kept on displaying negative performance figures.

The reality came to light at the beginning of the 2000; the Manhattan Investment Fund had lost more than $300 million, but Berger had failed to disclose these losses. His tricks were quite simple. The fund administrator used to calculate the fund's net asset value from daily statements sent by Bear Stearns Co. that summarized the securities held by Bear Stearns on the account of the fund. From September 1996 Michael Berger had started producing fictive statements from Financial Asset Management, supposedly another broker to the fund, and sent them to Bear Stearns. Bear Stearns used both statements to compute the net asset value, overstating the true value of the fund. As an illustration, the reported net market value for August 1999 was $427 million, whereas the true value was less than $28 million. As one might expect, the fund's auditor requested information from Financial Asset Management. Financial Asset Management forwarded the request to Berger, who simply responded to the auditors as if the information was coming from Financial Asset Management, again producing fictive reports and overstating assets.

Following the fund's collapse, several investors filed a lawsuit at the Securities and Exchange Commission (SEC) against Berger (the fund manager), Bear Stearns Co. (the prime broker), Deloitte and Touche Bermuda (the auditors) and Fund Administration Services (Bermuda), an Ernst and Young LLP affiliate (the administrator). Although the outcome is still unknown, the case resulted in closer monitoring by administrators, particularly when more than one broker is alleged to be holding the fund's assets.

In November 2000 Mr. Berger pleaded guilty to one charge of fraud, but he was never convicted. In August 2001 he changed his plea to one of "not guilty". A federal judge in New York first ruled on October 9, 2001 that Manhattan Investment Fund had to pay back $20 million to investors, representing fees collected. Since there is only about $240 000 left, it is hard to believe that investors would ultimately be in a position to receive some capital. Total legal costs are already above $9.5 million.

The case of David Mobley is even more striking. In 1993 he announced that he had created a "black box" timing tool to predict market movements and started a group of hedge funds (Maricopa Investment Fund, Ltd., Maricopa Index Hedge Fund, Ltd., Maricopa Financial Corporation, Ensign Trading Corporation, etc.). Until the end of 1999 he regularly provided statements to his investors showing stunning gains of above 50% per year without any losing year.

However, the performance was not audited, officially because it would be too easy to copy the proprietary trading system. The reality was that during these seven years, David Mobley used most of his clients' money to fund his lavish lifestyle and to actively invest in many of his own businesses as well as in local charities. All Mobley's close relatives held the fund's top positions, including his older brother William (president) and his 25-year-old son David Jr (vice president and head trader). Furthermore, it came out later on that David Mobley had a grand-theft indictment, was convicted of passing bad checks, made false representations on his application with the National Futures Association and had also previously declared personal bankruptcy.

Both Berger and Mobley headed up investment advisers that were not registered with the SEC through an exemption in the 1940 Investment Advisers Act. Conclusion: you get what you pay for.

Prime brokers' fees vary greatly, and obtaining comparable figures is usually hard, since there are different ways in which prime brokerage firms can be remunerated for services rendered. In addition, several prime brokers bundle their fees, so that circumscribing exactly what a fund pays for a particular service can be elusive.

The "soft dollars" concern

In the US, prior to 1975, brokerage commission rates were fixed at artificially high levels by the rules of various securities exchanges, so that brokers attempted to attract clients by offering them additional services, such as access to proprietary and third-party research. In 1975 Congress abolished fixed brokerage commission rates and introduced negotiated rates. Since then, with the emergence of prime brokers and the increase in competition, the popularity of "soft dollar" accounts has grown substantially.

"Soft dollars" and "hard dollars" refer to the payment of services by investment advisers. When the payment is made using the adviser's own funds, the industry talks of hard dollars. When investors subsidize these payments, the industry talks of soft dollars.

In a typical soft dollar arrangement, a hedge fund agrees to place a designated dollar value of trading commission business with a broker. In consideration for this promise, the broker provides the fund adviser with credits usually set as a percentage of the promised commissions. The adviser uses these credits to buy any third-party service (e.g. proprietary and third-party research, price and news delivery systems, portfolio management tools), and the broker pays the bill by canceling the appropriate number of credits from the fund's soft dollar account.

About one-third of all commissions in the US and around 10% in Europe are now soft. As the hedge fund industry continues to grow, the number of hedge funds using soft commission brokers is expected to grow in parallel, including particularly new hedge funds that need to focus their limited resources on asset gathering. However, there are two potential problems with soft dollars. First, the adviser may use the services he obtained through the soft dollar arrangement for purposes unrelated to the management of the accounts effectively paying for the brokerage service. Second, as a fiduciary, a hedge fund manager owes its clients undivided loyalty. The soft dollar agreement may conflict with a client's interest (e.g. a best execution policy) and therefore violates the investment adviser's fiduciary duty to his clients.

From an ethical viewpoint, investment advisers should not engage in activities that conflict with a client's interest. If they do, they should at least provide meaningful disclosure of such practices to their clients. Unfortunately, this is still wishful thinking for most of the hedge fund industry. The SEC has issued a negative report on soft dollar practices of broker-dealers, investment advisers and mutual funds, and has even settled charges for misappropriation of soft dollars from clients against Republic New-York Securities Corporation, a New York broker-dealer firm, and Sweeney Capital Management Inc., a San Francisco investment adviser. However, most hedge funds are not under SEC supervision.

ORGANIZATIONAL STRUCTURES

In addition to the complexity of their legal and operational structures, hedge funds also need to set up efficient organizational structures. In the following sections, we review the principal ones and describe their major advantages and disadvantages.

Side-by-side and master/feeders

In side-by-side structures, also called mirror funds or clone funds, several funds having identical or substantially similar investment policies invest in parallel in a group of cloned portfolios (Figure 4.2). These portfolios usually share a common investment adviser, portfolio managers and a custodian or administrator, and the cloning process essentially consists in facilitating bunched trades among the cloned funds and rebalancing cloned funds that have experienced different cash flows.

Mirror portfolios represent an effective solution to the problems inherent in reconciling inconsistent regulatory regimes, because each cloned portfolio maintains its distinct legal character and can implement individualized investment parameters. For instance, one clone could be structured as an FCP (*fonds commun de placement*) in one country, a second clone as a SICAV (*société d'investissement à capital variable*) in a second country, a third as a limited partnership in the US, and a fourth as a mutual fund in a fourth country. This would provide tax benefits for investors not subject to US tax laws.

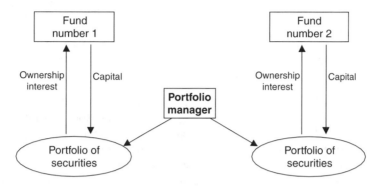

Figure 4.2   A typical side-by-side structure

The master/feeder structure (also known under the trademark Hub and Spoke or as a fund for fund, not to be confused with a fund of funds) is an efficient alternative to side-by-side funds. In this structure a series of funds (called feeders) sell their shares to investors under the terms of their prospectus and contribute their respective proceeds to another fund (called the master fund) rather than investing directly (Figure 4.3). The master fund has substantially the same investment objectives and policies as its feeders and will conduct all the investment activities. Each feeder participates in the profits and losses of the master fund according to its contributed capital. As one might expect, the flow of funds is reversed when an investor redeems his shares—the master fund makes a distribution to the feeder, which in turn pays back the investor. There are several advantages in using a master/feeder construction:

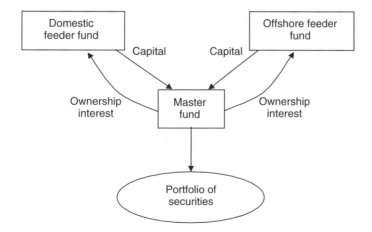

Figure 4.3   A typical master/feeder structure

- Since each feeder fund can have its separate identity, regulator, management, fee struct-ure and/or distribution channel, this allows several categories of investors to participate in the same investment strategy.
- It removes the burden of splitting trades or using average prices to allocate securities between several funds. In the master/feeder structure, all transactions are centralized in one place.
- It increases the critical mass of assets. This allows for a reduction in the number of transactions and reduces the trading costs. It also increases the collateral available for leveraged transactions, therefore yielding better terms for both feeders.

As an illustration of the first point, fund sponsors may find it desirable, for tax or any other reasons, to establish separate investment vehicles for US investors and foreign investors, respectively. Rather than establishing two separate investment vehicles (as is the case with the side-by-side structure), the sponsor may establish an offshore master fund with a domestic feeder for US investors and offshore feeders for foreign investors. Both feeders will yield exactly the same performance, regardless of the timing of inflows and outflows of capital. Another commonly used feeder is one for Japanese investors who want some form of hedging with respect to the yen.

The following disadvantages should be considered:

- Master/feeder constructions can result in a conflict of interests between onshore and offshore investors, for instance regarding the realization of capital gains or losses, or the payment of withholding taxes.
- Offshore investors and their feeders often have more favorable redemption terms than their onshore counterparts. When facing adverse market conditions, offshore investors may decide to redeem their shares, forcing the fund to realize losses and affecting the continuing onshore investors, who do not have the option to redeem.
- Due to the duplication of entities, master/feeder funds entail additional fees in terms of operations and organization. This will be negligible for large funds, but may signif-icantly affect small start-up funds.

An essential question in the master/feeder structure is where to establish the master fund, particularly onshore versus offshore. Offshore registration will eliminate the potential risk of being classified as an investment company and the necessity of blue-sky compliance, and will facilitate offshore financing from non-US lenders. Onshore registration will avoid dividend withholding for US investors in the domestic feeder, and will allow the fund to take advantage of existing US tax treaties. The final choice will therefore depend on the fund's strategy, assets and targeted investors.

Managed accounts

Several hedge funds offer managed accounts rather than fund shares to their largest clients, typically for accounts larger than $10 million. A managed account can be seen as a dedicated clone fund, but without any institutional structure. Operationally, it simply takes the form of an account opened by the client at a prime brokerage house. The fund manager gives orders to purchase and sell securities on behalf of the client, as if he were managing his own fund. The advantages for the client are full transparency and high liquidity, since the client receives daily reports from the prime broker about his position and can easily close his position within a few days.

Umbrella funds

Invented more than twenty years ago in Europe, the concept of an umbrella structure has become popular among hedge fund managers. An umbrella fund is simply a collection of subfunds with a common or central administration and brand (Figure 4.4). Each subfund has a separate investment policy and a separate portfolio of assets, and is run by a team of portfolio managers and analysts. A net asset value is calculated separately for each subfund, and shareholders are entitled only to the assets and earnings of the subfund in which they have invested.

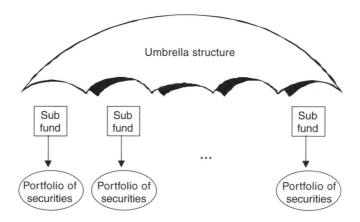

Figure 4.4   A typical umbrella structure

Umbrella hedge funds are tax-efficient, since investors can usually transfer shares from one subfund to another without creating a capital gain, which is taxable. Should investment objectives and needs change over time, investors in an umbrella fund can usually switch between the subfunds available, incurring reduced or minimal charges. They also provide fund managers with greater market proximity and quicker reaction to customer requests, as well as cost-effective sales within a standardized marketing concept.

Their danger is that under some regulations (e.g. British Virgin Islands) the rights of creditors against one of the subfunds would apply to all the assets of the fund vehicle, implying a potential risk of cross-liability for other subfund shareholders.

Multiclass/multiseries funds

Some hedge funds have a single portfolio of investments but issue different classes of equity to investors. This typically allows both distribution and accumulation shares to be offered, as well as for different expense charges to be applied, depending on the investor type, the amount invested and/or the redemption policy.

Another reason justifying the use of multiple shares is the fund's participation in the "hot issues" market. A hot issue refers to the securities of a public US offering that trade at a premium to their offered price immediately after public trading has started. According to the US National Association of Securities Dealers (NASD), certain categories of investors are restricted from participating in hot issues. Hedge funds have therefore the choice between staying away from hot issues, rejecting NASD restricted investors, or establishing a specific profit allocation procedure (e.g. separate brokerage accounts and independent verification) to isolate returns from hot issues and deny participation in hot issue profits to restricted investors. The latter of these choices is easy to implement with multiple shares.

Part Two
Hedge Fund Strategies

5

Introduction

The increasing investor interest in alternative investments has resulted in a phenomenal growth in the number of hedge funds available. Hundreds of traditional fund managers seeking higher wages have moved to the hedge fund industry and started their own funds. Several mutual fund management firms have launched hedge funds to serve their wealthiest clients and to preclude the defections of their best managers. Investment banks have aggressively hired the best academics to manage sophisticated hedge funds, and even commercial banks have followed the trend by creating and marketing funds of hedge funds.

The hedge fund industry represents 1–2% of global security markets. In relative terms, this is still quite small. However, in absolute terms, this means several thousand hedge funds are ready to welcome the assets of uninformed investors. And most of these funds are not allowed to advertise, cannot disclose performance results and must refrain from clearly positioning themselves on the hedge fund universe map. Consequently, for investors without much experience or time to devote to building their portfolio, selecting the right hedge fund seems an almost impossible task.

Nevertheless, the task of analyzing and comparing hedge fund performance is crucial. In comparison with other asset classes, hedge funds tend to display a high degree of heterogeneity. Although this often surprises investors, we believe it should be expected, at least for two reasons.

First, the term "hedge fund" just describes an investment structure. It does not represent an investment approach or even an asset class. Why then should we observe homogeneous behavior? To give an analogy, talking about hedge funds in general is like talking about vehicles in general, where vehicles would include bicycles, motorbikes, cars, trains, planes, etc. No one would compare a train and a bicycle in terms of speed limit, whereas similar comparisons are common for the performance of hedge funds. There are a large number of hedge funds comparing their performance to the S&P 500 to persuade investors that their hedge fund is better. Amusing, once we observe that they simultaneously claim to be noncorrelated with this index.

The second reason for the heterogeneity of hedge funds is that they are a skill-based industry. In a sense, each hedge fund manager is following a specific investment strategy, based on his proprietary tools and techniques, core competencies, specific expertise and experience. The uniqueness of the package is precisely what justifies the high performance fee. If hedge fund strategies were all alike and/or easy to replicate, hedge funds would turn into a commoditized investment product offered at a marginal cost, similar to mutual funds. Since this has not yet happened, there is no particular reason to expect two arbitrarily selected hedge funds to behave homogeneously.

Naturally, this heterogeneity in the hedge fund world may result in wide differences in investment returns and risks. These differences and their potential consequences need to be identified and explained before any asset allocation process can start. Fortunately, hedge fund returns are also driven systematically by market factors such as changes in credit spreads or market volatility, rather than only by the skills of individual managers. Relying on these factors may help in identifying homogeneous subgroups.

Clearly, the urge to classify the unruly tangle of hedge funds is irresistible. The goal is twofold: to compare the performance of a given hedge fund with that of managers pursuing the same strategy or a similar strategy; and to build representative indices to monitor the evolution of the industry or one of its divisions.

Several advisory firms have jumped on the bandwagon of measuring, monitoring and reporting the performance of hedge funds. Believing that investment objectives would be sufficient to provide a good surrogate for risk and return, these firms have identified dozens of different strategies, managed by some of the brightest and most sophisticated managers in the industry. Their initial intentions were certainly laudable, but the proliferation of hedge fund advisers has resulted in the absence of a real industry standard. Due to inconsistencies in the criteria of competing classifications, some hedge funds may be found in different category listings, despite identical fund category names that imply sameness. This is clearly misleading and unsatisfactory for end users. The time has come to begin taking "alternative" investing seriously and to start thinking about a new, rational and coherent approach to classifying hedge funds and their strategies.

This second part has a modest goal. It does not attempt to establish the ultimate hedge fund strategy classification, nor does it seek to exhaustively compare the pros and cons of the existing strategies. It adopts a more pragmatic approach.

First, it presents some of the tools that are used by hedge funds to implement their strategies. These tools include operations such as buying on margin and selling short, leveraging positions, and capturing arbitrage opportunities. Not surprisingly, all are considered rash by institutional investors and traditional money managers, but they are standard and essential in hedge funds.

Next come several hedge fund strategies, with the focus on how each one produces returns and controls risks. To simplify the analysis, I have arbitrarily decided to split the strategies universe into four broad categories: long/short, relative value/arbitrage, event-driven and directional.

The penultimate chapter in this part presents the major existing hedge fund indices; it compares their construction methodologies and their performance. Then the final chapter illustrates some of the major difficulties linked to the calculation of performance at the hedge fund level, as well as the practical solutions set up by most fund managers.

6

The tools used by hedge funds

Before going into detail about the various hedge fund strategies, I discuss the basic tools used to implement them: short selling, buying on margin, using derivatives, and leveraging. None of these tools is used in the traditional investment world, so most investors perceive them as being purely speculative and dangerous. As we will see, reality is more complex.

TWO TYPES OF TRANSACTION

Transactions using a cash account

The secret to successful investing—buy low and sell high—is one of the oldest pieces of investment advice on record. It sounds so simple that one could hardly argue with it. The profit simply equals the difference between the sale price and the purchase price. In terms of operations, the strategy involves two basic transactions, buying long and selling long at a later date, hopefully at a higher price.

Buying long

Buying long is the most common strategy, at least from an individual investor's perspective. A hedge fund buying long has some cash and simply exchanges it against a stock that he wants to hold (Figure 6.1). Once the transaction has been concluded, the hedge fund has no further commitment. It fully owns the stock.

Selling long

Selling long is simply the opposite of buying long. A hedge fund selling long has a stock that it no longer wishes to hold and simply exchanges it for cash (Figure 6.2). Once the transaction has been concluded, the hedge fund has no further commitment. It fully owns the cash.

Transactions using a margin account

Transactions using a margin account refer to the purchase or sale of securities relying on a credit extended to the hedge fund by a securities company (typically a brokerage firm). The securities company will use securities held in the fund's account as collateral for the loan. The collateral in this case is called margin and can be made up of cash, securities or other financial assets.

The two major margin transactions are *buying on margin* and *selling short*. Both are confusing for neophyte investors. While conventional security transactions involve two parties, the buyer and the seller, margin transactions involve a third party, the security lender. This is because both buying on margin and selling short imply borrowing an asset. When buying on margin, the hedge fund borrows some cash. When selling short,

Figure 6.1   Flows resulting from a long buy operation

Figure 6.2   Flows resulting from a long sell operation

the hedge fund borrows a security. In the following, we attempt to clarify the differences between these two strategies by looking at the detailed flows they generate.

Buying on margin

Let us start with the buying on margin transaction. Simply stated, a hedge fund buying on margin has no cash, but would like to buy a stock that it expects to appreciate in the future. It therefore borrows some money from a broker and exchanges it for the stock. Naturally, the broker will ask for some kind of collateral to secure the loan (Figure 6.3).

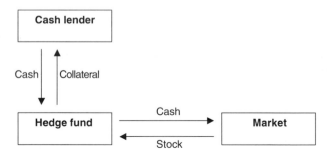

Figure 6.3   Flows resulting from initiating a buy on margin transaction

Later, once the hedge fund has enough cash, it will pay back the loan with interest, and receive back its collateral. The cash may come from the sale of the stock that was bought on margin, or from any other transaction (Figure 6.4). There are two basic reasons for a hedge fund to buy on margin:

- Trading on margin allows transactions to be conducted on a much larger number of shares than on a cash only basis. Indeed, the fund manager trades without fully paying for his purchase; he can buy or sell assets for a much higher value than the collateral amount. This results in leverage effects that we will discuss later on.
- Margin trade is a relatively easy and simple way of obtaining short-term financing to buy stocks that the fund could otherwise not afford to buy. In addition, margin loans charge lower interest rates than any other type of loan (e.g. bank loans), with very flexible repayment terms.

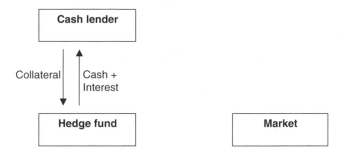

Figure 6.4   Flows resulting from closing a buy on margin transaction

Brokerage firms also find advantages in margin trading; they make money on margin accounts from the interest they charge on the loans and also from the higher commissions on the larger transaction sizes that leverage allows. Since margin loans are always secured by collateral, the default risk is limited. The residual risk is only that the collateral plus the securities held in the margin account decline in value to a point where they are worth less than the loan balance.

This raises two new problems. First, which type of collateral should be accepted? Lenders prefer stable collateral, such as cash or T-bonds, while hedge funds prefer using securities (including the shares they purchased on margin) to secure their loans. Second, what happens if, for any reason, the collateral fluctuates in value and becomes insufficient to cover the loan? To answer these questions and to prevent the excessive use of credit to purchase securities, most regulatory bodies and exchanges have enacted rules that govern margin trading. Whatever the country, the rules for margin trading usually cover three dimensions: minimum margins, initial margins and maintenance margins.

To open a margin account with a broker and before any trade takes place, investors must deposit a *minimum margin*. This first rule is targeted at small investors and is not really relevant to hedge funds, because the corresponding amount is small. For instance, in the US, the National Association of Securities Dealers (NASD) and the New York Stock Exchange (NYSE) now impose a minimum of $25 000 in cash or fully paid securities in order to open a margin account. It used to be only $2000 in the early days of e-trading. Of course, amounts differ in other countries and markets.

The *initial margin* requirement represents the minimum amount of funds investors must put up to purchase stocks on credit. For example, with a 50% initial margin requirement, the maximum amount of credit an investor can obtain from his broker to purchase stocks is 50% of the stocks' value. An investor willing to buy one share of common stock valued at $100 per share must do so with at least $50 of his own funds or additional collateral.

In the US, the Federal Reserve sets the initial margin requirement as part of its monetary policy. Since 1934 it has changed 23 times, and even at one time reached a full 100% payment. The current rate, set in 1974, is 50%. As a matter of comparison, the initial margin requirement in the 1920s was usually around 10%. This resulted in high levels of margin debt and unstable stock prices; it created perfect conditions to fuel the stock market crash in 1929.

The *maintenance margin* represents the minimum amount of funds investors must have on their margin account to maintain an open position. It is expressed as a fixed percentage of the total market value of the securities held on margin. For instance, in the US, the

NASD and the NYSE impose a minimum 25% maintenance margin requirement on their customers. Whenever this requirement is not met, the broker must issue a *margin call* to request additional collateral from the hedge fund. The fund manager can respond either by selling a part of his open position, or by depositing additional cash and/or new securities, until the maintenance margin requirement is met.

These buy on margin trading rules may be updated whenever market conditions justify such action. Brokerage houses must follow them and may establish more stringent requirements if they so wish. In practice, brokers request higher margins than the minima set by regulators and exchanges, but further differentiate their margin requirements by individual stocks and by the trading behavior of their customers.

Buying on margin: a detailed view

Let us now illustrate the mechanisms of buying on margin. Consider the case of a hedge fund buying on margin 10 000 shares at $10 each. Its broker applies the 50% initial margin and the 25% maintenance margin requirements.

The current market value of the purchase is $100 000. In accordance with the 50% initial margin requirement, the hedge fund would need to deposit collateral or safe securities worth $50 000 into its margin account. The broker would lend the remaining $50 000 and execute the purchase transaction. The hedge fund account would then appear as follows:

Assets		Liabilities	
Long stocks	100 000	Debit balance	50 000
		Equity	50 000

The debit balance consists of the amount due to the broker, plus interest on this loan amount, while equity is defined as the difference between the current market value of the long stocks and the debit balance. The fund's equity covers exactly 50% of the market value of the stocks held long. The basic accounting equation is

$$\text{Equity} = \text{assets} - \text{liabilities}$$

For margin investing, this equation changes slightly to

$$\text{Equity} = \text{market value of long stocks} - \text{debit balance}$$

The equity will therefore change as the current market value of the long stocks rises and falls and as interest is added to the debit balance. For the sake of simplicity, let us ignore interest and focus on stock price movements.

If the stock price goes up, say to $12, the value of the assets will increase to $120 000. On the liability side, the corresponding gain would be credited to the fund's equity. The fund's equity would then cover 58.33% (70 000/120 000) of the market value of the stocks held long. The hedge fund account would appear as follows:

Assets		Liabilities	
Long stocks	120 000	Debit balance	50 000
		Equity	70 000

If the stock price goes down, say to $8, the value of the assets will decrease to $80 000. On the liability side, the corresponding loss would be attributed to the fund's equity, which would fall to $30 000. The fund's equity would then cover 37.5% (30 000/80 000) of the market value of the stocks held long, which is still acceptable since it is above the minimum maintenance margin. The hedge fund account would appear as follows:

Assets		Liabilities	
Long stocks	80 000	Debit balance	50 000
		Equity	30 000

To trigger a margin call, the value of the hedge fund's equity needs to equal 25% (the maintenance margin) of the value of open positions. The corresponding threshold stock price can be calculated as

$$\text{Equity} = \text{long stock value} - \text{debit balance}$$

$$= 25\% \times \text{long stock value}$$

That is

$$(10\,000 \times \text{stock price}) - 50\,000 = 0.25 \times 10\,000 \times \text{stock price}$$

Solving yields a stock price equal to $6.6667. If the stock price reaches this threshold value, the hedge fund account will appear as follows:

Assets		Liabilities	
Long stocks	66 667	Debit balance	50 000
		Equity	16 667

The fund's equity then covers exactly 25% (16 667/66 667) of the market value of the stocks held long. Any additional drop in the stock price would further reduce the equity value, leading to insufficient coverage of the position. The broker would have to issue a margin call—a request to increase the amount of equity.

As an illustration, let us say that the stock price falls to $6 per share. The hedge fund account appears as follows:

Assets		Liabilities	
Long stocks	60 000	Debit balance	50 000
		Equity	10 000

If the fund decides to respond by depositing an additional amount of $5000 in its margin account, the cash deposit will be applied against the debit balance. The new account status will look like this:

Assets		Liabilities	
Long stocks	60 000	Debit balance	45 000
		Equity	15 000

The equity finances exactly 25% of the long stock position. However, any subsequent decrease in the stock price will prompt a new margin call from the broker. It would therefore be safer for the fund manager to deposit an amount larger than $5000, or to liquidate some shares.

Note that if the hedge fund manager ignores the margin call, the broker may sell a portion of the long stock position to bring the equity coverage into an acceptable range. The fund will be held responsible for any losses incurred in the stock during this process.

Selling short

Short selling is instrumental in a growing number of sophisticated investment models and vehicles. It can significantly expand the range of strategies available. In particular, it allows a hedge fund to profit from expected downturns in the market, which is not feasible with traditional cash account strategies.

Conceptually, selling short is just the opposite of buying on margin. A hedge fund selling short has no stock, but would like to receive some cash. Since the buyer of a stock will demand delivery on the settlement date, the hedge fund therefore borrows the stock for a fee and sells it for cash. Usually, the stock lender will demand some collateral to secure the loan, typically the cash proceed from the short sale (Figure 6.5).

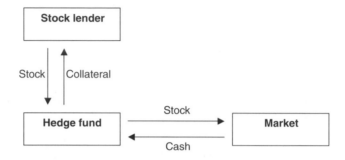

Figure 6.5   Flows resulting from initiating a short sale transaction

Since the lender now holds cash collateral for the market value of his stock, he has in essence turned his stock position into cash while still retaining ownership. This implies that there are in fact two stock positions in the market: a "real" position occupied by the buyer of the stock sold short, and a "phantom" position held by the entity lending the stock to the short seller. As a consequence, the stock borrower is responsible for any corporate action with respect to the stock lender. For instance:

- If the corporation whose shares are held short pays a dividend, the hedge fund must pay the amount of the dividend to the stock lender.
- If the corporation whose shares are held short splits two-for-one, the hedge fund owes the lender twice as many shares.
- If the corporation whose shares are held short spins off, the hedge fund is short two securities: the original security and the spin-off security.
- If the corporation whose shares are held short makes a rights offering, the hedge fund must go into the marketplace and deliver the rights to the lender.

Technically, selling short does not require an investment. It just requires collateral. Later the hedge fund will buy back the stock on the market and return it to the stock lender. It will also pay the renting fee and receive back its collateral (Figure 6.6). A gain will be realized if the security is repurchased for less than it was originally sold. A loss will be incurred if the repurchase price is higher than the sale price.

Securities lending is therefore nothing more than the practice of long-term holders of securities making their securities available for a small fee to sellers in the market, on

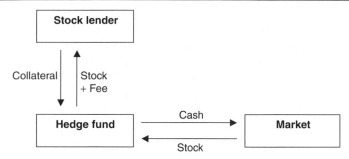

Figure 6.6   Flows resulting from closing a short sale transaction

condition that equivalent securities be returned to the lender at a future date. It had its roots in the United States in the 1960s but only really gained momentum in the seventies and eighties with the liberalization of regulations that had previously hampered the practice. Today, available official data suggest that the US market size of open securities loan positions is close to $2 trillion.

The group of share lenders will typically contain long-term investors, but also financial firms such as banks and broker-dealers acting as either agent or principal. Indeed, share lending has turned out to be a business in its own right, much more than an extension of firm's basic inventory management process. As an illustration, several firms borrow securities with the expectation that others will shortly be prepared to pay more to borrow them, and most prime broker contracts allow the lending of securities held in their margin accounts.

Another source of share lending are institutional investors, such as pension funds and insurance companies, which are willing to generate additional revenues on their long-term strategic holdings and are motivated by the desire to reduce custody fees for their portfolios. Although the returns on securities lending are relatively small, particularly for the most liquid securities, a few basis points may matter in a field as highly competitive as asset management. Here are three points to note:

- The standard stock lending practice is that the securities must be returned on demand. This creates a risk for the hedge fund, which might be compelled at the most disadvantageous time to replace borrowed securities previously sold short. If the hedge fund manager is unable to find an alternative lender, he may have to repurchase the shares in the open market at prices significantly higher than those at which the securities were sold short. This situation is called a short-squeeze. To help hedge funds assess the probability of a squeeze, brokers sometimes reveal the identity of the stock lender.
- A broker-dealer needs to explicitly obtain the right to borrow securities from one customer before lending them to another.
- Most brokerage firms require a stock to be trading above a given price level to be margined (typically $5 to $7 per share). Low-cost shares are therefore almost impossible to borrow.

Clearly, in addition to the renting fee, the collateral plays a crucial role in inducing lenders to lend their shares. To secure the transaction, the hedge fund must maintain in its margin account more money than necessary to buy back the stock at any time. This amount is referred to as margin.

Although short selling is regarded in some jurisdictions as a useful mechanism to improve liquidity, once again, regulators have stepped in. Their aim is twofold: to ensure the minimum margins are sufficient to prevent the collapse of lending institutions; and to prevent short sellers from feeding sell orders into a declining market and further eroding prices. In the US, for instance, the Federal Reserve (Regulation T) requires an initial margin deposit equal to the value of 50% of the short sale price, plus 100% of the proceeds of the short sale. And the NYSE and NASD maintenance margin requirement is 100% of the proceeds of the sale, plus 30% of the closing value of the security. In addition, short selling must be recorded in a short account, that is, a subaccount of the margin account, which is marked to market at the end of each trading day.

Finally, to prevent an uncontrolled decline in the market price of a security based on short selling, several countries require short sales on exchange-listed securities to be executed only on a plus-tick (last trade higher than the previous different price) or a zero-plus-tick (last trade the same price as the previous up-tick price) situation. The tick condition that a security is trading in at any given time is indicated on quotation terminals by a + or − next to the symbol. On the consolidated ticker tape, a + next to the price indicates a plus tick or zero-plus tick from previous trades. This is intended to prevent the short selling of stock that is already declining in price so as to avoid sending the stock price into a free fall.

Selling short: a detailed view

Let us now illustrate the mechanisms of selling short. Take the case of a hedge fund selling short 10 000 shares at $10 each. Its broker applies the 150% initial margin and the 130% maintenance margin requirements.

The current market value of the short sale is $100 000. First, the hedge fund would have to check with its broker if the securities are available for borrowing. Then, it would need to deposit safe securities worth $50 000 into its margin account, and leave the proceeds of the short sale as collateral. A less conservative broker could allow the fund to purchase risky securities with the short sale proceeds. The hedge fund account would then appear as follows:

Assets		Liabilities	
Cash	100 000	Short position	100 000
T-bills	50 000	Equity	50 000

The short position represents the market value of the short stocks, while equity is defined as the current market value of the assets minus the current market value of the short stocks.

If the stock price climbs from $10 to $11, the (absolute) value of the short position increases. Since the value of the assets does not change, the corresponding loss is absorbed by the equity. The new hedge fund account would appear as follows:

Assets		Liabilities	
Cash	100 000	Short position	110 000
T-bills	50 000	Equity	40 000

The new equity amount represents 36.36% (40 000/110 000) of the value of the short position, which is still above the 30% maintenance margin. Note that the equity is computed as a percentage of the short position, because this is what changes when market prices change.

One may wonder which stock price will create the first margin call. With a 30% maintenance margin, we have

Assets − market value of short position = 0.30 × market value of short position

That is

$$\$150\,000 - (10\,000 \times \text{stock price}) = 0.30 \times 10\,000 \times \text{stock price}$$

Solving for the stock price and rounding yields $11.54. As an illustration, let us say that the stock price climbs suddenly to $12 per share. The hedge fund account appears as follows:

Assets		Liabilities	
Cash	100 000	Short position	120 000
T-bills	50 000	Equity	30 000

The equity value represents 25% of the short position—a lower amount than the minimum maintenance margin. The broker will issue a margin call. If the fund manager decides to respond by depositing an additional amount of $6000 in the fund's margin account, the cash deposit will be added to the cash amount held on the assets side and to the equity on the liabilities side. The new account status will be as follows:

Assets		Liabilities	
Cash	106 000	Short position	120 000
T-bills	50 000	Equity	36 000

The equity represents exactly 30% of the short stock position. However, any subsequent increase in the stock price will prompt a new margin call from the broker. It would therefore be safer for the fund manager to deposit an amount larger than $6000. Alternatively, the fund manager may also use some of the cash to buy back some securities and return them to the stock lender, thereby reducing his short position.

Note that if a hedge fund ignores a margin call, its broker may use the cash to buy back and close the short stock position or to bring the equity coverage into an acceptable range. The fund will be held responsible for any losses incurred in the stock during this process.

Using prime brokers can significantly improve the buying on margin process. A hedge fund dealing with a single prime broker can have open lines of credit, and assets purchased on margin can be used (partly) as new collateral. Furthermore, when the fund wants to sell a stock short, it needs to borrow it from a brokerage, which itself needs to have the stock to lend. Since prime brokers are usually large institutions, they are more likely to have access to the required shares. The most efficient structure is one where the asset management and loan management activities are split between specialists in each respective field.

DERIVATIVES

Financial derivatives have changed the face of finance by creating new ways of understanding, measuring, managing and transferring risks. Unfortunately, the tremendous growth of the financial derivatives market and reports of major losses associated with derivative products have resulted in a great deal of confusion about these complex instruments.

The term "derivatives" refers to a large number of financial contracts in which a payment or delivery depends on the value of an underlying asset, interest rate or index. A derivatives contract therefore derives its value from the value of another asset, hence its name. In this sense, although most investors do not perceive them as particularly risky or speculative, simple bonds can be seen as derivatives because they derive their price from interest rates.

The most interesting feature of derivatives is that they are not limited by the market size of an underlying commodity or instrument. In particular, most derivatives positions are closed before maturity and never result in physical delivery. In some cases (e.g. weather and inflation derivatives), the underlying instruments do not even physically exist. Consequently, the size of any given derivatives market depends on the willingness and frequency of counterparties to enter into offsetting transactions to exchange financial risks.

Financial derivatives are not new. They have been around for years (Box 6.1). However, they became popular after the abandonment of the Bretton Woods system of fixed currency exchange rates by the United States and other industrial nations in 1973. The resulting fluctuations in foreign currencies followed by inflationary oil price shocks and wild interest rate fluctuations created a large demand for new hedging financial instruments. In 1973 the Chicago Board Options Exchange (CBOE) opened for business. This was the first time that an exchange itself acted as counterparty rather than being just the venue where the contracts were negotiated.

But trading options without a model is like wandering in the desert without a compass. Fortunately, the same year, Fischer Black, Myron Scholes and Robert C. Merton provided the first reasonable mathematical model for the pricing of options. The methodology that they introduced has since been expanded for use in pricing a wide variety of derivative instruments and contingent claims.

Box 6.1 THE FIRST DERIVATIVES USERS

Possibly the most ancient surviving story of two parties entering into a contingent claim contract can be found in Aristotle's writing. Aristotle mentions that Thales, the Greek philosopher from Miletus, used to forecast in the stars the quality of the next season's harvest. He then made option-like agreements with olive-press owners in Chios and Miletus, in which he undertook to pay them some money up-front in exchange for later exclusive access to their olive presses if needed. When the harvest came, all producers suddenly needed these olive presses and paid Thales high prices to use them. In a sense, Thales bought call options on the olive presses to speculate, while the olive-press owners were selling call options in order to secure their annual income. While this story is almost certainly apocryphal, there is no doubting its antiquity. This in itself would tend to indicate that option-like agreements were common in Ancient Greece.

The second well-known instance of derivatives occurred during the tulip mania that swept the Netherlands in the seventeenth century. Tulips originated in Turkey and were first introduced to Holland in 1593 by a famous botanist, Carolus Clusius. Rare and beautiful, they rapidly became a status symbol. Wealthy aristocrats and merchants vied with one another to buy them. Several hobbyists created intriguing colors by breeding the plants. And speculators actively traded existing and nonexisting bulbs.

Buyers had to place orders with money up-front for delivery at a later date, which is nothing else than a forward contract. This in turn led to a trade in "tulip futures," where notarized paper orders were traded at the Amsterdam Bourse and the East India Company for higher and higher prices pending delivery of the bulbs themselves. This forced tulip retailers to buy call options and futures to protect themselves against sudden price rises imposed by their suppliers. Finally, growers also bought put options and sold futures contracts in order to make sure they would receive good prices for their bulbs.

Around 1636 the tulip speculation reached its peak. Some single tulip bulbs sold for 4600 florins, roughly the price of 460 sheep. In February 1637, tulips crashed. People who thought of themselves as extremely rich were reduced to poverty overnight.

In general, derivatives markets are split into a regulated exchange-traded sector, and an unregulated over-the-counter sector. Exchange-traded contracts are transacted through a regulated exchange. They are standardized and cannot be specially tailored to specific situations. They have three major advantages:

- The exchange or its clearing house acts as the counterparty for each transaction, which ensures sufficient liquidity and reduces default and settlement risks.
- All contracts are marked to market on a daily basis by margin calls and margin requirements, so that default risk is minimized.
- As a result of the standardized maturities, contract sizes and delivery terms, all contracts are entirely fungible.

Fungibility means that contracts dependent on identical terms are totally interchangeable. This allows buyers and sellers to close out a position through a closing transaction in an identical contract.

Contracts identified as over-the-counter (OTC) are negotiated between two parties, typically an end user and an investment bank. They may be customized to address the end user's specific exposures, but carry legal risk and credit risk. Legal risk is usually reduced when using International Swaps and Derivatives Association (ISDA) master agreements that define the general terms and conditions for trading. The actual trades are documented in confirmation sheets, which are then filed as attachments to the master agreement. They are not marked to market, and if the end user wishes to modify or reverse the transaction, he must renegotiate the change with the original dealer, which is not always feasible or efficient.

Today, the most common types of exchange-traded derivatives are forwards, futures and options:

- *Forwards* are over-the-counter agreements to purchase or sell a given quantity of an underlying asset at a fixed price determined at the outset, with delivery or settlement at a specific future date. The settlement can be made by physical delivery or by a net cash payment.

- *Futures* are exchange-traded contracts similar to forwards. They are marked to market on a daily basis, via postings to the parties' margin accounts maintained at a futures broker. They are most commonly settled through an offsetting 'reversing' trade rather than by delivery of the underlying item or cash settlement.
- *Options* are over-the-counter and exchange-traded contracts that give their purchaser the right, but not the obligation, to buy (call option) or sell (put option) a given quantity of an underlying asset at a specified price (strike price) during or at the end of a specified period of time. Since an option is a right and not an obligation, the purchaser of an option has to pay the seller (writer) of the option a premium. The premium will vary depending on several parameters, such as the moneyness of the option (i.e. where is the strike price with respect to the underlying asset price), the volatility of the underlying asset, the interest rates, and the time period over which the option can be exercised.

Of course, there are many variations and combinations of the contracts described above. For instance:

- *Swaps* are over-the-counter contracts to exchange cash flows as of a series of specified dates. These cash flows are often based on an agreed notional amount and agreed fixed and floating interest rates. They can be synthetically recreated by combining several forward or futures contracts.
- *Caps and floors* are over-the-counter interest rate options. An interest rate cap will compensate the purchaser of the cap if interest rates rise above a predetermined rate (strike rate); an interest rate floor will compensate the purchaser if rates fall below a predetermined rate (strike rate).
- *Swaptions* are options to enter into swaps.

It is essential to understand that, unlike spot transactions, all derivatives transactions are settled in the future. The initial amount needed to enter into a derivatives contract varies from nil (over-the-counter products) to the initial margin deposit (exchange-traded contracts). This is exactly where their risk lies.

LEVERAGE

The term "leverage" is cited so often and in connection with so many different types of financial arrangements that it is easily misunderstood. Simply stated, leverage denotes an investment that is higher in value than the available equity capital. Leveraging is an aggressive investment strategy because it magnifies both profits and losses. For instance, say a hedge fund invests $1000 of its equity capital in a stock that rises by 10%. The fund earns $100—a 10% return.

By contrast, if the fund had borrowed $10 000 and invested it along with its original $1000, it could have earned $1100—a 110% return, before factoring in the borrowing costs. Now, what if the same stock dropped by 10%? If the fund had invested $1000, it would have lost $100, i.e. 10%, and its shares would be worth $900. But if the fund had borrowed another $10 000 and put it into the stock, the total investment of $11 000 would have fallen to $9900. Instead of losing $100, the fund would have lost $1100 plus the borrowing costs—more than its initial equity capital. Clearly, although leverage creates an opportunity for increased income and gain if the market moves on expected lines, it also creates certain risks if the market trend is contrary to the expectation.

Leverage can take several forms:

- Explicitly borrowing external funds to invest more or sell short more than the equity capital.
- Implicitly borrowing through a margin brokerage account. Margin accounts allow the hedge fund to use the brokerage firm's money to buy additional shares.
- Using financial instruments (such as repurchase agreements, futures and forward contracts and other derivative products) to establish positions by posting margins rather than the full face value of the position.

When using leverage, the amount borrowed is treated as a negative asset allocation. It actually becomes a liability of the portfolio as opposed to an asset. For instance, when a hedge fund borrows an additional 25% against its portfolio holdings, it has a 25% liability that must be paid for, but also has 125% of the original capital to allocate to investments. Of course, the operation only makes sense when investments offer a higher rate of return than the cost of borrowing.

Leveraged investing is often dismissed as gambling. I personally disagree with this assertion. In my opinion, leverage plays a positive role in the financial system. It results in greater market liquidity, lower credit costs, and a more efficient allocation of resources in the economy. It allows younger people to invest more in equities, rather than waiting until they are older and have sufficient resources to do so. And why, one might ask, is borrowing to buy a new home a perfectly natural thing to do, while funding one's future through an investment loan is apparently another story?

The unpopularity of leverage can be traced back to the numerous disasters encountered by overleveraged speculators. Once an initial investment is financed by leverage, the new asset (e.g. the stock) can be used as collateral for another loan. The only leverage constraint is therefore the degree to which banks and broker-dealers will finance additional trades. Albeit overcollateralization may become an eventual constraint in the same way that a reserve requirement on deposits limits the creation of new money, this credit exposure is subtle and a function of the mark to market exposure and liquidity rather than an outright loan. For instance, Long Term Capital Management's counterparties had placed too much reliance on their collateral agreements. Because they did not take these risks into account, they granted LTCM huge trading lines in a variety of products, and LTCM took advantage of those lines to achieve its exceptional degree of leverage (Box 6.2).

Box 6.2   LONG TERM CAPITAL MANAGEMENT

Long Term Capital Management (LTCM) was indeed a very particular hedge fund. John Meriwether, a legendary Wall Street figure that had to leave Salomon Brothers after its 1991 Treasury bonds trading scandal, founded LTCM in 1994. It allied 16 partners, including Nobel prize winners Myron Scholes and Robert C. Merton, the former Federal Reserve vice-chairman David Mullins, and a group of superintellects who had tamed the business of money management with the most elegant models from academia.

The LTCM strategy consisted in taking advantage of small price differences in nearly identical bonds. In particular, the fund placed bets on the euro convergence. These were extremely profitable until 1997, and the equity capital grew from $1 billion to more than $7 billion. However, to maintain the high return on investment, LTCM returned $2.7 billion of equity capital to its investors, while maintaining the size of its positions. This resulted in a significant increase of leverage, and therefore of risks.

The Russian "debt restructuring" in August 1998 plunged LTCM into deep water. The fund was basically playing on convergence between various pairs of government bonds and other credit instruments, while credit spreads jumped sharply on the market. The cost for LTCM was $550 million on August 21 alone. A call for new investors on September 2 did not provide any additional capital. But portfolio losses accelerated. The fund had also sold several long-term US equity options, but the sudden increase in equity market volatility led to another $500 million loss on September 21. Bear Sterns, the fund's prime broker, started issuing margin calls. They remained unanswered.

As evidenced later by the President's Working Group on Financial Markets (1999), the situation was scary. One dollar invested with LTCM in March 1994 was worth about 10 cents in December 1998. LTCM had used its $2.2 billion in capital as collateral to establish bets on about $125 billion in securities, half in long positions and half in short positions. It then used those securities as collateral to enter into off balance sheet transactions to a total notional amount of more than a trillion dollars. Among these were futures ($500 billion), swaps ($750 billion) and options, as well as other over-the-counter derivatives ($150 billion). In total, the fund had more than 60 000 trades on its books and a leverage of more than 500 : 1. This situation might not have been considered problematic if LTCM had not faced liquidation. Of course, the leverage before the crisis was "only" about 25 : 1. According to LTCM partners, the fund was targeting a 1% return on assets, leveraged 25 times, which would result in a 25% return. This leverage was less than the 34 : 1 leverage common at securities firms and comparable to the 24 : 1 leverage common at money-center banks. But one could also argue that money-center banks have much fewer volatile assets.

So big was its portfolio, so leveraged and so intertwined with so many institutions on Wall Street that liquidating the fund would have blown up the world's financial system. In addition, LTCM could have had recourse to Cayman bankruptcy law protection, which does not allow for an immediate liquidation of the collateral. The Ferrari had suddenly become an Oldsmobile. Fortunately, the New York Federal Reserve finally stepped in and organized a bailout. After two days of rancorous debate, a consortium of 14 securities firms and banks agreed to invest $3.6 billion for a 90% equity stake in the fund. Month after month, the consortium took back its money, plus a modest profit, and closed shop. To prevent another collapse, several banks scaled down their proprietary trading desks and imposed higher margin requirements in lending to hedge funds. It seemed as if Wall Street was learning from its losses.

However, since December 1999 John Meriwether has been managing a new relative value hedge fund, called JWM Partners. Also based in Greenwich, Connecticut, it manages $850 million and pursues bond arbitrage strategies similar to those used by

LTCM, but with leverage limited to 20 : 1. Most of Meriwether's partners in LTCM joined JWM Partners, with a few notable exceptions. Robert C. Merton returned to Harvard. Myron Scholes started advising Oak Hill Platinum Partners, a hedge fund affiliated to Texas billionaire Robert Bass and whose founding principal is Chi Fu Huang, a renowned derivatives modeler and fellow alumnus of LTCM. And James McEntee and Gregory Hawkins joined Caxton Corporation to set up a relative value bond hedge fund. The world is definitely small.

After the debacle of LTCM, it is hard to maintain that leverage is not dangerous. Nevertheless, to illustrate its benefits, let us look at the annual return of three investment strategies: investing in LTCM, investing in an index fund mimicking the S&P 500, and buying the same index fund on margin using a 2:1 leverage (Figure 6.7). In the 2:1 leverage we assume that interest is paid on debit balances at the rate of 10%.

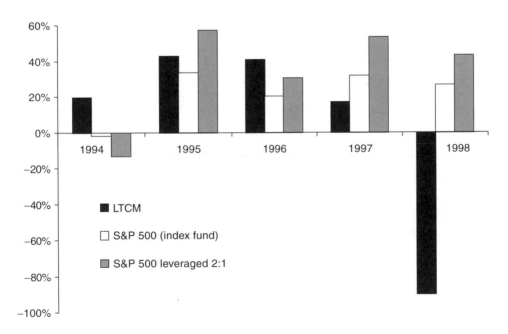

Figure 6.7 Comparing annual returns on three strategies

As can be seen, while LTCM averaged a 29.62% return between 1994 and 1997, the indexed fund achieved an average of 20.17%, and the leveraged strategy 28.67%, net of interest. If we include the year 1998 (which is obviously unfair), the average return drops to −22.35% for LTCM, and rises to 21.44% for the index fund and 31.47% for the leveraged strategy. Had we taken the risk of leveraging our index fund 50:1, as did LTCM, our returns would have been nothing short of spectacular.

7

Long/short strategies

Long/short strategies involve the combined purchase and sale of two securities. Their roots are to be found in the original Alfred Winslow Jones hedge fund model and, despite their age, they are probably still today among the most popular hedge fund strategies. In addition, they form the basis of more specialized strategies, such as arbitrage and relative value, that we will come to later.

MECHANICS OF INVESTING

Let us first illustrate the mechanics of long/short investing with a simplified example detailing all the steps of the process. We consider a hedge fund that has a hypothetical initial equity capital of $1000 to invest. Its manager has identified two potential investments; according to him, stock A is undervalued, while stock B is overvalued. The manager therefore wishes to engage in a long/short strategy to profit from both mispricings. The process can be structured as follows:

1. The fund manager deposits the $1000 at a custodial prime broker.
2. The fund manager starts by purchasing $900 worth of stock A that he perceives as being undervalued. He pays for these shares with the fund's equity capital, so that his situation with respect to his broker will be a long position in stock A for $900 and a long cash position of $100. So far, this is very similar to a traditional investment fund's position.
3. The manager sells $900 worth of stock B that he perceives as being overvalued. This increases his cash balance by $900. However, since the fund does not own any B shares, this is a short sale. It is therefore necessary to borrow these shares from a third party in order to deliver them to the buyer.
4. The prime broker arranges to borrow $900 worth of the required shares from a stock lending institution or a large institutional investor. The share lender will typically ask for a collateral (for instance the $900 that the fund just cashed in) as well as for a rent (say a 1% fee, i.e. $9 at the end of the lending period).
5. The $900 collateral will only secure the current value of the borrowed shares. If the share price increases, the hedge fund will actually have to return shares worth more than its collateral. The prime broker will therefore retain a liquidity buffer, typically about 10% of the invested capital, to cover the potential losses and mark-to-market requirements on the short position. Then, if the share price increases, the liquidity buffer will have to dry up first before the fund receives a margin call.

It should be clear from Figure 7.1 that the key element in the long/short position is the ability to sell short—the ability to borrow shares at a reasonable cost. The choice of a good prime broker can be of great help here and may also influence the amount of collateral that the hedge fund needs to supply.

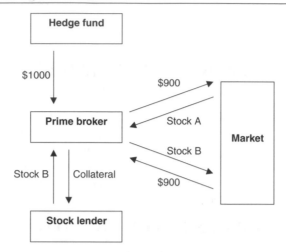

Figure 7.1 Flows in long/short investing

It should also be clear that long/short investing results directly in leverage effects. At the end of the process, our fund's assets consist of $900 of stock A (long), $900 of stock B (short), plus $900 as a collateral and $100 as a liquidity buffer. That is, a total of $2800, compared with its initial $1000 of equity capital.

SOURCES OF RETURN

Traditional long-only strategies have only one source of return—the appreciation of the purchased stock. Long/short strategies, in contrast, have four potential sources of return:

- The spread in performance between the long position and the short position. Ideally, the stocks on the long side should appreciate in value while the shorted stocks should decrease in value. This is why long/short investing is often referred to as a "double alpha" strategy. The term "alpha" is commonly used for the outperformance of an investment. In long/short investments, one alpha may come from the long side (the undervalued stock appreciates in value) and the other alpha may come from the short side (the overvalued stock depreciates in value).
- The interest rebate on the proceeds of the short sale that are used as collateral. The lending fee is usually taken as a haircut (that is, as a deduction) on the interest on the proceeds paid to the fund, but this haircut is usually extremely small for most liquid shares.
- The interest paid on the liquidity buffer that remains as a margin deposit to the broker. The interest rate is usually very close to the Treasury bill rate.
- The spread in dividends between the long position and the short position. Stock borrowers need to reimburse stock lenders for dividends paid on borrowed stocks, while they cash in dividends on the long position. Although the difference may be small, it should be taken into consideration when calculating the total return.

Consequently, a short position in long/short investing can serve three purposes:

- It can represent a bet on an overvalued asset that should decrease in value in the near future.
- It can be used to hedge the market risk of the long position. This is typically the case when the short position is made up of futures contracts while the long position consists of stocks.
- It collects interest on the short amount.

The strategies used to identify long (undervalued) and short (overvalued) positions vary enormously. Some funds use purely quantitative factor-driven models or fundamental value approaches, while others prefer qualitative or judgmental approaches. Many long/short funds focus on a specific industry, country, or capitalization range.

A remarkable property of long/short investing is that the manager may be partly wrong in his choice of securities, but the position may still be profitable even though both the long and the short positions decline or appreciate in absolute terms. Indeed, what matters is that the long position outperforms the short position on a relative basis. This explains why long/short funds have the ability to perform well in bear markets as well as bull markets.

Let us return to our example. We assume a one-month holding period. The stock A share price increases from $10 to $11 and pays in addition a $1 dividend at the end of the month. The stock B share price increases from $10 to $10.25 and pays in addition a $0.25 dividend at the end of the month. The interest rate on margin accounts and collateral is 0.5% per month.

	Rate (%)	Profit/loss ($)
Variation in A shares (including dividends)	20	180.00
Variation in B shares (including dividends)	5	45.00
Interest on collateral	0.5	4.50
Interest on liquidity buffer	0.5	0.50
Renting fees	0.1	−0.90
Total profit		139.10

At the end of the month, the hedge fund's profit, based on a $900 long position and a $900 short position, would be $139.10. As a proportion of the initial capital, which was only $1000, the total return is therefore 13.91%.

One could object that a long-only portfolio invested equally in shares A and B would have achieved a return of 12.50%, very close to the return of the long/short equity position. So why bother? This argument misses two important points.

First, in our example the manager was wrong on the short side: stock B can be considered a winner, with a monthly performance of 5%. Suppose the stock B share price had fallen by 5% over the month, the gain on the long/short position would be as follows:

	Rate (%)	Profit/loss ($)
Variation in A shares (including dividends)	20	180.00
Variation in B shares (including dividends)	−5	45.00
Interest on collateral	0.5	4.50
Interest on liquidity buffer	0.5	0.50
Renting fees	0.1	−0.90
Total profit		229.10

The return now looks much more favorable, at 22.91% for the long/short position, versus 7.5% for the equally weighted long-only portfolio.

Second, the long/short portfolio has a much lower risk than the long-only position. The reason for that is simply the diversification of risks. There is a good chance that securities A and B are somehow positively correlated, so that grouping them in a long-only portfolio will only result in a limited diversification. The long/short portfolio, on the other hand, mixes a long position in A and a short position in B. Since A and B are positively correlated, the correlation between the long and the short positions will be negative. This enhances the risk diversification. The phenomenon is further strengthened if securities A and B are strongly correlated. Then the two positions in the long/short portfolio will have a large negative correlation, which will result in higher risk reduction through diversification. This clearly shows why, to diversify risk, long/short hedge fund managers prefer to take positions in highly correlated securities.

Figure 7.2 shows the set of portfolios that can be created by combining two stocks called "positive" and "negative." The "positive" stock has a positive 20% expected return and 30% volatility. The "negative" stock has a negative 3% expected return and 20% volatility. The correlation between the two stocks is 0.5, the overnight deposit rate is 4.5% per year, and the lending rate to borrow shares is 0.50% per year. We consider two possible strategies. The first (continuous line) corresponds to long-only portfolios. The second (dotted line) corresponds to various mixes of long "positive" and short "negative" positions. Clearly, the long/short strategy provides a much better risk/return trade-off, mostly because of the negative correlation between the long position and the short position.

RISKS AND DRAWBACKS

Five downsides

- A long/short fund trades in a much larger amount than its initial capital, which means the overall costs compared to the initial capital are usually high. In our example the fund would face trading costs on a $1800 position, plus the borrowing costs for $900 worth of shares. To reduce these costs to an amount comparable to the long-only position, the manager would need to reduce the size of each position to $450.
- The values of the long position and the short position will usually vary over time, meaning that some rebalancing may be necessary to face margin requirements and avoid significant drops on the liquidity buffer.
- Although investing in equities, the fund manager does not capture the equity risk premium, nor can he offer the long-term upside potential of equity investing.

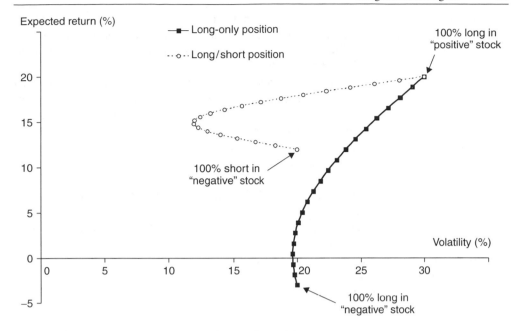

Figure 7.2   Comparing long/short and long-only positions

- The fund will generally lag in a bull market.
- Some exchanges require selling short to be done only on an up-tick—when the last traded price is higher than the previous one. In a bearish market, this may significantly delay the trading of short positions.

Net market exposure

Note that long/short equity hedge fund managers often maintain net positive or negative market exposures. For instance, in the long/short portfolio that we structured in the previous example, although the position was $900 long and $900 short, it was not necessarily market neutral. Everything depends on the sensitivity of the two stocks with respect to the market, which is measured by a statistical coefficient called beta. If the betas of the two stocks are not equal, the overall portfolio will have a small residual degree of market exposure.

MARKET NEUTRAL INVESTING

An interesting variant of the long/short strategy is the market neutral strategy. It aims at balancing long and short positions to ensure a zero or negligible market exposure and consequently a performance pattern that is independent of market movements. The term "market exposure" should be taken in a broad sense here, because there are usually several market factors that may be neutralized. A fund may be neutral to a specific exchange rate, a stock index, a series of interest rates, etc. As more factors are hedged away, the opportunity set for the manager to add value is reduced. In theory, a perfectly hedged portfolio should yield the risk-free rate, minus transaction costs. In practice, since the portfolio is not hedged against some residual factors, the strategy will yield returns slightly above the T-bills, but with much less risk than unhedged positions and with a very low correlation to the market. Note that several market neutral fund managers tend to use leverage to magnify the performance.

Choosing the right factors to hedge and hedging them correctly are therefore crucial to the results of the strategy. For instance, let us consider a portfolio that is long technology stocks and short an equal amount of utilities. The resulting portfolio may appear on paper as being market neutral, but this is just an illusion. Most of the risk is concentrated in two sectors, technology and utilities, so the combination of long and short positions effectively hedge some market risk, but this is minor with respect to the residual risk. Indeed, to be market neutral, the characteristics of longs and shorts should match precisely, and the fund should only contain securities whose relationship is proven and established. A good illustration of this is the pair trading strategy—the combination of long and short positions that trade in the same market, are from the same industry and from the same economic sector (Box 7.1).

Market neutral investing has a major disadvantage with respect to other long/short strategies. It requires an increased number of transactions to maintain the position hedged. These transactions are costly, and they have potential consequences in terms of undesirable tax effects.

Box 7.1   MARKET NEUTRAL OR SECTOR NEUTRAL?

In May 2000 ABN Amro Asset Management launched its first hedge fund, the ABN Amro Europe Neutral Fund. Relying on its in-house team of global analysts, the Irish-based fund categorizes itself as a "market neutral pan-European equity hedge fund." Its major particularity is that it combines long and short positions to offset market risk within sectors. For instance, if the fund purchases an industrial stock because it is expected to outperform, it must simultaneously sell another industrial stock that is expected to underperform. The overall result is therefore a sector neutral fund.

8
Arbitrage and relative value strategies

We now turn to the arbitrage and relative value strategies, which are also very popular among hedge funds. Unfortunately, I believe there is no more confusing name than the term "arbitrage," at least for someone with an academic background. Strictly speaking, an arbitrage is a risk-free trade that does not require any cash outflow and results in an immediate profit and no future losses. The typical example of an arbitrage is the simultaneous purchase and sale of the same security on different markets at different prices. By buying low and immediately selling high the same underlying asset, one makes an instantaneous profit without taking any risk. For the sake of simplicity, we have neglected here all the delivery and settlement risks.

However, in the world of hedge funds, "arbitrage" often has a different meaning. An arbitrage is a term used rather loosely to describe a financial transaction or strategy that seeks to profit from a price differential perceived with respect to related or correlated instruments in different markets. It also involves the simultaneous purchase of an instrument on one market and the sale of the same or a related instrument on another market. However, the resulting position is usually not risk-free, but is often a play on factors other than the market risk of the original position. As an illustration, consider the following examples of arbitrage transactions:

- A corporate bond combines interest rate risk and credit risk in a single package. A hedge fund buying the corporate bond and selling short Treasury bonds with similar characteristics (coupon rate, maturity, etc.) would be hedging its interest rate risk, but it would still be exposed to the credit risk of the corporate issuer. Its position is therefore not risk-free. Nevertheless, its strategy would be categorized as fixed income arbitrage, or possibly as credit arbitrage.
- A hedge fund buying 1-year Treasury bills and selling short 30-year Treasury bonds is typically betting on an increase in the slope of the yield curve in the near future. Lower short-term rates will result in higher Treasury bill prices, and higher long-term rates will decrease the value of long-term Treasury bonds. However, its position is not risk-free, because interest rates could move in the opposite direction. Nevertheless, its strategy would be categorized as yield curve arbitrage.

When correctly examined, most strategies called arbitrage strategies are in fact nothing more than directional spread bets. They attempt to exploit irregularities or discrepancies in the relative pricing of closely related securities, based on the premise that these irregularities should disappear over time. The essential point is therefore to realize that arbitrage does not necessarily imply freedom from risk, or guaranteed profits. In particular, the key to arbitrage when combining long and short positions is the fungibility of two positions. With fungibility, a pure arbitrage can take place. Without it, the corresponding strategies may entail some risk. As an illustration, Long Term Capital Management used to buy Danish bonds and sell German bonds. In this case the Danish bonds are not fungible with

German debt. If the market perceives more credit risk for the Danish bond, the spread will widen and the position will sour.

Nevertheless, most of the arbitrage and relative value hedge funds are rather conservative. Their aim is to deliver a "risk-free rate plus something" payout, with low volatility and no correlation with traditional markets. As we will see throughout this chapter, most of these funds are in fact long/short funds or even market neutral funds, but they tend to specialize in particular niches such as convertible arbitrage and fixed income arbitrage.

CONVERTIBLE ARBITRAGE

Convertible arbitrage funds attempt to profit from mispricing of convertible securities and/or expected trends in factors influencing convertible securities prices.

Convertible bonds in simple terms

Convertible securities are fixed income instruments issued as either debt or preferred stock. They give their holders fixed coupon/dividend payments and cash redemption at maturity, as well as the right to "convert" them into a fixed number of shares of common stock. These shares are typically shares of the issuer, but occasionally they are shares of another company. The latter is likely to happen when a company chooses to dispose of its stake in another company by issuing a convertible. Of course, if a holder decides to convert his convertible into shares, he gives up the right to any further coupon and redemption payments from the bond.

The exact terms of the conversion are set forth in the bond indenture. The most important one is the *conversion ratio*; this is the number of shares into which a fixed amount of bond (face value) may be converted. For instance, in the US, a conversion ratio of 10 means that $1000 face value can be exchanged for 10 shares of common stock. Alternatively, one may use the *conversion price*, which is the face value of the bond divided by the number of shares each bond is convertible into. It remains fixed during the entire lifetime of the bond.

Convertibles are hybrid securities in the sense that they simultaneously exhibit features of several instruments. A convertible bond can be seen as debt, since it pays its holder a regular coupon until maturity, and then repays its face amount. Like any other debt security, it ranks senior to equity in case of default, and its value depends on prevailing interest rates. A convertible bond can also be seen as equity, because its holder has the right to convert the face amount of the bond into shares. Conversion becomes attractive as soon as the quoted share price exceeds the conversion price. Finally, a convertible bond can also be seen as an option to exchange a bond against a share. This option is granted to the convertible bondholder, who can decide if and when he wishes to convert.[1] Note that there are often several other options embedded in a convertible, such as *call provisions*, which allow the issuer to call back the convertible issue at a fixed price, and *put provisions*, which allow the bondholder to require the issuer to redeem the convertible issue at a fixed price.

At maturity, convertibles are worth either their cash redemption value or the market value of the shares into which they are convertible, whichever is the greater. Before maturity, things are much more complicated. The valuation requires a fairly elaborate pricing model and the identification by the holder of an optimal conversion policy. Both

topics are far beyond the scope of this book and the interested reader should consult the
original research by Ingersoll (1977) and Brennan and Schwartz (1977, 1980). However,
I will try to indicate the reasoning behind these models.

The value of a convertible bond as a function of the stock price can be represented
as shown in Figure 8.1. The value is always bounded below by conversion value and
straight bond value:

- *Conversion value, or parity*, is the market value of the stock position obtained if the
  bond is converted immediately. It is usually quoted as a percentage of the par value.
  This value constitutes a lower bound because investors would otherwise purchase the
  bond and convert it immediately, cashing in the difference as a pure arbitrage profit.
  Obviously, the conversion value will change as the stock price changes.
- *Straight bond value, or bond floor*, is the price of a nonconvertible, but otherwise
  equivalent corporate bond. This value constitutes a lower bound because it only prices
  purely the fixed income aspects of the convertible bond and neglects all the upside
  equity potential. Note that since we are talking about corporate bonds, credit risk
  matters in the bond floor pricing.

In addition to these lower bounds, the price of a convertible bond should include the
time value of its embedded option—the option to convert. This option is usually of an
American type; that is, it may be exercised at any time until expiration. Its value—and
therefore the convertible bond value—will depend on both the time remaining to maturity
and the volatility of the underlying stock. This results in four potential stages in the life
of a convertible bond:

- *Distressed*: when the stock price is very low, the issuer's ability to finance its debt
  obligations is called into question, and the convertible security is considered distressed.
  This corresponds to area 1 in Figure 8.1, with parity between 0 and 40% of the face
  value.
- *Bond proxy*: when stock prices are low, the conversion is unlikely. The exposure to
  the equity upside will remain small or even negligible, so that the bond floor matters

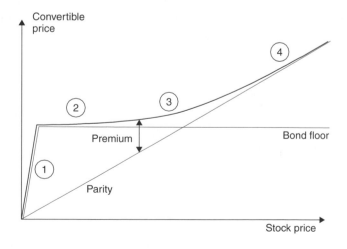

Figure 8.1 The four stages in a convertible bond

more. This corresponds to area 2 in Figure 8.1, with parity between 40% and 80% of the face value. Such convertibles are said to be "out of the money."

- *True convertibles*: when stock prices are close to break-even, the option to convert starts being valuable. This is area 3 in Figure 8.1. Parity is typically between 80% and 120% of the face value, and the convertible is said to be "at the money."
- *Equity proxy*: when stock prices are very high, the conversion is very likely and it is solely conversion value that matters. Parity is typically above 120% of the face value, and the equity premium is less than 10%. This corresponds to area 4 in Figure 8.1.

As an illustration, let us consider the case of Telewest Communications, one of the leading broadband communications and media groups in the UK, providing cable television, telephone and internet services to homes and businesses. On June 30, 2000 Telewest issued a 5-year US dollar convertible bond with a 6% coupon paid semiannually. The denomination was $1000 and the conversion ratio was 228.436 shares per bond; that is, the conversion price was $4.378 per share.

Although the convertible bond was quoted in US dollars (USD), the underlying stock was quoted in British pounds (GBP). On September 14, 2001 the stock price was quoted at GBP 0.3525 per share, and the exchange rate was $USD1 = GBP0.6806194$. The conversion value was therefore equal to $0.3525 \times 228.436/0.6806194 = \$118.31$. This conversion value corresponds to $1000 face value—11.831% of the face value of the convertible bond.

On September 14, 2001 the Telewest convertible bond was quoted on the market at 60.93% of its face value. This represents a 415% premium over the conversion value. On the same date, Telewest was facing a credit spread of 1700 basis points above the London inter-bank offered rate (Libor). The bond floor was 60.54% of the face value, and the yield to maturity 21.528%. This allowed the bond to be classified as a high-yield convertible bond.

In practice, convertible bonds often have specific features that make them hard to value, at least for inexperienced investors. These features include exotic clauses such as the conversion into a time-varying combination of shares and cash or reset features that allow the conversion price to be changed. There may also exist provisions for the issuer to call back the convertible if the underlying share price or the average underlying share price over some period is above a certain barrier, Pricing such bonds is probably the toughest of one-dimensional pricing problems. It combines the difficulties of bond pricing, stock pricing, barrier option pricing and American option pricing.

Basic arbitrage of convertibles

Convertible securities are generally undervalued relative to their theoretical value. There are three reasons. First, the majority of convertible issuers are rated below investment grade, which makes them suitable only for a limited set of investors and significantly reduces their liquidity on the market. Second, several convertible issues are small in size and analysts do not necessarily follow them. This is confirmed by the observation that the degree of undervaluation usually increases as the market capitalization decreases. Finally, there is some evidence that markets for different types of securities, such as stocks and bonds, are not closely integrated. Investors tend to prefer a security whose type is clearly identified, and discount securities such as convertibles can change type several times during their life.

Given this mispricing, most convertible arbitrage trades are implemented by combining a long position in the convertible and a short position in the underlying stock. The long position captures the underpricing and the short position reduces or offsets as much underlying equity exposure as practically possible. The combination maximizes the probability of profiting from the price discrepancies while not being dependent on the evolution of the underlying stock price.

The key parameter in this strategy is called delta. It is the equity sensitivity of the convertible bond, in the sense that it measures the bond's price sensitivity to movements in the share price. Mathematically,

$$\text{Delta} = \frac{\text{change in convertible bond price}}{\text{change in stock price} \times \text{conversion ratio}}$$

Saying for instance that a convertible bond with a $100 face value and a conversion ratio equal to one has a delta of 52% means that a $1 change in the underlying stock price will result in a $0.52 increase in the convertible bond price. Consequently, a long position in such a convertible bond could be hedged against stock price variations by selling short 0.52 shares. By doing this, a $1 change in the stock price will result in a $0.52 gain on the convertible bond, which is offset by a $0.52 loss on the short stock position. Practitioners say that they are delta hedged or delta neutral.

If we consider again our Telewest issue, its delta on September 14, 2001 was 21.21% and its conversion ratio 228.436. This means that a long position in the convertible bond could be hedged by a short position in 48.45 shares (21.21% of the 228.436 shares).

Some insight into delta can be gained from a graphical analysis (Figure 8.2). Delta can be represented as the slope of the tangent drawn on the convertible price curve at a given share price. In practice the delta of a convertible bond is influenced by the conversion ratio and the moneyness of the option embedded in the convertible. In particular, it will change with time and with the underlying stock price variations. This implies that the size of the short position will need to be adjusted dynamically to ensure that an effective delta hedge is maintained. As the stock price increases and the embedded option moves more into

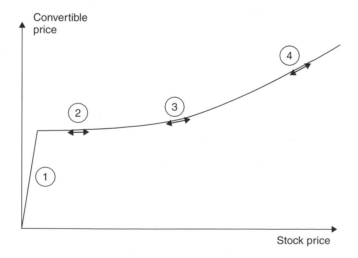

Figure 8.2   Delta as the slope of a tangent drawn on the convertible price line

the money, the convertible bond becomes more equity sensitive, so the arbitrager must adjust the hedge by selling short more shares. Conversely, as the stock price declines and the option moves out of the money, the arbitrager must reduce the hedge by buying back some shares. This corresponds to delta hedging in options terminology.

Hedge fund managers also monitor other sensitivity parameters. Here are the most important:

- *Gamma* is the expected move in delta for a one-point movement in the conversion value.
- *Vega* is the expected points move in the convertible price in response to a one basis point move in the volatility of the underlying stock or the volatility of interest rates.
- *Rho* is the expected points move in the convertible price in response to a one basis point movement in interest rates.
- *Theta* is the expected points move in the convertible price over one day.

These sensitivity parameters are usually small with respect to delta. For example, in the case of our Telewest bond, gamma was 0.222, vega was 0.005, rho was 0.019 and theta was 0.033. Hull (1989) is an excellent technical reference on how to compute these sensitivities and how they vary.

As a general rule, convertible hedges will typically make money if the expected volatility increases (long vega position) or if the stock price increases significantly (long gamma position). The reason is that delta is a linear approximation that is only valid for small variations of the underlying stock. The delta hedge will break out for large price movements, because the convertible is obviously not linearly related to the stock price. However, the convexity effect plays in favor of the arbitrager. If the stock price increases by a large amount, the convertible bond price should increase more rapidly than the losses on the short position. And if the stock price decreases by a large amount, the convertible bond price should decrease less rapidly than the gains on the short position. This provides a hint that profits can be realized on the hedged position if the volatility of the underlying stock increases.

However, volatility gains are just the icing on the cake. The major sources of profit are elsewhere. First, the convertible bond position pays a regular coupon, which is cashed in by the arbitrager. Second, the short stock position generates interest income on the sales proceeds. And third, the mispricing of the call option embedded in the convertible relative to the hedging instruments is captured as soon as it becomes fairly valued.[2] By adding a bit of leverage to this, hedge fund managers can often offer an attractive, stable and regular performance.

A more advanced arbitrage strategy

Delta hedging protects the arbitrager against any decline in the value of the underlying equity. However, the strategy is not a true arbitrage, because it still carries some risk. First, there are potential interest rate variations. Because the convertible bond is indeed a bond, the position will lose value if interest rates rise. Arbitragers may hedge this risk by using interest rate futures, forwards and swaps. Second, there are credit risk and credit spread changes. If the underlying stock price falls steeply, the convertible will be evaluated as a straight bond and reach its floor price. However, this is precisely the situation where the underlying company's financial situation may have deteriorated,

Convertible market

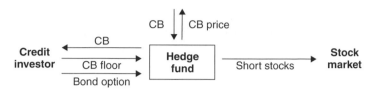

Figure 8.3 Typical flows in an asset swap

meaning larger credit spreads, a higher discount rate and therefore a lower bond value. This point is particularly important for unsecured, subordinated convertible bonds issued by firms with high volatility of earnings, higher leverage, more intangible assets and higher growth rates.

Until recently it was almost impossible to hedge the credit risk of a specific issuer. Nowadays, to hedge the credit risks of their books, convertible arbitragers may use an asset swap. This is a generic term for a transaction that actually repackages a convertible bond into an equity option component and a fixed income component. The "credit seller" will keep the equity option, while a "credit buyer" will acquire the fixed income component. This unlocks the theoretical value of the convertible bond and allows for the implementation of arbitrage strategies.

Although asset swap arrangements can be technically complex, the basic idea is very simple. The process can be summarized in two steps (Figure 8.3):

1. A hedge fund manager identifies an undervalued convertible bond. He verifies with his prime broker that the underlying stock can be borrowed. If so, he purchases the convertible bond, which generally bears a fixed rate coupon and an option for its holder to convert into equity. In terms of risk, the manager is now exposed to rising interest rates, falling equity prices, and widening credit spreads.
2. The fund manager enters into an asset swap with a credit investor. This swap usually consists of two transactions:

    — The fund manager sells the convertible bond to the credit investor at a large discount with respect to its market price. The selling price is typically set at the bond floor value; that is, the present value of the bond's future cash flow (coupons and repayment) discounted at Libor plus a fixed credit spread.
    — In exchange for the discount on the sale price of the convertible bond, the credit investor gives the fund an over-the-counter bond option. This option allows the fund to purchase back the convertible bond at a higher fixed strike price. The higher strike price is also typically set at the present value of the bond's future cash flow (coupons and repayment) discounted at Libor plus a fixed recall spread. The recall spread is tighter than the one used for calculating the selling price to discourage rapid turnover of position and to deliver a minimum return to the credit buyer. The swap terms often allow for a call at par value at the maturity of the bond.

Before going any further, we need to verify that each party has only the desired exposures. After the asset swap, the hedge fund still has the equity upside exposure inherent in the convertible bond by virtue of owning the call option but is no longer exposed to the risk of widening credit spreads. This option is useless as long as the convertible bond is out of the money, but will allow participation in the upside potential of the stock. The good news is that if the convertible bond was underpriced on the market, the floor value (at which the bond was sold to the credit investor) was correctly priced. This means that the hedge fund now holds an option whose final purchasing price was much less than its theoretical value. To capture the price difference, most hedge funds will simply delta hedge this option until its maturity. Note that the hedge fund's loss is limited to the option premium, whose strike price depends on the credit spread initially agreed in the asset swap. On the other hand, the hedge fund can benefit if the credit trades to a tighter spread by calling the initial asset swap and simultaneously establishing a new one at a tighter spread.

After the asset swap, the credit investor holds a synthetic straight callable bond. The term "synthetic" is used because the position is not a straight callable bond, but it behaves exactly as a straight callable bond. He is solely interested in betting that the credit quality of the issuer will improve in the future. He has no equity exposure, but faces credit risk and interest rate risk. Several credit investors will eliminate the interest rate risk by entering into another swap, in which they will pay a fixed rate equal to the convertible bond coupon and receive a floating rate, typically Libor plus a spread. This leaves them with only the credit exposure of the original convertible bond.

Now, let us consider what can happen at expiration. There are five basic cases to be considered:

- If the convertible bond matures out of the money, the hedge fund manager lets his option expire. The credit investor will redeem the convertible bond and will be repaid at par by the issuer.
- If the convertible bond matures in the money, the hedge fund manager will call back the convertible bond and pay the par value to the credit investor. The hedge fund manager will then exercise the convertible bond and receive the parity value, which is higher than his payment to the credit investor.
- If the convertible bond is called out of the money by the issuer, the hedge fund manager lets the option expire. The credit investor will be repaid at the call price by the issuer.
- If the convertible bond is called in the money by the issuer, the hedge fund manager will call back the convertible bond and pay the agreed call value to the credit investor. The hedge fund manager will then exercise the convertible bond and receive the parity value, which is higher than his payment to the credit investor.
- If the issuer defaults, the hedge fund manager lets his option expire. The credit investor will receive the recovery value of the convertible bond, if any, from the issuer.

In practice, asset swaps may take several alternative forms, but the basic principles remain the same: the asset swap allows a hedge fund to split a convertible into its core components and to maintain equity exposure to the company while reducing credit and interest rate risk.

Risk control

In terms of risk, when correctly implemented and monitored, a convertible arbitrage strategy is expected to yield low-volatility returns, typically equal to a few hundred points above the T-bill rate. However, leverage is often used to magnify returns and may significantly increase risk. Convertible arbitrage has four major dangers:

- *Event risk* may be a sudden dividend payment or capital distribution; even when they are delta hedged, convertible arbitragers may face abrupt variations in their hedge ratios that are costly to follow.
- *Liquidity risk*: the liquidity of convertible bonds is considerably lower than the liquidity of equivalent straight bonds, and bid/ask spreads can widen significantly; in addition, the short sale position is also subject to stock-borrow risk.
- *Screw clauses* state that bondholders converting into shares will not be paid the accrued interest on their bonds by the issuer.
- *Cleanup clauses* state that if a certain percentage of bonds has been converted into shares, the issuer may force conversion of the rest.

Portfolios of convertible arbitragers are typically diversified across a large number of issues from different issuers and different industries in order to reduce these risks. Research is also a critical step to assess the risk of default.

A market overview

Convertible bonds have existed for more than 150 years in the United States, where the first issues were used to finance railroad companies. However, the practice of convertible arbitrage is much more recent. Initially set up as a niche business for dedicated proprietary trading desks in large investment banks, convertible arbitrage has become a popular strategy within the alternative investments world.

Hedge funds, ironically, are now more important than ever as the primary liquidity providers to convertible buyers and sellers. According to some estimates, convertible bond arbitrage trades currently represent more than half of the secondary market trading in convertible securities at the institutional level, and US hedge funds are said to own around 30% of all convertible bond issues outstanding in the US.

The Japanese convertible bond market is the largest in the world. It consists essentially of a large number of very small domestic issues listed and traded on the Tokyo stock exchange, as well as a series of larger issues on the European convertible market. According to market participants, Japanese convertible bonds exhibit the most pronounced mispricing, primarily because of the presence of numerous retail investors and unsophisticated institutional investors. It is therefore not surprising that Japan has become the focus of many hedge fund managers and investors.

The US convertible bond market comes second in size. It is essentially structured as an over-the-counter market animated by market makers. Most issues come from young technology and telecom issuers. They are issued under SEC Rule 144A (private placement), which means they are not fully registered and can only be purchased by qualified investors at issue. The mispricing is slight, because of the presence of more sophisticated investors.

The European convertible market is now booming, but it has not yet reached its full potential. Unlike the situation in the US, most European convertibles are issued by investment grade names. Most of the European issues are from large companies, with market capitalization in excess of $10 million, versus only 25% in the US.

Finally, the Asia-Pacific region is also becoming an important source of convertible issues, mostly driven by the asset swap community. Pricing errors are quite large in some countries, due to the unavailability of adequate stock borrowing facilities.

FIXED INCOME ARBITRAGE

Fixed income arbitrage attempts to profit from observed relative pricing inefficiencies between related fixed income securities and/or expected changes in intermarket spreads. It typically involves taking long and short positions in interest rate sensitive securities to neutralize exposure to interest rate fluctuations.

Fixed income arbitrage strategies rely heavily on mathematical and/or statistical valuation models. Interest rate sensitive securities fluctuate in accordance with yield curves, call covenants, expected cash flow, credit ratings, volatility curves, etc., and therefore often generate pricing anomalies that dynamic, sophisticated arbitragers can capture. The generic types of fixed income arbitrage trades include yield curve arbitrage, corporate versus Treasury yield spreads, municipal bond versus Treasury yield spreads and cash versus futures. Let us describe some of these.

Yield curve arbitrage

Yield curve arbitrage involves taking long and short positions at various points (maturities) on a yield curve, typically a Treasury bond curve. The goal is to profit from unusual patterns and/or expected future deformations of the yield curve. For instance, during the first half of 2000 there were several forecasts of a diminishing supply of long bonds as a consequence of the US Treasury's plans to use the growing budget surplus to buy back the national debt. This created an excess number of buyers for these very long bonds. Consequently, the price of US Treasury bonds was such that the yield on a 30-year issue was lower than the yield on a 10-year issue, resulting in a negative spread (Figure 8.4).

This is clearly an abnormal pattern because longer-maturing securities are usually considered more risky and therefore investors should demand a higher yield for a 30-year bond than for a 10-year bond. In addition, both 10-year and 30-year T-bonds are

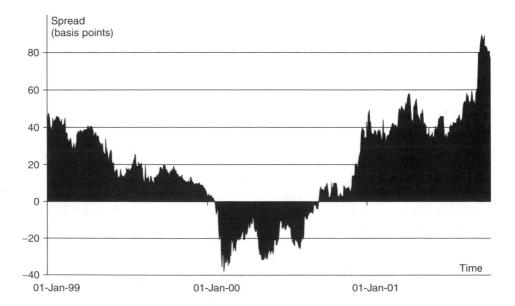

Figure 8.4   The 30-year/10-year US T-bond spread

extremely liquid, so the liquidity argument seems hard to sustain. An arbitrager would therefore typically buy the lower priced 10-year bonds and short sell the higher priced 30-year bonds. His bet is that the 10-year yield will go back below the 30-year yield. The outcome of the strategy does not depend on the absolute level of the interest rates, but just on the relative level of 10-year and 30-year rates.

If we look at what happened in this particular case, we can see that the markets did indeed end up by pushing the 30-year yield above the 10-year yield. However, the time it took to make the correction, about 8 months, is surprisingly long. This constitutes a hint that "arbitrage" profits may take some time to materialize. As an illustration, there are other anomalies that have still not been rectified, such as the spread between the 30-year and the 20-year T-bond yields, which has been negative for more than six years.[3]

Corporate spreads

Another popular fixed income arbitrage strategy focuses on corporate spreads. Corporate bond spreads measure the difference in yields between corporate bonds of various credit grades and Treasury bonds of comparable maturity. This spread is essentially attributed to the credit risk of corporate bonds, although there has never been a consensus as to how much of the corporate/Treasury yield spread is actually due to credit risk and how much to other factors such as liquidity and call features. Nevertheless, several authors (e.g. Alessandrini 1999; Pendergast 2000) claim there is some form of predictability in corporate spreads, and this opens the door to speculative strategies that capitalize on this predictive power.

A spread that is often considered is the difference between the yield on BAA corporate bonds, the lowest investment grade corporate bonds, and 10-year Treasuries. As can be seen from Box 8.1, this spread has widened dramatically in recent years and has become very volatile.

Depending on his forecast concerning the evolution of a particular corporate spread, an arbitrager will take a long position and a short position in a particular corporate bond and T-bonds (or T-bond futures). If he expects the spread to widen, the arbitrager will be long the T-bond and short the corporate bond. If he expects the spread to narrow, the arbitrager will be short the T-bond and long the corporate bond. What matters is not the absolute level of the interest rates, but just the level of the spread.

Spread arbitrage may also take the form of relative value trades between two sectors of the fixed income markets. For example, European telecom debt trades at historically high credit spreads to European Treasuries, given investor fears that Vodafone, Mobilcom, etc., are overpaying for new license auctions in the UK (Box 8.1).

Box 8.1   THE LUCENT TECHNOLOGIES AND ALCATEL MERGER

Fixed income arbitrage hedge funds closely watch the creditworthiness of companies as a potential source of profits. Over recent months the telecommunications sector has been the subject of intense scrutiny, since default rates of telecom companies are expected to peak over the forthcoming years. An interesting illustration of fixed income arbitrage deals were the merger talks between the French equipment maker Alcatel SA and its US rival Lucent Technologies. If successful, the merger was expected to strongly benefit Lucent's debt, which totaled about $3.6 billion and was at the bottom end of investment grade (BBB−). In contrast, Alcatel would probably have lost its A− rating on its $4.6 billion debt.

Merger talks between Alcatel and Lucent were confirmed on April 30, 2001. Merger arbitragers jumped on the deal, immediately followed by fixed income arbitragers. The fixed income arbitragers typically played the convergence by buying Lucent Technologies bonds and selling short Alcatel bonds. Consequently, Lucent's 5 1/2 bonds due in 2008 gained 7.57 cents on the dollar, from 67.66% to 75.23%, and kept on increasing in the following days (see figure). Alcatel's bonds remained relatively stable. But about a month later, the two companies issued a statement announcing that they had ended merger talks. Within minutes, Lucent bonds plummeted and came back to a more reasonable quote of 66.9%.

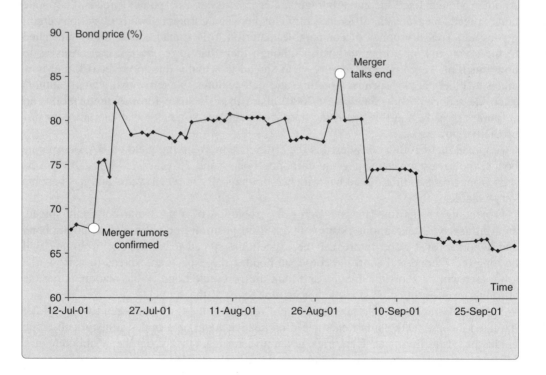

Another common arbitrage strategy focuses on the Treasury/Eurodollar spread (TED spread). The TED spread is defined as the difference between yields on US Treasury bills and those on Eurodollars (certificates of deposit in US dollars in a non-US bank). It reflects investors' views of the relative credit quality of the US Treasury and of the highest-quality international banks. It typically widens during times of international banking stresses, such as a spike in the Libor or the collapse of a major bank.

The TED spread arbitrage is usually implemented using Eurodollar futures contracts. It is a pure bet on the direction of movements of a futures price related to the interest paid on a Eurodollar deposit. For example, assume that the rate of a US T-bill is 94.20 (implied discounted rate of 5.80%) and the Eurodollar future[4] is trading at 93.10 (implied Eurodollar deposit rate of 6.90%). In this case the TED spread would be $94.20 - 93.10 = 1.10$, and would be quoted at 110. An arbitrager expecting the TED spread to widen to 125 would buy the TED spread—he would buy T-bill futures and sell Eurodollar futures. An arbitrager expecting the TED spread to contract to 100 would sell the TED spread—he would sell T-bill futures and buy Eurodollar futures.

Suppose the arbitrager expects the TED spread to widen. Say he buys 10 September T-bill contracts at 94.20 and sells 10 September Eurodollar contracts at 93.10. Later, the spread widens to 126, with the September T-bill contracts at 93.95 and the Eurodollar contracts at 92.70. The arbitrager then sells 10 September T-bill contracts and buys back 10 Eurodollar contracts. His profit is 40 basis points $\times$ \$25 $\times$ 10 contracts = \$10 000, and his loss is 25 basis points $\times$ \$25 $\times$ 10 contracts = \$6250, leaving a net profit of \$3750.

The key assumption in fixed income arbitrage is a correlation hypothesis: the future behavior of the fixed income securities under consideration should remain related over some interval of time. Once this hypothesis is accepted, the next step is to find securities that differ in terms of relative valuations. However, determining what will drive the bond market next and/or even the future direction of long rates is a risky business. Any of the above trades would potentially lose money if the spreads and/or the correlation do not evolve as expected.

OTHER TYPES OF STRATEGY

Closed-end fund arbitrage

Closed-end fund arbitrage attempts to capture the variations in the premium or discount between the net asset value and the trading price of closed-end fund shares. When correctly identified, these variations can lead to large profits. The Quota Fund, for example, had a 56% premium before its manager, Nick Roditi, decided to retire for an unspecified period. After Roditi's retirement, the premium collapsed to 0% in less than three months.

Mortgage-backed securities arbitrage

Mortgage-backed securities arbitrage focuses on mortgage-backed securities (MBS) and their derivatives. MBS are a form of ownership in a pool of mortgage loans made by banks and other financial institutions. Essentially, a number of individual mortgage loans are grouped together and ownership interest in this mortgage pool is sold to investors.

One of the primary advantages of investing in MBS is that their yield tends to be higher (historically about 125 basis points) than the yield on US Treasury notes and bonds with comparable maturities (about 10 years on average), even though there is little or no additional credit risk.[5] Some hedge funds try to capture this spread by being long MBS and hedging interest rate exposure by the short sale of treasury securities or other mortgage-backed securities, or through the use of fixed income derivatives. However, this is not a free lunch, since the position is exposed to liquidity risk and to prepayment risk, particularly in a declining interest rate environment.

Stock index arbitrage funds

Stock index arbitrage funds trade typically on the spread between index futures contracts and the underlying basket of securities. They also actively trade around announcement dates of index modifications. A classic strategy is long the stocks to be added to the index and short the index itself to hedge market risk. It is based on the observation that most index funds rebalance their positions at or very close to the market closing time on the effective date of the reconstitution (Box 8.2).

Box 8.2   THE FREE FLOAT TRANSITION: A TYPICAL INDEX ARBITRAGE TRADE

Since October 1, 2001 all Swiss indices have adopted a new calculation method. It follows the recent trend toward the "free float" method, which was initiated earlier by Morgan Stanley Capital International for all its indices. Before October 1 the market capitalization and the weights of each security in the Swiss index were based on the total number of outstanding shares. In the new method, they are now based on the number of free-floating shares—shares that are not closely held. They therefore reflect the tradable segment of the market more accurately.

Consequently, several securities saw their official market capitalization, and therefore their weight in the indices, rise or fall. Serono, a biotechnology company, saw its weight in the Swiss Market index reduced from 2.04% to 0.65%. The resulting difference in market capitalization represented the equivalent of 205 trading days (calculated as the difference in market capitalization divided by the average turnover over the last six months). For the Swatch Group, a Swiss watchmaker holding company, the weight in the Swiss Market index was reduced from 0.49% to 0.24% (153 trading days) and for Baloise Holding, an insurance company, it went from 0.92% to 0.62% (127 trading days). In contrast, other companies saw their weight in the index increase. For instance, Nestlé went from 17.57% to 19.15% (35 trading days) and Roche from 10.23% to 11.10% (26 trading days) of the Swiss Market index.

These index changes were announced long before they became effective. All index trackers had to adjust their positions to the new weightings just after October 1. This created a significant market impact, particularly for smaller companies, due to the flows of a vast range of investors implementing the announced shift. Several hedge funds participated in the index arbitrage by buying long shares whose weight was increased and selling short shares whose weight was decreased. Similar arbitrage profits were also captured when MSCI indices switched to free float and increased their number of constituents to cover 85% rather than 60% of market capitalization in each country.

Statistical arbitrage funds

Statistical arbitrage funds (also called relative value arbitrage or quantitative arbitrage) seek to profit from systematic or occasional pricing discrepancies between securities (including equities, debt, options and futures) that are detected by mathematical models. The corresponding strategies are designed to be effectively market neutral,[6] and have generally been successfully back-tested. Back-testing essentially entails gathering the historical data and performing the calculations thereon necessary to determine whether the opportunity would have been profitable had it been pursued in the past. However, their success is not always guaranteed. In particular, model breaks and model errors may result in mispredictions and large losses. This is often exacerbated by the high leverage these funds must use to magnify the impact of the very small spreads they attempt to capture. As an illustration, much of what the late Long Term Capital Management and its managers were doing was modeling the spreads of various fixed income markets and trading as soon as these spread diverged significantly from levels predicted by their models. The failure of their model to account for market liquidity combined with their excessive leverage brought them to default in 1998. Risk control is therefore critical, particularly model risk control.

ADR arbitrage funds

ADR arbitrage funds trade essentially in American depositary receipts (ADRs) and their underlying shares. An ADR is a certificate issued in the US, quoted in US dollars and traded on a US exchange that represents and is backed by shares of a foreign company held at a US bank. ADRs sometimes diverge from the value of their underlying shares, essentially because of the segmentation between US markets and local markets, as well as the relatively low liquidity of the underlying shares. This opens the door to arbitrage for hedge funds that specialize in the ADR market (Box 8.3).

Box 8.3   ADR ARBITRAGE

As an illustration of American depositary receipt (ADR) arbitrage, consider the case of Biora AB. This Swedish company develops, manufactures and markets products for the treatment of periodontal disease and oral surgery. It trades on the Stockholm Stock Exchange and has ADRs listed on the Nasdaq. Each ADR represents two ordinary Swedish shares. On October 26, 2001 one could observe the following situation. The Biora ADR was quoted $1.70 while the stock traded at SKr10.5, with the currency exchange rate at SKr10.54 per US dollar. That is, the underlying share value of the ADR (2 shares) was equal to $1.99, while its market price was $1.70. An arbitrage trade consisted in buying a given quantity of ADRs, selling short twice more Swedish shares, and waiting for the two prices to converge.

NOTES

1. In practice there could be a forced conversion case if the convertible is callable by the issuer and the value of the stocks receivable upon conversion is higher than the call redemption amount.
2. This will occur, at the latest, at the convertible's maturity date, since the convertible will be worth exactly its theoretical price at this date. Thus, convertible market value and theoretical prices must finally converge.
3. A possible explanation is that true 7-year and 20-year Treasuries are not issued, but instead the yields for these maturities are based upon 10- and 30-year Treasuries

that were issued 3 and 10 years ago. Since 10-year and 30-year bonds are more popular, there may be a small liquidity premium embedded in the price of these bonds.

4. The Eurodollar price is based on the 3-month Libor for deposits of US$1 million. The Libor is quoted as an annual interest rate. The futures price is quoted as 100 minus the interest rate, in percentage terms, of a 3-month Eurodollar deposit for forward delivery.

5. Most securities have the same "full faith and credit" backing that the US government gives to Treasuries. For instance, in the US, the mortgages in Ginnie Mae (Government National Mortgage Association) pools are either insured by the Federal Housing Administration or guaranteed by the Veterans Administration.

6. This explains why statistical arbitrage is sometimes classified as a subcategory of the market neutral strategy. As an illustration, it is only in 1999 that Hedge Fund Research disaggregated statistical arbitrage from equity market neutral in its classification.

9
Event-driven strategies

Event-driven strategies focus specifically on corporations involved in special situations or significant restructuring events. Examples include spin-offs, mergers and acquisitions, bankruptcy reorganizations, capital restructuring and share buybacks. The securities issued by such companies are often more influenced by the uncertainty about the particular event or the situation itself rather than by rational market behavior. Very logically, hedge funds step in and attempt to capitalize on expected price fluctuations.

The most popular event-driven substrategies are distressed securities investing and merger arbitrage. Other strategies offer additional opportunities for event-driven funds. They are often employed alongside merger arbitrage or distressed security investing.

DISTRESSED SECURITIES

The interest in distressed securities dates back to the end of the nineteenth century, when a few investors purchased falling railway stocks at ridiculous prices. They actively participated in the restructuring process and ended up making large profits.

Today distressed securities are no longer restricted to railway stocks. They now include several types of securities, depending on whether one uses a narrow or a broad definition. In a narrow sense, distressed securities are all publicly held securities issued by companies that have effectively defaulted on their debt obligations and/or have filed for protection during their reorganization process. A more comprehensive definition would also include all types of publicly held debt securities that yield a significant premium over US Treasury bond yields, as well as the stocks, bank loans and trade debt of those same companies.

An interesting case is that of high-yield bonds, also known as junk bonds. They embrace all fixed income securities issued by organizations that do not qualify for investment grade ratings, that is, with a Standard and Poor's rating lower than BBB. They are therefore considered as predominantly speculative, and to compensate investors, their yield to maturity includes a risk premium over Treasury bonds. Should high-yield bonds be included in the category of distressed securities? Analysts' views diverge on this point. Some only include the lowest-grade bonds, e.g. those rated C or D, since most other high-yield bonds will not default or come close to bankruptcy. The C rating covers a situation where a bankruptcy petition has been filed or similar action taken, but payments on the obligation are being continued; the D rating is used when payments on an obligation are not made on the due date. Others include all high-yield bonds, arguing that the spread over Treasury bonds is nothing but an early signal of financial distress.

Investing in distressed debt

Hedge funds investing in distressed securities essentially attempt to profit from market pricing inefficiencies, which can be absolute or relative. Absolute inefficiencies refer to differences between the market price and the intrinsic value of a distressed security.

The intrinsic value is estimated by discounting the security's expected cash flows at an appropriate discount rate, or by using a more complicated pricing model. Relative inefficiencies refer to price differences between two securities issued by the same distressed company. Both inefficiencies have their origins in several sources:

- *Investor irrationality*: most individual investors react emotionally and prefer to sell distressed securities at a cheap price rather than remaining invested in a financially troubled company.
- *Risk aversion*: many trade vendors prefer to use the cash to reinvest in their businesses rather than speculate on the outcome of reorganization.
- *Legal restrictions*: many institutional investors become forced sellers because their charters or regulators bar them from buying or holding bonds below investment grade, even if the company is a viable one.
- *Lack of knowledge*: valuing distressed claims is a labor-intensive process requiring numerous skills and continuous access to the most up-to-date information. Creditors often prefer to sell their claims at much lower prices than they would ultimately be worth because they do not have the knowledge, interest, ability, or time to make the necessary analysis.
- *Low analyst coverage*: analyst coverage tends to decline significantly as a firm becomes distressed and is almost nonexistent in bankruptcy. Clearly, the low interest from investors and the specific nature of the bankruptcy process reduce the incentive for equity analysts to spend time collecting and analyzing information.

The result is a market for distressed firms' securities that is disorganized, illiquid and has no firm bid price structure. Most of the order book is concentrated on the sell side, with traditional investors reluctant to buy. In contrast, hedge funds act as liquidity providers and attempt to profit from the market's lack of understanding of the true value of these securities. The hedge fund investment process is usually a three-step procedure:

- The fund manager performs a thorough analysis to assess the fundamental value of the distressed company, the likely recovery by each creditor constituency and the timing thereof.
- He purchases the distressed security at a discount with respect to its estimated fundamental value. The security may be bank debt, corporate debt, trade claims, lease contracts, private placements, common or preferred stock and/or warrants.
- The hedge fund actively or passively waits for a price recovery. Active hedge funds usually attempt to obtain a significant position in the outstanding debt. They then use the size of their holdings to influence the restructuring efforts, and to participate in the reorganization, refinancing and even acquisition process, if any. When markets are not transparent, some hedge funds may even engage in bond mailing activities; that is, threatening the other claimants and forcing them to make concessions, even though the size of their ownership stake does not make them a pivotal claimant. See Gilson (1995) and Schifrin (1991) for examples of bond mailing activity, and Noe and Rebello (1996) for a theoretical analysis.

Passive hedge funds simply follow a buy and hold approach and try to free ride on the coattails of the reorganizers. However, investing in distressed securities remains a niche activity, which requires a lot of know-how and connections. In a sense, it is very similar to the huge less-developed countries loan market, which grew up during the last decade. Its only advantage is that it is easier to force restructuring of a company than of a country.

Distressed securities markets

After enduring years of snickering, distressed securities finally gained mainstream acceptance in the US in the 1980s with the wave of leveraged buyouts and hostile takeovers. Much of the credit for their take-off is given to Drexel Burnham Lambert and particularly its trader Michael Milken. Milken gradually transformed the junk bond market from a highly illiquid bazaar for a few specialist buyers into a robust secondary market for deeply discounted debt.

In the early 1990s, following the collapse of Drexel Burnham Lambert, a record number of junk bonds became distressed. Large issuers such as LTV, Eastern Airlines, Texaco, Continental Airlines, Allied Stores, Federated Department Stores, Greyhound and Pan Am filed for the protection of Chapter 11 of the US Bankruptcy Code. A few others (e.g. Maxwell Communication, Olympia & York) became involved in more complex multijurisdictional workouts. In both cases their cast-off assets started attracting several vulture investors. The junk bond market resulted in the creation of a highly distressed securities market.

Today, with about $600 billion face value of assets, the United States clearly dominates the landscape of the distressed securities market. According to Moody's Investors Service (2001), it also continues to be the largest single source of corporate defaults: of the 167 rated and nonrated defaults observed worldwide in the year 2000, 125 (that is, 75%) were based in the US. In dollar terms, this represented a total of $49.07 billion, of which 59.3% belonged to US issuers. The largest US defaulters were Owens Corning ($1.3 billion), Paging Network Inc. ($1.1 billion), ICG Holdings, Inc. ($1.3 billion) and ICG Services, Inc. ($0.9 billion).

In comparison with the US, the situation of distressed securities in Europe is quite different. In the 1990s, the market for distressed securities was essentially composed of bank debt and it attracted a limited set of specialists. It was only with the emergence of the European Union (EU) that the market for distressed securities began to take off and achieved respectability. The euro transformed companies' attitudes toward financing their operations, with the high-yield bond market emerging as a viable alternative to banking finance. It halted the trading of currencies and interest rates between EU members, and forced investors to develop new strategies based on credit spreads to a much greater extent.

Today the European distressed securities market still lags far behind the United States in terms of both experience and market size ($15 billion). However, it experienced a 100% growth in 2000 and should continue its expansion, supported by strong demand from European as well as US investors and issuers. Issuance in euros and British pounds, primarily targeted at a European investor base, is growing rapidly, although large issues are still overwhelmingly denominated in US dollars.

So far, growth has been driven primarily by the telecommunication sector, essentially for two reasons. First, the birth of the EU coincided with a boom in telecommunication financing requirements (with GSM mobile phones and UMTS, the next generation of wireless network licenses). Second, the entire telecom sector has been slipping toward the lower end of the credit ratings spectrum. In a single year, the seven largest European phone companies have issued more than $170 billion of debt. In an industry where capital expenditure remains the key to staying ahead of the competition, the burden of huge interest payments could significantly affect issuers and create a new pool of truly distressed securities.

However, there are two major curbs on the growth of a European distressed securities market. First, European distressed securities are typically issued by a holding company, in contrast to the US where issuers are operating companies. This makes it harder to force a default. Combined with the rights of secured bank lenders, it also limits the ability of distressed securities holders to participate in restructuring. Second, the US Chapter 11 legislation (Box 9.1) is typically more transparent and straightforward than the multitude of bankruptcy legislations and judicial procedures in European jurisdictions. A European consensus on bankruptcy procedures, accounting standards and reporting requirements combined with a single body of regulatory rules and practices could be the signal for the market for subinvestment grade paper in euros to take off.

Box 9.1   CHAPTER 11 BANKRUPTCY

In the US, investors often use the corresponding chapter of the US Bankruptcy Code as a generic name for distressed companies. In particular, Chapter 11 describes companies legally protected from their creditors while they restructure their debt, and Chapter 7 refers to companies liquidating.

It is interesting to mention a few aspects of Chapter 11, because unlike Europe, the US has substituted an administrative bankruptcy process for a market process. When filing for Chapter 11, a debtor has the exclusive right to put to creditors an initial reorganization plan. This plan must include an estimate of the value of the restructured firm. Creditors then have to discuss and vote on the plan. If they disagree with it, they may attempt to sell their claims to exit from the restructuring process or acquire more claims to influence the management or even gain control. In particular, reorganization plans often convert large debt holdings into controlling equity stakes. In any case, a debt holding that represents more than one-third of the claims in a class can block the approval of the plan. More rarely, creditors petition the court to file a competing reorganization plan or request a formal valuation.

In Europe different bankruptcy processes exist under the various national jurisdictions and there is no single body of regulatory rules and practices. The system is therefore less transparent and straightforward than the Chapter 11 system.

Several other countries are also occasional providers of distressed securities. For instance, in 2000 the Republic of Korea ran second to the US in the number of corporate defaults with 13 totaling $6.2 billion. Among these were Daewoo Motor Company ($2.5 billion) and Hyundai Engineering and Construction ($2 billion). Canada registered the largest rated single-issuer default with Laidlaw Inc. ($2 billion). On the sovereign side, Ukraine ($1 billion), Côte d'Ivoire ($2.3 billion), and Peru ($4.8 billion) defaulted, following the 1999 default by Ecuador ($6.6 billion) on Brady bonds. However, these defaults were often linked to sector-specific problems and/or regional economic stresses. In general, defaults outside the US and, to a lesser extent, outside Europe tend to be quite dispersed around the globe.

Finally, an interesting case is that of Japan. As of March 2001, Japanese bankruptcies officially totaled more than $200 billion of liabilities. The purchase and sale of these has become a profitable business. However, Japanese institutions are still extremely reluctant to disclose information on these activities, in order to spare the original borrowers embarrassing publicity. Nevertheless, some estimates even mention a trillion dollars of present and prospective nonperforming Japanese loans. If we use a conservative 10% recovery rate, this implies a $100 billion universe, of which probably 20–45% will change hands in the near future. This scenario is likely, because it would give the Japanese economy a new start. Box 9.2 looks at a Chapter 11 bankruptcy in California utilities.

Box 9.2   THE LIGHTS GO OUT FOR CALIFORNIA UTILITIES

The California energy crisis attracted a great deal of attention at the beginning of 2001. Its major event was the filing for bankruptcy under Chapter 11 by Pacific Gas and Electric Company (PG&E), one of the two major California utilities and a large debt issuer. Based in San Francisco, PG&E runs all the regulated distribution activity of Pacific Gas and Electric Corporation (PG&E Corp.), a vertically integrated utility publicly listed on the New York Stock Exchange (NYSE). It serves 13 million people throughout a 70 000 square mile service area in Northern and Central California.

On April 6, 2001 PG&E announced it was filing for reorganization under Chapter 11 of the US Bankruptcy Code. The distress of the company was entirely attributable to the deregulation of the electricity industry in California. Deregulation resulted in extraordinarily high wholesale electricity prices, far higher than the retail consumer rates that remained frozen by state regulators. The imbalance was exacerbated by supply shortages that lasted throughout 2000.

Several PG&E requests for price adjustments to the California Public Utilities Commission were not followed by any action. In the meantime, the company had to use all its available cash and credit to finance the shortfall between customer rates and wholesale costs. By the first quarter of 2001, the cumulative shortfall had soared to about $9 billion. PG&E lost its investment grade status. This broke existing debt covenants and forced the company to default on an $850 million credit facility and $1 billion of commercial paper. As bailout talks between PG&E and the State of California were unsuccessful, Chapter 11 became the only viable solution to give PG&E a breathing space to continue operating while at the same time developing a reorganization plan to pay back its creditors.

Chapter 11 froze all debts for goods and services provided to PG&E prior to the filing date. Among the largest creditors were Bank of New York ($2.21 billion, bonds), California Power Exchange of Alhambra ($1.97 billion, power purchases), Bankers Trust Co. ($1.3 billion, bonds), California Independent System Operator ($1.13 billion, power purchases), and Bank of America ($938.5 million, unsecured revolving credit). Robert D. Glynn Jr, chairman of PG&E, declared, "Our objective is to proceed through the Chapter 11 process as quickly as possible, to develop and implement a court-approved plan of reorganization, and to emerge and rebuild value for our shareholders."

> Whatever the final outcome, California's electricity future remains a daunting challenge. It is not unrealistic to project that it will have harmful effects on the rest of the country in the form of higher electricity prices, credit problems for related lenders and deteriorating credit quality for affected municipal borrowers. Since California represents 13% of the US GDP, is the largest state economy, and even the sixth–largest economy in the world, a lights-out scenario there could spell plenty of trouble elsewhere.

The risks of distressed security investing

- *Specific risk*: the specific risk of the underlying company is an essential element of the risk.
- *Liquidity risk*: a weak pricing environment provides ample buying opportunities, but also meager exit opportunities. Once purchased, a distressed position often needs to be held until the end of the restructuring process. This may take several months or even years. Moreover, if the hedge fund holds a controlling position, regulators can prohibit it from selling the position immediately. This often results in the fund applying a very strict redemption policy, with investors' commitments often superior to one year.
- *Model risk*: fund managers often rely on models to identify undervalued distressed securities, but also to compute the net asset value of their funds when there are no market prices available. This can result in a potential mark to model bias and lower official risk figures.
- *Credit risk*: distressed security investing often conveys some sort of credit risk.
- *Legal risk*: the final restructuring decisions often need some court validation.
- *Interest rate risks*: since the expected profits are usually long term, an increase in interest rates will decrease the present value of these expected profits. It may also impair the chances of successful restructuring.

How about economic cycle risk? It is true that the likely supply of new defaulted and distressed paper is cyclical in nature. It depends on several factors such as the current business cycle, industry trends, and competitive forces. However, distressed securities are only slightly cyclical, since bankruptcies are permanent in nature and each industry sector may be in a different cycle. In addition, distressed securities are relatively unaffected by equity market swings, mostly because they have a high priority in a company's capital structure. This is particularly true when comparing senior debt to more junior securities such as subordinated debt or equity. In many cases, however, the original debt security will evolve into some equity interest via either a distressed exchange or bankruptcy reorganization.

To reduce the overall risk, hedge fund managers diversify their portfolios between several companies, sectors and securities. They partially hedge their market and/or interest rate risk exposure using futures contracts or short selling T-bonds. They also tend to use a low leverage ratio, so that their volatility ranges from low to moderate.

MERGER/RISK ARBITRAGE

Merger arbitrage, also called risk arbitrage, focuses on firms involved in mergers and takeovers. Its invention is usually credited to Gustave Levy, a partner at Goldman Sachs in the middle of the 1940s. Although very profitable, it remained inconspicuous for several years until the merger mania of the 1960s.

Mergers and acquisitions: a historical perspective

A historical perspective shows how extraordinary the current wave of megamergers really is and sheds light on the development of merger arbitrage activities. Economists usually identify five waves of takeovers, mergers and consolidations that have transformed business structures in developed economies.

The first wave occurred between 1895 and 1903 and culminated in the trust movement, when numerous small and medium-sized firms were consolidated to build monopolies in oil, steel and other heavy industries (e.g. Standard Oil, US Steel). The second wave took place between 1920 and 1929. It could be called mergers for oligopoly, as many industries consolidated, particularly electricity and gas utilities as well as manufacturing firms (e.g. Bethlehem Steel).

The third wave swelled between 1960 and 1973. Fueled by a bullish stock market and the emergence of new sources of financing (e.g. issues of convertible preferred stocks and debentures), it resulted in the creation of large conglomerates, essentially through the merging of companies engaged in nonrelated activities. Several large investment banks started creating their merger arbitrage desks at this time and generated very large profits. Unfortunately, most of these conglomerates generated power and prestige for their managers, but made no economic sense, so the third wave ended in a severe decline in conglomerates' market values and the oil crisis.

Merger arbitrage effectively gained prominence during the fourth merger wave, which took place between 1978 and 1989. Supported by an accommodating regulatory environment and low interest rates, the number of hostile predatory takeovers exploded, followed by the breakup of inefficient conglomerates and the dismembering of undervalued companies. Junk bonds and initially depressed stock markets resulted in cash purchases being the preferred and cheaper medium of expansion rather than acquisitions through stocks.

Fueled by the utter euphoria of leveraged buyouts and excited by the unprecedented set of opportunities offered by the numerous corporate-control deals, the market reached one of the greatest paroxysms of speculation and usury that the world has ever seen. As an illustration, the RJR Nabisco leveraged buyout generated senior bank debt of about $15 billion, $5 billion of subordinated debt, and an additional $5 billion of junk bonds that paid interest not in cash but in other junk bonds. Legendary figures, such as Michael Milken and his Wall Street associates Ivan Boesky, Dennis Levine and Martin Siegel, were the symbols of the decade of greed (Box 9.3).

However, in October 1989 the bull market suddenly came to an end when the proposed leveraged buyout of United Airlines fell apart because the management team and employees could not get the proposed financing. Several leveraged companies declared bankruptcy in late 1989, followed by Drexel Burnham Lambert, the leading investment bank on the junk bond market. Although this was the end of the golden age, the gains on equity to shareholders caused by takeovers and restructuring from 1976 to 1990 had totaled over $750 billion.

Box 9.3   IVAN BOESKY: THE WORLD'S MOST INFAMOUS ARBITRAGER

Ivan Boesky, on whom Michael Douglas's character of Gordon Gekko was modeled in the Oscar-winning movie *Wall Street*, is probably still today the most famous merger arbitrager. Boesky originally graduated from a law school no one on the Street had ever heard of. When he came to New York, he rapidly entered the merger arbitrage business and started making investments in announced takeover deals, with moderate success. However, in May 1982 Gulf Oil announced the failure of its takeover of Cities Service. Boesky lost $24 million in the deal, which convinced him that he did not exactly have the magic touch in selecting deals to invest in. He therefore decided to switch tactics.

Illegally obtaining tips about impending mergers through a network of contacts he had set up, Boesky started buying and selling stock before the mergers became public knowledge. Among his major sources was the investment banker Martin Siegel of Kidder Peabody. Boesky rapidly accumulated personal profits estimated at more than $200 million and became one of the guru investors on Wall Street. He created the Hudson Fund, the first hedge fund specializing in merger arbitrage, for which Dennis Levine of Drexel Burnham Lambert agreed to raise over $600 million through a junk offering. This resulted in almost $24 million in fees for Levine and a new source of insider tips for Boesky.

However, Boesky's activities finally attracted the attention of the Securities and Exchange Commission (SEC), who became suspicious of unusual transactions on stocks prior to public announcements of pending mergers. Convicted of crimes relating to insider trading, Ivan Boesky was sentenced to three years in prison, a $50 million fine and $50 million disgorgement. He agreed to cooperate with the SEC in its investigations. This led to several other major court cases and cast a pall over the arbitrage community.

On February 13, 1990 the investment bank Drexel Burnham Lambert, which had made a fortune masterminding corporate takeovers, filed for bankruptcy and went into liquidation. Its guru, Michael Milken, was indicted, much to the distress of junk bond holders who saw him as a buyer of last resort.

The fifth wave of mergers began in 1993 and is still under way. It is the greatest merger cycle in history, in terms of both number and size of deals. For instance, the years 1996 and 1997 each had more mergers and acquisitions by value than the years 1990, 1991, 1992 and 1993 combined. And in 1999, worldwide mergers and acquisitions reached a whopping $4.4 trillion volume, with the US alone accounting for a record $1.8 trillion, with over 200 deals above $1 billion (Table 9.1). Most of these transactions were driven by consolidators and focused on strategic rather than purely financial reasons. Companies were responding to changing technology, globalization of the economy, industry upheaval, or deregulation. Stock rather than cash became the preferred medium of payment. European and transborder mergers have also begun to represent a significant part of merger activity. This trend is expected to continue, with the increasing integration of the world's financial markets over the last two decades.

Table 9.1   Largest mergers over the period 1997–2001

	Acquirer	Target	Sector	Size	Premium	Offer	Type
1997	Bank of America Corp.	Barnett Banks Inc.	Finance	15.1	45.79	S	Friendly
	First Union Corp.	Corestates Financial Corp.	Finance	16.6	11.37	S	Friendly
	Union Bank Corp.	Swiss Bank Corp.	Finance	19.7		S	Friendly
	WorldCom Group	MCI Communications Corp.	Telecom	36.1	55.23	S	Friendly
	Diageo plc	Grand Metropolitan plc	Food/beverages	39.0		S	Friendly
1998	Bank of America Corp.	BankAmerica Corp.	Finance	57.5		S	Friendly
	SBC Communications Inc.	Ameritech Corporation	Telecom	68.2	23.05	S	Friendly
	Citigroup Inc.	Citicorp	Finance	69.9	8.06	S	Friendly
	Verizon Communications Inc.	GTE Corporation	Telecom	71.1	3.84	S	Friendly
	Exxon Mobil Corp.	Mobil Corp.	Energy	80.3	26.23	S	Friendly
1999	Total Fina Elf SA	Elf Aquitaine	Energy	52.3	29.98	S	Hostile
	AT&T Corp.	MediaOne Group Inc.	Telecom	55.4	24.25	C, S, D	Friendly
	Vodafone Group plc	Vodafone Americas Asia Inc.	Telecom	57.4	38.97	C, S	Friendly
	Pfizer Inc.	Warner-Lambert Co.	Medical/drugs	88.6	30.18	S, D	Friendly
	Vodafone Group plc	Mannesmann AG	Telecom	185.1	104.63	S, D	Friendly
2000	JDS Uniphase Corp.	SDL Inc.	Telecom	36.2	62.01	S	Friendly
	Pacific Century Cyber-Works	Cable & Wireless HKT Ltd	Telecom	38.4	10.38	S	Friendly
	Vivendi Universal SA	Seagram Co. Ltd	Multimedia	44.6	56.14	S, D	Friendly
	GlaxoSmithKline plc	SmithKline Beecham plc	Medical/drugs	72.4	−0.61	S	Friendly
	AOL Time Warner Inc.	Time Warner Inc.	Multimedia	186.2	81.09	S	Friendly
2001	Halifax Group plc	Bank of Scotland	Finance	14.1	0.77	S	Friendly
	E.ON AG	Powergen plc	Energy	14.9	9.62	C	Friendly
	Allianz AG	Dresdner Bank AG	Insurance	20.7	19.06	C, S	Friendly
	American International Group	American General Corp.	Insurance	23.2	21.58	S	Friendly
	Echostar Communications Corp.	Hughes Electronics Corp.	Telecom	30.1	11.08	S	Hostile

Note: the size of each merger is expressed in billion US dollars; the premium is expressed as a percentage of the target market price; the offer can consist of shares (S), cash (C) and debt (D); mergers for 2001 are still pending and subject to completion

Arbitrage spread in cash offers

Unlike Ivan Boesky, most merger arbitragers are not insider traders. Rather, they simply take positions based on the likelihood and terms of a takeover or a merger. Let us illustrate their activities in the case of a cash takeover; that is, an acquiring company offering a fixed amount of cash (say $100) in exchange for each share of a target company. To convince investors to tender their shares, the bid price usually includes a premium (say $20) with respect to the target's current share price on the market ($80 in our example).

Following the announcement and filing of the acquisition bid, the market price of the target firm should naturally adjust upward. In practice it does, but it does not reach the bid price. Let us say for instance that the new market price is $95. The remaining gap between the bid and the market price ($5) is called the *merger arbitrage spread*. Technically, it is usually defined as the percentage difference between the initial bid price and the target's closing price on the day after the acquisition announcement. It will fluctuate over time, reflecting the unwillingness of other market participants to take on transaction-based risk, i.e. the risk that the transaction may not be completed. This could occur because of regulators, unsatisfied shareholders, management actions or any other reason.

Merger arbitragers are specialists in evaluating this transaction risk. If they are confident that the takeover will succeed on time and on the terms originally announced, they just buy some target company's shares and wait to capture the corresponding spread. However, if the takeover is delayed, renegotiated or abandoned, the price of the acquired company usually falls and arbitragers incur a loss, usually much larger than the profits obtained if the deal succeeds (Figure 9.1).

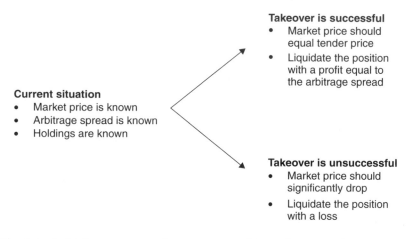

Figure 9.1   A typical takeover process from a merger arbitrager's perspective

In reality, things are far more complicated. The probability of a deal succeeding depends on several factors, such as the approval of the management, any antitakeover devices used by the target company, the number of small shareholders willing to tender, the attitude of regulators, and the reaction of arbitragers. Indeed, the number of risk arbitragers trying to capture the spread will also influence the final outcome, since they are usually more likely to tender and favor the bidder. This results in an asymmetry of information in favor of large arbitragers, because they know the exact number of shares that they control. This also explains why, after a tender offer, the trading volume usually increases dramatically, largely because of risk arbitragers accumulating shares.

Stock offers and other transactions

Another profitable situation for merger arbitragers is the case of stock mergers, where the bidder offers its common stock in exchange for target shares, in lieu of cash (Box 9.4).

This case is slightly more complicated than the cash offer (Box 9.5), because the reference price for the target (used to calculate the arbitrage spread) is no longer fixed, but depends on the bidder's stock price. It is therefore not sufficient simply to buy the target stock and have it converted into the bidder's stock. The reason is that the bidder's stock may fall significantly, so the converted shares once the merger is completed will be worth less than the initial purchase price.

Empirically, in most cases, the bidder's stock price is seen to fall while the target stock price rises. The arbitrage strategy therefore consists in buying the target company's stock (which sells at a discount with respect to the offered value) and short selling the bidder company's stock (which is expected to decrease in value). The proportion of the two shares of stock should be the same as the one used in the bidder's offer. Note that since this is a long/short position, the arbitrager does not care about the absolute price variations of the target and the bidder shares, but only cares about their relative variation.

Box 9.4   A STOCK OFFER ARBITRAGE: MICROSOFT AND VISIO

On September 15, 1999 Microsoft Corp. announced that it would acquire Visio Corp., a supplier of enterprise-wide business diagramming and technical drawing software quoted on the Nasdaq. The terms of the acquisition were a fixed share exchange ratio of 0.45 share of Microsoft for every Visio share. Any fractional shares that resulted from the exchange would be paid in cash based on a Microsoft share average closing price for each of the 20 trading days ending December 31, 1999. Although the acquisition received the support of Jeremy Jaech, president and chief executive officer of Visio, the success of the acquisition depended on approval by both regulators and Visio shareholders.

Figure 1 shows the movement of the Visio share price from September 1999 to January 2000. On September 15, Visio shares closed at $39.875 and Microsoft at $92.625. According to the terms of the merger, a Visio share was worth $41.681— there was a $1.806 merger spread.

Note that a typical Visio shareholder should disregard this spread, since what matters for him is the price at which Microsoft will trade once the merger has closed and he has received his Microsoft shares. His attention will focus on the absolute variations in the Microsoft share price, hoping that it will increase. A merger arbitrager, however, has a different approach. To capture the spread, he will buy Visio shares and sell short 0.45 Microsoft share for any Visio share purchased. His only concern will be the price difference between his long position and his short position, that is, the narrowing or widening of the spread.

The deal was completed successfully on January 10, 2000 for a total amount of $1.5 billion. Looking at the trading volume (Figure 2) confirms the unusual activity around the announcement date and just before the exchange of securities.

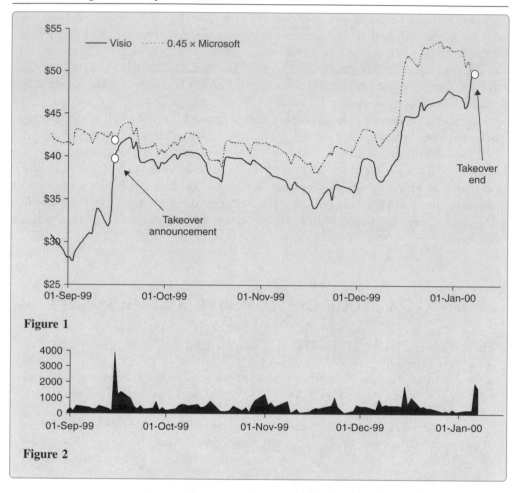

Figure 1

Figure 2

Box 9.5   A CASH OFFER ARBITRAGE: FIRST DATA CORP. AND PAYMENTECH, INC.

On March 22 1999, First Data Corp., a provider of electronic commerce solutions, announced that it was offering $25.50 in cash for each publicly held share of Paymentech Inc., a company providing full-service electronic payment solutions. The expected closing date for the deal was July 27, 1999. The deal failure risk was limited, since Bank One was the major shareholder of Paymentech with 52.5% of the company and had a merchant processing alliance with First Data.

Figure 1 shows the change in the Paymentech share price in 1999. It can be seen that the shares closed at $24 on March 22, and even went down to $23.25 on March 23. We can therefore realistically assume that arbitragers were able to buy shares at $24 just after the deal announcement. This represents a 6.25% discount with respect to the bid price. Figure 2 shows daily trading volume (thousands of shares); it confirms record high trading activity between March 22 and March 24, probably due to risk arbitrage activities.

It was only after the May 13 that the share price started converging significantly towards $25.50. The deal was closed successfully on July 27, 1999. It generated an annualized return of about 19.5% without any leverage. Of course, not all risk arbitrage investments are as easy and attractive.

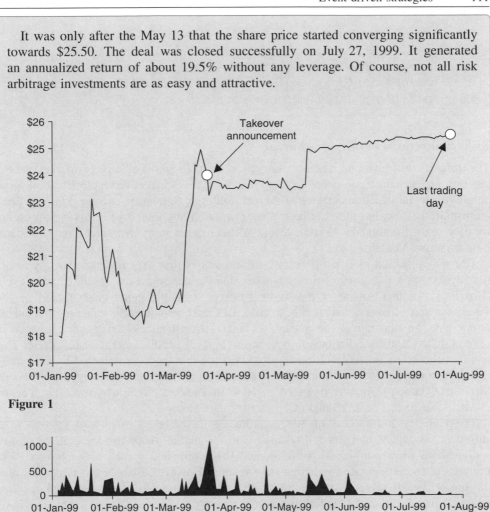

Figure 1

Figure 2

Of course, there are also more complicated deal structures involving preferred stock, warrants, debentures, and other securities concerned in the takeover. There are also takeovers or mergers that result in multiple bids (Box 9.6).

Box 9.6   A MÉNAGE À TROIS SITUATION

In 1999 General Dynamics Corp., a manufacturer and supplier of defense systems to the US government and its allies, launched a friendly takeover to acquire Newport News, but the deal was thwarted by the Department of Defense. In 2001 the prospects for approval were expected to be more favorable under the new Bush administration.

General Dynamics agreed again to acquire Newport News in a cash transaction valued at $2.1 billion. Immediately, Northrop Grumman Corp. launched a counter offer at the same price, paid 50% in cash and 50% in stock. On August 5, 2001 the arbitrage spread was 6.1% ($63.60 closing price versus $67.50 deal value), essentially reflecting the prospects of approval by the Department of Justice.

Risks and returns of merger arbitrage

The primary objective of merger arbitrage is to maintain a relatively market neutral position and generate consistent returns (Box 9.7). Investments are typically short term, although special situations may entail longer holdings. Spreads in merger arbitrage deals are usually narrow, but they can be captured in much less than a year, freeing up capital for new deals. Combined with some leverage, this modest short-term total return translates into attractive annualized returns.

The major source of risk for merger arbitragers is that of a deal breakup, typically for regulatory reasons, lack of agreement, shareholder rejection or unexpected event (Box 9.8). Another source of risk is deal delay, since the gains made would be the same, but spread over a longer time period, therefore significantly reducing annualized returns. As an illustration, the September 2001 terrorist attacks on the US resulted in several delays and cancellations in most of the biggest pending merger/sales offers. This includes the offers on AT&T Broadband (AT&T's cable business, targeted by Comcast), Brooks Brothers (a unit of Marks & Spencer), Hugues Electronics (owned by General Motors), Compaq Computer (targeted by Hewlett Packard), Tempus Group (targeted by Havas Advertising) or Telemundo Communications Group.

The viability and success of merger arbitrage therefore relies on two factors: (a) a sufficient volume of mergers and takeovers on the market to permit the construction of a diversified merger arbitrage portfolio; and (b) a sufficient spread on each successful transaction to compensate for failing transactions. However, one should remember that the larger the arbitrage premium, the more attractive the deal, but also the larger the potential loss if the deal fails for any reason.

The use of leverage among risk arbitragers varies enormously. Most risk arbitragers prefer to hold diversified portfolios and leverage their positions to enhance returns, while others prefer to concentrate their positions on specific deals, but use leverage in a more reasonable way.

Risk arbitrage returns are impacted essentially by the deal flow, not by market returns. Nevertheless, there remains a little market-related risk in the portfolio. Falling equity markets or an uncertain economic outlook can put a large number of transactions in jeopardy, particularly those that are linked to a stock merger—where the bidder is offering to pay with shares.

Box 9.7   JULIAN ROBERTSON: HOW TO BECOME AN INVOLUNTARY MERGER ARBITRAGER

When Julian Robertson decided to shut down his Tiger Fund, he announced that he would liquidate most of its holdings and return to investors about 80% of their stakes within two months, mostly in cash and the rest in stocks. The remaining 20% would be paid later on from the sell-off of large stakes in five companies (including US Airways) that had contributed significantly to the fund's poor performance over the preceding year. When UAL, the world's largest airline, announced its intention to take over and merge with US Airways, Julian Robertson found himself in the very comfortable position of a merger arbitrager, holding an estimated 26% stake in the target company. However, the merger finally fell through when US antitrust authorities scuttled the deal on the grounds that it would damage competition, and Julian Robertson ended up distributing the fund's 24.8 million shares in US Airways.

Box 9.8   A DEAL FAILURE: GENERAL ELECTRIC AND HONEYWELL INTERNATIONAL

On October 22, 2000 General Electric announced its intention to buy Honeywell International in a stock-for-stock transaction. The terms of the offer were 1.055 shares of General Electric for each share of Honeywell International. The transaction came 10 months after the former Allied Signal bought Honeywell and assumed the name. Honeywell's shares had since dropped by one-third. Discussions on another offer to acquire Honeywell from United Technologies had just terminated a few days before. The merger was supposed to generate more than $1.5 billion in annual cost savings, and was favorably welcomed by most analysts. Given the size of the two companies, most merger arbitragers jumped on the transaction.

At the beginning of October, Honeywell was trading at $35–37 a share, with a daily volume of 3–4 million shares (Figures 1 and 2). On October 20, two days before the announcement, the share price jumped to $46 with a daily volume of 22 million shares. On October 23 it reached $49.9375 with a daily volume of 39.3 million shares. In contrast, General Electric was trading at $58–59 a share at the beginning of October, with a daily volume of 9–10 million shares (Figures 1 and 3). On October 20 the share price dropped to $52.25 with a daily volume of 14.6 million shares. On October 23 it sank to $49.75 with a daily volume of 50.2 million shares.

On May 2, 2001, after close scrutiny of the competition effects in the production of jet engines, automation controls and industrial sensors, the US Department of Justice approved the merger. This reinforced the likelihood of the merger, with the result that on May 18 Honeywell peaked at $53.25 and General Electric at $52.99—an arbitrage spread of $2.65 per share (taking into account the 1.055 coefficient for the exchange of shares). Investors were short 130 million shares of General Electric, five times more than before the deal was announced. Financial analysts estimated that about $1 billion worth of Honeywell shares were held by risk arbitragers.

However, on June 14, 2001, after several rounds of negotiations, Mario Monti, the European Union's competition commissioner, surprised the entire financial community. He announced the commission's intention to reject the proposed merger between General Electric and Honeywell International, despite the General Electric offer to divest $2.2 billion in assets. The official motive was the European Union's concern that the combined company might use its airplane-leasing units to dominate the market for jet engines and aviation electronics. This was the first time that the European Union had reached a conclusion different to that of the US antitrust authorities. Honeywell stock sank from $42.26 to $37.10 in a record volume of 71 million shares, while General Electric shares gained $1 at $48.86, also in a record volume of 50 million shares.

The deal's collapse created a climate of risk aversion and dampened deal activity for several months. It also caused merger spreads to be extremely sensitive to rumors, particularly for transactions with regulatory issues (e.g. GPU/First Energy, Ralston Purina/Nestlé, Quaker Oats/Pepsi Co.)

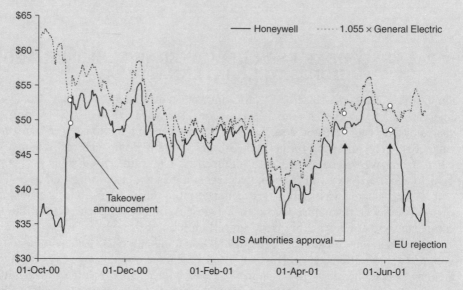

Figure 1

Figure 2

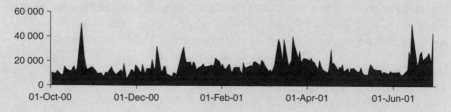

Figure 3

10

Directional strategies

Directional strategies constitute a substantial departure from the original hedge fund philosophy. Rather than hedging market risk and leveraging selection skills, they rely on the direction of movement in a security or market in order to profit. Some of them also rely aggressively on leverage to achieve large positions and to boost returns.

GLOBAL MACRO FUNDS

Global macro funds have long been the most successful and most visible category of hedge funds. Their reputation is essentially due to the phenomenal success of a few star managers. Despite their popularity (or unpopularity), they represent only a very small percentage of the hedge fund universe, but they manage a large proportion of the corresponding assets.

Macro hedge funds started developing in the 1980s with managers coming from other investment styles, in particular long/short equity and managed futures. These managers had very different backgrounds and investment approaches. The long/short equity people were typically managers who had been very successful in taking long and short positions in underresearched small capitalizations. As the size of their portfolios increased, they needed to move to bigger and more liquid markets where larger bets could be placed. This was the case for George Soros (Quantum Fund) and Julian Robertson (Tiger Fund).

The managed futures people, on the other hand, came from the derivatives and managed futures industry, which are global and macroeconomic in nature. This was the case of Louis Moore Bacon (Moore Global) and Paul Tudor Jones (Tudor Investments). Despite their differences, both types of manager capitalized on the number of investment and trading opportunities that emerged with the freeing up of the global currency markets, the subsequent development of non-US financial futures markets, and later the creation of the European Union.

The strategies of macro hedge funds depart radically from the original concept of Alfred Winslow Jones. These funds do not hedge anything. Rather, they make very large directional bets that reflect their forecasts of market directions, as influenced by major economic trends and/or particular events. In a sense, one could say that macro hedge fund managers attempt to anticipate price changes before they occur. They then take a leveraged position and wait until the expected price adjustments occur. Consequently, their performance depends uniquely on the quality and timing of their forecasts.

Macro hedge funds are usually not specialized. They tend to invest globally, wherever they see value, in both developed and emerging markets. They switch from one investment opportunity to another, from one asset class to the next. They use leverage and derivatives extensively to hold large market exposures and to boost returns. Consequently, their risks and returns are often very volatile in comparison with other hedge funds.

Consider, for instance, George Soros and his flagship, the Quantum Fund. In 1992 he went short for about $10 billion of British pounds, because he was expecting a currency devaluation. Despite the attempts of the British Chancellor of the Exchequer to borrow $15 billion in order to defend sterling, Soros's action precipitated a humiliating currency drop and the UK's subsequent withdrawal from the European Monetary System. Conversely, the Quantum Fund and its investors ended up with a comfortable profit of almost $1 billion. However, Soros's later failures were just as spectacular. In 1998 the Quantum Fund lost $2 billion when Russia defaulted on its debt. In 1999 a bet that internet stocks would fall came basically one year too early and resulted in a $700 million loss. In 2000 a bet on the rise of technology stocks resulted in an embarrassing $3 billion loss when the Nasdaq sank. Clearly, success was not always the outcome.

A key factor in the success of a macro hedge fund is the ability of its manager to identify and capitalize on macro trends. There are several books available that describe the techniques of macro hedge fund managers. The most famous one is undoubtedly *The Alchemy of Finance* by George Soros himself. Not surprisingly, Soros does not accept the theory prevailing among economics and finance professors that markets are rational and efficient. He claims, rather, that there are some systemic conditions of macroeconomic disequilibrium that are worth looking for and betting on. For instance, the combination of a huge government deficit, an expansionary fiscal policy (higher government spending and taxation) and a tight monetary policy (higher interest rates to stem borrowing) should result in the appreciation of a currency. Soros is prominently interested in such discontinuities and in deploying the best assortment of financial instruments to profit from them. But this is probably not the only key to his success. Stanley Druckenmiller, a former manager of the Quantum Fund, confessed [admitted] that they were also using technical analysis for investing in Japanese equities. Felix Zulauf, another famous macro manager, anticipated the 1987 stock market crash by looking at shifts in monetary policy. Therefore, the reality is probably that (i) there are as many approaches as there are macro hedge fund managers; (ii) these approaches are not static, but evolve over time, as does the world around us; and (iii) these approaches need to be conducted on a global basis, given the increased interaction between the various countries' economies.

The mid 1990s was the golden age of global macro investing. Since then the combination of increased transparency and better information flows have reduced the volume of profitable trading opportunities. Indeed, large leveraged macro bets are out of fashion. Julian Robertson brought down the curtain on the Tiger funds and retired after a wrong-way bet on the yen in 1998, followed by several other losses and investor withdrawals that dwindled assets from $21 billion to $6 billion in 18 months. A few months later, Stanley Druckenmiller, portfolio manager of the Quantum Fund, and Nick Roditi, portfolio manager of the Quota Fund, decided to retire from active management and left the Soros Fund Management group. In his April 2000 letter to shareholders, George Soros himself wrote: "My own needs are for a more reliable stream of income to fund my charitable activities. To meet those needs, we shall convert the Quantum Fund into a lower risk/lower reward operation." One of the most profitable and well-known global hedge funds is now just history. However, hedge fund investors tend to jump on what is hot. The tide may therefore turn back for macro funds.

EMERGING MARKET HEDGE FUNDS

As might be expected, emerging market hedge funds primarily take positions in all types of securities that are quoted on emerging markets. What constitutes an emerging market is frequently a matter of opinion. The World Bank classifies as emerging any country with an annual per capita income of less than $9266. In the following analysis, we adopt a looser definition and consider as an emerging market any country that has public securities markets with a reliable source of data, and a low annual per capita income. Examples of emerging markets are usually to be found in Latin America, Eastern Europe, the former Soviet Union, Africa and parts of Asia.

Investing in emerging markets is often justified by three empirical characteristics: high average returns, high volatility, and low correlation both across the emerging markets and the emerged markets. However, these arguments should be treated with caution because emerging market indices are often poor indicators of the actual performance of portfolios. There are three reasons for this:

- Several emerging market indices were launched recently and their past performance was recomputed using only surviving securities. This resulted in a strong survivorship bias and resulted in an overestimation of the average returns and an underestimation of risks.
- Most index providers focus on carefully selected countries, that is, markets with a proven track record. This creates a selection bias and an overestimation of the average returns for all emerging markets.
- Some markets have emerged, collapsed, and reemerged later. For instance, in the 1920s Argentina had a larger market capitalization than the UK. Most indices only consider such markets during their reemergence phase.

However, most actors acknowledge that emerging markets are typically less efficient and less liquid than emerged markets. This opens the door to mispricing, and therefore to hedge funds, which are better suited than traditional mutual funds to exploit inefficiencies while still being able to withdraw from the market whenever necessary.

Investments in emerging market equities are primarily long, because short selling is not permitted in many emerging countries. Nor do viable futures markets exist to hedge market risk, so that hedge funds willing to hedge often need to use over-the-counter products such as equity swaps or warrants. Some managers invest solely in individual regions, while others shift their weightings among these regions according to their market perception.

On the equity side, an increasing number of transactions are implemented using American depositary receipts (ADRs). These are certificates issued in the US, quoted in US dollars and traded on a US exchange (such as the New York Stock Exchange) that represent and are backed by shares of a foreign company held at a US bank. They have several advantages over trading the original shares directly: a more liquid market, lower transaction costs, no foreign exchange fees and a larger potential pool of investors.

On the fixed income side, most securities are usually below investment grade. They consist essentially of three types of instrument:

- Local bonds in local currencies offer the highest yields, but also the greatest credit and currency risk exposures. Their liquidity and the potential to hedge them are usually extremely limited.
- Eurobonds are issued in the Eurobond market and denominated in any of the major currencies. They are more liquid and can be hedged using several instruments, such as interest rate futures and emerged markets' government bonds for the interest rate

risk, asset swaps or credit derivatives for the default risk, and currency forwards for the exchange rate risk.

- Brady bonds are dollar-denominated, zero-coupon bonds backed by the US Treasury, at least for the repayment of principal at maturity. Their risks can be partially hedged via US Treasury futures and currency forwards.

Market risk, currency risk, country risk and liquidity risk are clearly high with emerging markets. The Mexican crisis of 1994, the Thai devaluation of 1997, and the Russian default of 1998 were reminders that emerging markets, far from remaining isolated, were an integral part of the world economic and financial system. The shock waves emanating from these events were felt deeply even in the most stable and developed economies.

An interesting open question is the impact of hedge fund transactions on emerging markets. In particular, during the 1997 Asian crisis, several governments accused hedge funds of attacking Asian currencies and causing their downfall. The supporting argument was that the convergence of leveraged bets by large hedge funds resulted in sizable transactions with respect to the small market capitalization of emerging markets. Several studies focused on the question (e.g. Eichengreen *et al.* 1998; Brown *et al.* 1998; Fung *et al.* 1999). They concluded that (i) hedge funds did not play a central role in causing the Asian crisis; and (ii) the major hedge funds' exposures and profits during the Asian crisis were not much different from usual. However, since excessive speculation is often at the origin of market crises, there is no doubt that the finger will again be pointed at hedge funds in the next market crash.

SECTOR HEDGE FUNDS

Sector hedge funds specialize in long and short investments in particular sectors of the economy. They justify their sector-oriented approach by the increasing homogeneity of the macroeconomic frame, the lower interest rates and the weakening of the home country bias. Some examples of specialization are given below, though there are several other investment themes that are actively followed, such as entertainment and communications, media, and financial institutions. Managers may also use a wide range of primary focus (e.g. large-cap, mid-cap, small-cap, microcap, value growth, opportunistic) and investment approaches (e.g. bottom-up, top-down, discretionary, technical).

Life sciences

Life sciences include e.g. pharmaceutical, biotechnology, medical equipment and health-care companies. The last ten years have witnessed an explosion in the understanding of the mechanisms underlying biological processes. Given the favorable demographics, new discoveries in biomedical science will have enormous commercial value. The demand for new and effective treatments is insatiable and shows little price sensitivity. Hedge funds active in life sciences tend to focus on younger and smaller companies for their ability to take the discoveries of fundamental biomedical research and translate them into products. They spread the risks by investing in several companies and holding a somewhat diversified portfolio. The key to success is of course the identification of winners and losers, a hard task since about 50% of biotechnology and medical technology products fail in clinical trials.

Technology

Technology hedge funds tend to mix long and short positions in segments where their manager has specific expertise. Fueled by the widening scope of scientific breakthroughs, the promising development of the internet and the benefits ensuing from productivity enhancement and cost reductions, this has been one of the most explosive growth opportunities in history. However, the sector was hard hit by the collapse of technology stocks in 2000 and 2001.

Real estate

The real estate sector has evolved gradually from very conservative holdings of stand-alone real estate assets to dynamic investments in companies operating in real estate as well as publicly traded and securitized real estate securities (e.g. real estate investment trusts). Securitized real estate is particularly important for hedge funds, because it allows taking both short and long positions; that is, investing during up and down cycles of the market as well as hedging existing positions. The market is still small but the growth potential is large, particularly when one considers the enormous pool of real estate assets suitable for securitization.

Energy

Energy funds fall into two major categories. There are those that invest on both the long and short sides of the energy equity markets, and those that are structured more like commodity pool operators and invest essentially in commodity-related futures. The major investment themes are linked to technological innovation, exploration and development, as well as mergers and acquisitions. Their portfolios tend to be correlated with commodity prices, but remain uncorrelated with stocks.

REGULATION D AND PIPES FUNDS

The search for new avenues to make money is inexorable. Regulation D is a part of the Securities Act 1933 that allows securities sold exclusively through private placements to avoid the rigorous filing requirements of the Securities and Exchange Commission (SEC). Most domestic US hedge funds rely on Regulation D to place their securities directly to a selected set of individuals. But Regulation D is also widely used by small public companies experiencing difficulties to raise additional equity in the US, essentially through private deals. In particular, private investments in public equities (PIPEs) allow companies with publicly listed shares to issue new restricted shares and sell them against cash in a private transaction. This type of transaction became popular in the US since January 2000, when Janus, the $240 billion Denver-based mutual fund giant, announced that it had just bought $930 million worth of securities issued by Healtheon/WebMD, the first end-to-end internet healthcare company connecting physicians and consumers to the entire healthcare industry. Since then Regulation D securities have spawned a new hedge fund category.

More generally, the issue of Regulation D securities takes essentially two forms:

- *Equity issues*: investors purchase the company stock at a discount with respect to the market price. As an illustration, the Healtheon/WebMD issue was discounted by about 6%, but smaller offerings are often forced to issue at much larger discounts. A SimPlayer.com issue in February 2000 was even discounted by 34%.

- *Convertible issues*: investors purchase a convertible bond that converts into a specific dollar value of the underlying stock, whatever happens to the stock price during the holding period. This means that the number of shares received when converting is not known, but the value of these shares is known. In a sense, the investment is "market neutral." The convertible security is usually sold at a discount with respect to the value of the shares.

The profit from Regulation D securities comes from the discount between the purchase price and the market value at the issue. In exchange for this price concession, investors, who must be accredited, are taking a risk, because (i) the underlying shares are not registered on an exchange, (ii) the issuer may default and (iii) there is virtually no liquidity. Legally, the required holding period before public sale of privately placed securities is two years. However, the issuer usually files the necessary registration statements with the SEC within 180 days. In between, the shares can only be traded among accredited investors.

DEDICATED-SHORT FUNDS

Short-only investing is essentially traditional asset management flipped upside down. Dedicated-short hedge funds seek to profit from a decline in the value of stocks by taking short positions. A fund needs to borrow the corresponding securities from a third party in order to make delivery to the purchaser. It then returns the borrowed securities to the lender by purchasing securities in the open market at a later date and at a lower (anticipated) price. If the anticipation was right, a profit results. If prices rise, however, a loss results. The result therefore depends purely on the security selection and timing skills of the manager.

Short seller funds were popular at some periods (e.g. just after the 1987 or the 2000 crash), but the long bull markets gave them a tough time. Funds that focus solely on short selling stocks are now rare. Most of them migrated to the long/short strategy, where they still have a systematic short bias.

TRADING FUNDS AND MANAGED FUTURES

Trading funds, commodity trading advisers (CTAs) and managed futures form an industry made up of professional money managers who use their own proprietary trading methods and money management techniques to establish positions on behalf of their clients on a discretionary basis. They essentially use commodity, financial futures and foreign currency markets around the world as an investment medium.

The popularity of trading funds, CTAs and managed futures started rising in the early 1970s, with the introduction of futures contracts that were not linked to traditional commodities but to interest rate and currencies, and later to stock indices. Individuals or companies willing to participate in the futures and/or options markets often lacked the time and knowledge to trade these markets themselves. This is why they started hiring experienced managers, typically former traders, to trade on their behalf.

There are numerous substrategies in the world of trading funds and managed futures. According to Billingsley and Chance (1996), 58.1% of these funds are trend followers, in the sense that they play on market momentum (i.e. they tend to buy when the market goes up and sell when the market goes down), because they believe that some form of trend will subsist; 26.1% are discretionary traders that can implement whatever strategy they like; and 6.7% follow some sort of systematic strategy. The rest use quantitative analysis (4.9%), arbitrage (1.1%), technical (1.1%) or statistical analysis (0.9%), fundamental analysis (0.5%), mechanical approaches (0.2%), pattern recognition techniques (0.2%) and stochastic analysis (0.1%). Most of them use leverage explicitly or implicitly (through futures contracts) to accentuate the impact of market moves on their portfolios.

Charles Darwin's theory of natural selection applies perfectly to the domain of trading and managed futures funds—only the fittest and the best-performing survive. However, they suffer from a lack of consolidation, mostly because of the entrepreneurial nature of the business and the desire for independence shown by some managers. Indeed, many CTAs have been losing their customers and a significant portion of their assets to hedge funds during the last few years. Consequently, relying on the increasing globalization of markets and the development of financial derivatives, CTAs have started to apply their skills to individual equities as well as other markets and launched long/short equity funds. The distinction between hedge funds, trading funds and managed futures funds is therefore becoming blurred.

11
Hedge fund indices

As hedge funds are increasingly accepted as mainstream investments, the industry has launched a range of indices for tracking their performance and comparing funds. Broadly stated, an index is a number published at regular time intervals that measures the price movements of a particular group of financial securities. It is usually stated in relative terms, that is, with respect to a base-day figure arbitrarily set at 100 or 1000. It can focus on a certain asset class (stocks, bonds, commodities, etc.) or a mix of those. It can also be broad in scope (e.g. measuring a large group of stocks in different industries) or quite narrow (e.g. measuring selected stocks in a particular sector such as utilities). It can be general or focus on securities sharing specific characteristics (e.g. large capitalization, growth stocks, high-coupon bonds).

Indices are useful for investors and managers alike because (i) they inform on current and historical market trends, and (ii) they can be used as benchmarks, or in other words, as a point of reference by which the relative performance of a particular investment can be determined. Given the ample academic and practical evidence for the long-term superiority of indices over active managers, an increasing number of investors prefer indexing their portfolios; that is, they minimize trading costs and only track the performance of a market index. This has in turn given rise to a large number of structured products that provide just this kind of tracking service.

While indices are common in the areas of stock and bond investment, it is only in recent years that a number of indices tracking the performance of hedge funds have come into being. In the world of hedge funds, the situation used to be different. A few years ago, hedge fund investing was still the preserve of an elite. Very high net worth individuals used to entrust their assets to hedge fund managers whom they knew personally, a process that was similar to private banking at the beginning of the 19th century. The hedge funds of these managers had an absolute target return, and there was no need for indices, comparative performance or due diligence whatsoever. However, with the increasing interest in alternative investments, the set of available strategies has significantly expanded. A very large number of unknown managers have launched their own hedge fund, so that investors are now confronted with a wide range of competing products that are hard to distinguish from each other.

Hedge fund indices are particularly useful in such a situation. They provide a reference point that is crucially important, particularly for institutional investors and private bankers who are responsible for large sums of other people's money and are accustomed to looking for relative returns measured against a benchmark. Individual investors need to know if the managers they hired are performing well or badly. And managers themselves may still have an absolute return target in mind, but they like to know how their performance compares with that of their peers. Combined with the increasing number of third-party agencies and consultants that collect and distribute data on hedge fund performance, this explains the growing importance of hedge fund indices over recent years.

Indeed, after several years without any reference point, investors now have the opposite problem. The proliferation of hedge fund listings and analysis services has created confusion, in the absence of industry-standardized fund categories. Since hedge fund information providers have slightly different methods of categorizing funds and computing indices, a number of problems can arise.

CALCULATING HEDGE FUND INDICES

Today several hedge fund indices are available. They differ from one another essentially in four respects: their sampling rules, their mapping strategy, their weighting methods and their maintenance policies (Figure 11.1). The sampling rules specify the criteria for a given hedge fund to be included in an index. Three points of view clash here:

- An index is supposed to be representative of a particular investment strategy or asset class, so it is necessary to include as many funds as possible. This gives birth to indices that contain several hundred hedge funds, most of which are totally unknown to the index builder.
- A hedge fund index may only consider a relatively small percentage of the total number of hedge funds in the category and still be representative of a given strategy. The justification is that the quality of the available data deteriorates rapidly as one moves away from the largest players in the industry. Smaller or newer funds typically tend to compute their net asset values later in the month, to disclose the corresponding figures with some delay and even to come back and adjust the net asset values published in the previous months. They are also more likely to switch strategy without necessarily disclosing it. Therefore, some index builders prefer to select a few established managers whom they know well rather than raking over as many managers as possible.
- A compromise is to rely on a predefined set of criteria to filter the mass of hedge funds and retain only some of them in the final index. Examples of such criteria are a minimum size of assets under management, a minimum track record, a performance that is audited, and a minimum redemption policy. The number of funds selected will therefore vary depending on the category considered. For instance, a minimum size of $300 million will not be a problem for global macro funds, but it may eliminate a significant number of convertible arbitrage funds.

Other important issues when building a set of indices are (i) the selection of the investment strategies for which an index is needed, and (ii) the mapping process between the funds in the universe and the various strategies considered. The first step is rather arbitrary, and each firm can provide investors and investment professionals with its own

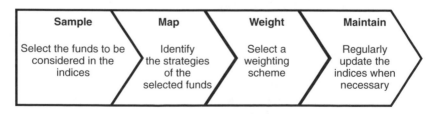

Figure 11.1 The four steps for building hedge fund indices

perceived categorizations. However, due to the low level of disclosure, it is very difficult to assess precisely the investment strategy followed by a hedge fund manager. Consequently, a wide diversity of policies are used in the industry. Some index builders rely on the hedge funds' self-reported styles. Others send due diligence questionnaires and conduct interviews with managers in order to get more insight. Very few attempt to have access to the funds' underlying positions to properly identify their strategies.

Once funds have been selected and mapped on a given strategy, the next step is to give them weights in the corresponding index. Almost all index builders use an equal weight for each fund—they simply take an arithmetic average of the fund performances. While this may appear acceptable at first glance, it is counterintuitive from an asset allocation viewpoint. Let us explain why. Say the index is calculated on a monthly basis. We can imagine the index as being a portfolio of hedge funds, each of them having an equal weight in the portfolio. The portfolio is set up at the beginning of the month and the initial index value is calculated. One month passes, and the end-of-the-month value of the index is calculated and published. Now, the portfolio is not equally weighted any more. Some funds have dropped in value, while others have risen. Resetting an equal weighting for the next month simply means that one has to sell winners to buy more losers at the end of each month. In asset allocation terms, this corresponds to a contrariwise strategy, which most investors will be reluctant to implement.

A much better approach is provided by the asset-weighted index, in which the weight of each fund depends on the size of its assets relative to the size of the assets of all funds in the index. Larger funds thus have more influence on the overall performance, which is in line with the idea of measuring the performance of an industry from a "dollar invested" perspective. It is also consistent with the capitalization-weighted approach used in the large equity and bond indices, such as the S&P 500. If we return to our example, at the end of the month, winners have grown in the index, while losers have naturally reduced their weight. The drawback of this approach, however, is that the size of the assets managed by each fund has to be known at each calculation date, since subscriptions and redemptions will influence the weighting.

The final step to consider is the maintenance of the index, which is an ongoing process. It includes operations like these:

- *The exclusion of funds from the index*: an index deletion typically occurs when a fund is no longer representative (e.g. if the manager changes its strategy), stops reporting, goes bankrupt, merges with another fund, or is acquired by another company.
- *The inclusion of new funds in the index*: an index addition can be made only if an index vacancy is created by an index deletion, or as soon as a new hedge fund enters the universe or changes categories.
- *The monitoring of newly included funds*: since new funds have neither holdings histories nor performance histories, they are often classified according to their stated investment objectives. After a while, these funds may be reviewed and their performance (and possibly their underlying holdings, if available) will be used to determine the appropriateness of their classification.
- *The creation of new categories*: once a universe of managers emerges in a new strategy, a new subindex should be created and the corresponding hedge funds grouped together.

Indices are useful, quick tools for measuring the performance of a given system. While they certainly do not provide an absolute measurement of all the capabilities of the system, they do provide useful information. However, there is no "correct" absolute method for constructing a hedge fund index. In fact, several types of indices may be devised for the same set of funds. Each serves a valuable function, but depending on the usage, it may be more or less relevant in different situations.

AN OVERVIEW OF MAJOR INDEX PROVIDERS

There are more and more third-party agencies that collect and distribute data on hedge fund performance. I list only the major ones, indicating the major characteristics of each index and highlighting their principal differences.

Altvest

Altvest is a subsidiary of InvestorForce Inc., an information-providing company that targets institutional investors, consultants and money managers. Since 2000 Altvest has produced a family of 14 hedge fund indices from a database of about 2000 hedge funds, with data going back to 1993.

Altvest's indices consist of a master index, which is built from all funds in the database, and 13 subindices comprising funds that are included in the master index (Table 11.1). To

Table 11.1 Hierarchy of Altvest, CSFB/Tremont and EACM indices

Altvest	*EACM*
Altvest Hedge Fund Index	EACM 100 Index
Currency Trading	Relative Value
Emerging Markets	Long-Short Equity
Event Driven	Convertible Hedge
Merger Arbitrage	Bond Hedge
Distressed Securities	Multi-strategy
Fund of Funds	Event Driven
Health Care	Deal Arbitrage
Macro	Bankruptcy/Distressed
Relative Value	Multi-strategy
Long/Short Equity	Equity Hedge Funds
Capital Structure Arbitrage	Domestic Long Biased
Short Selling	Domestic Opportunistic
Technology	Global/International
	Global Asset Allocators
CSFB/Tremont	Discretionary
Hedge Fund Index	Systematic
	Short Sellers
Market Neutral	
Emerging Markets	
Event-Driven	
Fixed-Income Arbitrage	
Global Macro	
Dedicated-short bias	
Convertible Arbitrage	
Dedicated Short Bias	
Long/Short Equity	
Managed futures	

map funds with categories, Altvest assigns each fund to the category in which the largest percentage of its assets is invested. If a fund changes category, its past performance remains with its previous subindex and future performance is included in the new index. Note that a fund can be simultaneously included in several subindices. For example, a fund of funds specialized in technology stocks would appear in both the "fund of funds" and the "technology" subindices. Additionally, the "event driven" subindex includes all funds from both the "merger arbitrage" and "distressed securities" subindices, and the "relative value" subindex includes all funds from the "long/short equity" and "capital structure arbitrage" subindices.

Although only recently created, Altvest became popular when Calpers, the largest public pension plan in the US, announced that it would be using Altvest's capabilities to manage its $1 billion position in alternative investments. Since then Altvest has also created an innovative technology platform that allows investors and consultants to search for alternative assets information online. The information is updated online on a daily basis and provided through the web, which means it is available as soon as managers report their performance. Historical data are frozen after a month, so they will never be modified by the addition or removal of new funds.

CSFB/Tremont

CSFB/Tremont Index LLC is a joint venture between Credit Suisse First Boston (CSFB) and Tremont Advisers Inc. CSFB is one of the world's leading global investment banking firms and Tremont is a diversified financial services company specialized in hedge fund consulting, information and research, and investment products. Oppenheimer Funds, a US-based provider of traditional investment products managing assets of $127 billion, recently acquired Tremont Advisers Inc. for $140 million. The two companies have joined forces to produce a series of hedge fund indices (Table 11.1).

The selection of funds for the CSFB/Tremont indices is done every quarter. The process starts by considering all 2600 US and offshore hedge funds contained in the TASS database, with the exception of funds of funds and managed accounts. Founded in London in 1990, TASS Investment Research is the information and research subsidiary of Tremont; it is a leading provider of data, information and market intelligence to the hedge fund industry.

To qualify for inclusion in an index, a hedge fund must (i) have at least $10 million under management, (ii) provide audited financial statements, and (iii) meet the CSFB/Tremont Index LLC reporting requirements. As of July 1, 2001 only 375 funds met these three requirements. These funds are then separated into various categories based on their investment style, with the final constraint that the index in all cases should represent at least 85% of the assets under management in the corresponding universe.

The weight of each fund in an index is given by the relative size of its assets under management. This makes the CSFB/Tremont indices the only asset-weighted indices in the industry. The composition of the indices are public and available on the web.

Evaluation Associates Capital Markets

Evaluation Associates Capital Markets (EACM) is an investment advisory firm based in Norwalk, Connecticut. It specializes in hedge funds and multimanager investment programs for institutional and high net worth clients. In January 1996 EACM launched a

new benchmark for alternative investment strategies called the EACM 100 index, as well
as indices for five broad strategies and 13 underlying substrategies, with data going back
to 1990 (Table 11.1). EACM's indices are computed from an equally weighted composite
of nonaudited performance information provided by a set of about one hundred hedge
funds. These funds are selected by EACM as being representative of their style, and the
index may be rebalanced at the beginning of each calendar year. However, EACM does
not disclose individual fund names or their weightings.

HedgeFund.net (Tuna)

Based in New York, HedgeFund.net is a consulting company owned by Links Holdings
LLC and Capital Z Investments LP, and operated by Links Securities LLC. These firms

Table 11.2 Hierarchy of Tuna and HFR indices

HedgeFund.net (Tuna)	*Hedge Fund Research*
Hedge Fund Aggregate Index	HFRI Fund Weighted Composite Index
Aggressive Aggregate Index	
Equity Hedge Aggregate Index	HFRI Convertible Arbitrage
Relative Value Aggregate Index	HFRI Distressed Securities
	HFRI Emerging Markets (Total)
Aggressive Growth	HFRI Emerg. Mkts: Asia
Convertible Arbitrage	HFRI Emerg. Mkts: Eastern Europe/CIS
Country Specific	HFRI Emerg. Mkts: Global
CTA	HFRI Emerg. Mkts: Latin America
Distressed	HFRI Equity Hedge
Emerging Markets	HFRI Equity Market Neutral
Energy Sector	HFRI Equity Non-Hedge
Event Driven	HFRI Event-Driven
Finance Sector	HFRI Fixed Income (Total)
Fixed Income	HFRI Fixed Inc.: Arbitrage
Fixed Income Arbitrage	HFRI Fixed Inc.: Convertible Bonds
Fund of Funds	HFRI Fixed Inc.: Diversified
Healthcare Sector	HFRI Fixed Inc.: High Yield
Long Only	HFRI Fixed Inc.: Mortgage-Backed
Long/Short Hedged	HFRI Macro
Macro	HFRI Market Timing
Market Neutral	HFRI Merger Arbitrage
Market Timer	HFRI Regulation D
Opportunistic	HFRI Relative Value Arbitrage
Options Arbitrage	HFRI Sector (Total)
Options Strategies	HFRI Sector: Energy
Other Relative Value	HFRI Sector: Financial
Regulation D	HFRI Sector: Health Care/Biotech
Risk Arbitrage	HFRI Sector: Miscellaneous
Short Bias	HFRI Sector: Real Estate
Short-term Trading	HFRI Sector: Technology
Small/Micro Cap	HFRI Short Selling
Special Situations	HFRI Statistical Arbitrage
Statistical Arbitrage	HFRI Fund of Funds
Technology Sector	
Value	
Venture Capital/Private Equity	

combine management expertise, capital, and execution capacities: Capital Z Investments is an investment fund that holds a diversified portfolio of hedge funds and private equity, and Links Holdings is the holding company of Links Securities LLC, a US broker-dealer registered with the National Association of Securities Dealers. HedgeFund.net produces a set of 33 hedge fund indices (also called the Tuna indices) from a database of around 1800 funds, with data going back to 1979. It also produces three aggregated indices using the same data (Table 11.2). The Tuna indices are calculated as an equally weighted average of the performance of all funds within the corresponding category. Fund managers themselves select the category to which they want to be assigned.

Hedge Fund Research

Hedge Fund Research (HFR), a veteran of the hedge fund industry, is a Chicago-based performance measurement and consultancy firm. Since 1994 it has computed and published a total of 33 monthly performance indices based on a large number of onshore and offshore hedge funds (Table 11.3). The available data was backfilled until 1990. These indices are net of fees, free of survivorship bias after 1994, and equally weighted. The weighting scheme is revised on a monthly basis to include new funds and to eliminate defunct ones. Funds are assigned to categories based on the descriptions in their offering memorandums.

In addition, HFR has published a series of five daily indices since the beginning of 2000. They cover the major investment styles according to HFR: convertible bond arbitrage, equity hedge, event driven, merger arbitrage and distressed securities arbitrage. Each index is based on an equally weighted portfolio of hedge funds. These must have at least $5 million under management and agree to disclose detailed positions to HFR. The information is used to assign funds to a category, to estimate the net asset values on a daily basis using multiple price sources, and to unleverage performance according to debit balances. For instance, a $500 000 debit balance in a $1 million portfolio would indicate 50% leverage, so the performance for that portfolio would be reduced by 50% for that particular day.

Hennessee Group

The Hennessee Group LLC is a New York research and consulting firm. It produces a set of 23 indices, based on a sample of about 500 hedge funds selected from a database of about 3000 funds. The indices were created in 1987 and became publicly available in 1992. Funds are assigned to categories based on "manager's core competency" (Table 11.3). An interesting feature of the Hennessee indices is that they include several funds that are closed to new subscriptions, hence they do not report to other agencies. This is possible only because clients of the Hennessee Group are effectively investing in these funds.

LJH Global Investments

LJH Global Investments is a consulting and advisory firm based in Naples, Florida. It has developed a set of 16 indices of various hedge fund styles (Table 11.3). Each index is calculated as the performance of an equally weighted sample of 25 to 50 hedge funds. These funds are selected and mapped to a specific strategy by LJH Global Investments.

Table 11.3 Hierarchy of HFR (daily), Hennessee and LJH indices

Hedge Fund Research (daily indices)	Hennessee
Equal-Weighted Aggregate Index	Hennessee Hedge Fund Index
Asset-Weighted Aggregate Index	
	Convertible Arbitrage
Convertible Arbitrage	Distressed
Equity Hedge	Emerging Markets
Event-Driven	Europe
Merger Arbitrage	Event Driven
Distressed Securities	Financial Equities
	Fixed Income
LJH Global Investments	Growth
LJH Global Hedge Index	Healthcare
	High Yield
Asian Hedge	International
Convertible Arbitrage	Latin America
Distressed Securities	Macro
Domestic Hedge	Market Neutral
Emerging Markets	Merger Arbitrage
Emerging Markets Fixed Income	Multiple Arbitrage
Event Driven	Opportunistic
Fixed Income Arbitrage	Pacific Rim
European Hedge	Short Biased
Global Macro	Regulation D
Hedge	Technology
Market Neutral Equity	Value
Risk Arbitrage	
Risk Arbitrage	
Short Only	
Technology Fund	

They must provide audited statements and pass some due diligence tests. The composition of each index is revised on a regular basis but is not disclosed.

Van Hedge Fund Advisors International

Van Hedge Fund Advisors International is a research and advisory services firm based in Nashville, Tennessee. It maintains a database of about 4000 funds, primarily used to identify hedge funds for investors, and on request, to design custom hedge fund portfolios. Van Hedge tracks the performance of 14 strategies, plus a global index, based on a subsample of about 750 offshore and onshore hedge funds (Table 11.4). Funds are assigned to categories based on their offering memorandums and interviews with their managers.

Zurich Hedge Fund Universe/Managed Account Reports LLC

Founded in 1979, Managed Account Reports (MAR) is a subsidiary of Metal Bulletin plc, a London Stock Exchange listed publishing and information providing company. It has tracked managed futures investments since 1979 and hedge funds since 1994. MAR used to publish a series of hedge funds and managed futures monthly indices that had the particularity of considering the median performance rather than the average (Table 11.4).

Table 11.4   Hierarchy of Van Hedge and Zurich indices

Van Hedge Fund Advisors	*Zurich Hedge Fund Universe/Managed Account Reports LLC*
Van US Hedge Fund Index	Zurich Event-Driven Median
Van Offshore Hedge Fund Index	Distressed Securities Sub-median
	Risk Arbitrage Sub-median
Aggressive Growth	Zurich Global Emerging Median
Distressed Securities	Zurich Global International Median
	Zurich Global Established Median
Emerging Markets	Global Established Growth Sub-median
Fund of Funds	Global Established Small-cap Sub-median
Income	Global Established Value Sub-median
Macro	Zurich Global Macro Median
Market Neutral—Arbitrage	Zurich Market Neutral Median
Market Neutral—Securities Hedging	Market Neutral Arbitrage Sub-median
Market Timing	Market Neutral Long/Short Sub-median
Opportunistic	Mortgage-Backed Sub-median
Several Strategies	Zurich Sector Median
Short Selling	Zurich Short-Sellers Median
Special Situations	Zurich Fund of Funds Median
Value	Fund of Funds Diversified Sub-median
	Fund of Funds Niche Sub-median
ZCM/HFR Hedge Fund Indices	
Merger Arbitrage	
Convertible Arbitrage	
Distressed Securities	
Hedged Equity	
Event Driven	
Zurich Hedge Fund Indices	
Merger Arbitrage	
Convertible Arbitrage	
Distressed Securities	
Hedged Equity	
Event Driven	

Since the acquisition of the company's alternative investment fund databases and related intellectual property by Zurich Capital Markets in March 2001, MAR's range of managed futures and hedge funds benchmarks has been rebranded under the Zurich name. Zurich has announced its intention to significantly increase support for the MAR databases by "improving reported performance data, modernizing the technological platforms behind the databases and expanding the hedge fund categories, strategies and styles."

ZCM/HFR Index Management

In October 1999 Zurich Capital Markets (a wholly owned New York subsidiary of the Zurich Financial Services Group of Switzerland) and Hedge Fund Research created a joint venture named ZCM/HFR Index Management for the purpose of offering hedge fund indices as well as funds of funds tracking these indices. The new company designed the methodology and started publishing indices tracking five strategies: merger arbitrage, convertible arbitrage, distressed securities, equity hedge and event driven (Table 11.4).

However, the concept never attracted more than $300 million from investors, mostly from Zurich Capital Markets. The major problem was that the methodology was rather opaque: "Each index is constructed as a diversified allocation to a collection of separately-managed accounts, weighted and rebalanced via a proprietary methodology developed by the joint-venture." The joint venture terminated in December 2000. Zurich Capital Markets bought back the investment platform of ZCM/HFR for an undisclosed sum and stopped calculating these indices.

Zurich Capital Markets

In March 2001, following the acquisition of the alternative investment fund database and intellectual property from Managed Account Reports LLC, Zurich Capital Markets in partnership with Schneeweis Partners LLC again started offering five hedge fund indices. The five strategies selected were the same as the former ZCM/HFR hedge fund indices: merger arbitrage, convertible arbitrage, distressed securities, hedged equity, and event driven (Table 11.4).

Each index is built from an equally weighted portfolio of 10 to 15 hedge funds. These funds are carefully selected for the "purity" of their investment style, which manifests itself primarily in manager correlation with other pure style managers as well as specific style-related benchmarks. In addition, each selected fund must have at least $25 million under management for at least two years, and must be likely to be considered for investment by institutional investors or sophisticated investors. The composition of the portfolio is public, and rebalancing occurs on a quarterly basis, under the supervision of an independent committee.

In parallel, ZCM launched the Zurich Institutional Benchmark Series, a fund of hedge funds, with the goal of replicating the performance of the indices with modest tracking error and at relatively low cost. It collected $315 million the first month, and has a target size of $2–3 billion by the end of 2002. One of its particularities is that it invests with the managers represented in each index through managed accounts, in order to have a complete view on the assets (Zurich acts as a custodian).

Newcomers

Besides the above providers, there are lots of newcomers to the world of hedge fund index providers. For instance, Deutsche Bank Asset Management has also announced the creation of the Deutsche Bank 100 index, comprising 100 hedge funds selected by the bank. It is quite popular in Germany because index certificates are offered on this hedge fund index.

A major player should soon enter the arena. Morgan Stanley Capital International (MSCI), the world's leading index provider for equities, has teamed up with Financial Risk Management (FRM) to investigate jointly the development of a set of new hedge fund indices. Very little is known about these indices, except that they should be designed and structured by MSCI, while FRM will handle the day-to-day operational matters, including data collection, rule setting and manager relationships. MSCI has announced it will use a three-dimensional classification system:

- The first dimension should cover the process employed to generate returns, such as stock selection, relative value, credit specialist and directional trading. It should include several subcategories within each process, such as the long or short investment bias and the industry bias for the stock selection; distressed debt, positive carry and private placements for the credit specialist; convergence, merger and statistical arbitrage for the relative value; and discretionary, strategic, systematic and fund timing for the directional trading.

- The second dimension will cover the asset class used to generate returns. This should include equities (split into equity and convertibles), fixed income (split into credit sensitive, credit insensitive and mortgage-backed securities), commodities, currencies (split into developed and emerging markets), real estate and options.
- The third dimension will be the location of the funds' investments. The announced categories are Europe, North America, Japan, Pacific ex-Japan, emerging markets, as well as broader global developed and global categories.

This gives a very large number of potential combinations, but it allows for a very precise definition of the strategy followed by a hedge fund, such as relative value, convergence arbitrage, fixed income, global, developed; or directional trading, long bias, equity, Europe, financial sector, mid-cap. Given the prominence of the sponsor, these indices should become widely accepted benchmarks.

Finally, there has been an updated proposal from the Investor Risk Committee of the International Association of Financial Engineers (IAFE). It suggest a new framework for hedge funds to classify themselves based on their asset class, direction (long, short, neutral), type (e.g. relative value, convertible arbitrage, macro), region, liquidity and turnover. The last two measures are relatively innovative in the usual hedge funds taxonomies, but they would help to differentiate performance in a particular strategy. If the IAFE's suggestions are accepted and implemented by hedge funds, then investors will be able to compare hedge funds with their true peers in the market and better benchmarks could be developed.

STATISTICAL BIASES IN INDICES AND DATABASES

Hedge fund indices are subject to several statistical biases. Among the most important are survivorship bias, selection bias, backfill bias, double counting bias, and reporting bias. Most of these biases are spurious, because they are embedded in the data collection process that is necessary to build up a database. All benchmarks and indices built on a database will therefore inherit its biases.

Survivorship bias

Survivorship bias arises when a hedge fund sample contains only surviving funds. Funds that have gone out of business in past years, typically for poor performance reasons, are excluded from the sample. A very natural bias, it is present in almost all databases; when data vendors decide to start publishing a new performance index, they tend to collect information on the set of existing, and therefore surviving, hedge funds. With respect to the historical universe of funds, their sample characteristics therefore represent winners' characteristics, creating an upward bias in performance.

Some data vendors (e.g. TASS and HFR) attempt to correct for survivorship bias by leaving dead funds in the index for the duration these hedge funds operated. However, since they only started doing this in 1994, their data prior to 1994 still contains significant survivorship bias. Other databases (e.g. HedgeFund.net) do not care about survivorship bias and prefer to remove a fund from the index if it is shut down for whatever reason.

Survivorship bias is well documented and easy to quantify for mutual funds, where the entire fund population is known and observable (Grinblatt and Titman 1989; Brown *et al.* 1992; Malkiel 1995). One simply computes the average performance of all funds that operated during some period, and compares it with the average performance of the subsample of funds that survived until the end of the period. The difference is the survivorship bias; it is usually in the range 0.5% to 1%, expressed on an annual basis.

Unfortunately, there are several reasons why survivorship bias is harder to quantify for hedge funds. First, due to the nonreporting requirement, the set of all hedge funds that operated during a given period is not observable, and even the set of all databases does not coincide with the universe. Second, there are two reasons that cause hedge funds to disappear from databases:

- Poor performance may result in unhappy investors withdrawing their funds, but also in managers having to work for free. Managers working for free arises when there are high water mark provisions in the performance contracts, so that managers have to recover the losses before charging performance fees. It is sometimes easier for them to cease operations and start a new virgin fund under a new name.
- An excellent performance by a fund may result in a substantial increase in the size of its managed assets. Several niche managers report to database vendors at the beginning of their activity and wait until they reach an optimal size of assets under management with respect to their investing style. They then close their funds to new subscriptions and stop reporting, because they do not want to attract new investors. Their fund still exists, but it has simply disappeared from the observable population.

Consequently, it is very difficult to distinguish between the two types of fund and, unlike the case of the mutual fund universe, a hedge fund that disappears has not necessarily stopped its activity.

A few studies have attempted to quantify the survivorship bias for hedge funds, with widely differing results (Table 11.5). The major reason for these differences is the use of different data samples containing different numbers of dissolved funds, as evidenced by Liang (2000).

Selection bias

Self-selection bias arises because of the voluntary nature of hedge fund reporting. Numerous hedge funds lack the incentive that other funds have to report to data vendors, hence they are excluded from any index calculations.

Table 11.5 Impact of survivorship bias on annual performance of hedge funds

	Annual bias (%)	Sample
Ackermann *et al.* (1999)	1.5	Hedge funds
Fung and Hsieh (1998)	3.54	Hedge funds
Fung and Hsieh (2000b)	3	Hedge funds
Brown *et al.* (1999a)	3	Offshore funds

The problem is particularly delicate for funds whose performance rating lies at each end of the sample. At one end, funds performing consistently well and funds from top managers have enough equity capital and do not need additional promotion. Consequently, they simply refuse to disclose their numbers to any index compiler, and this biases the performance of the index downward. At the other end, for very different reasons, it is natural to expect that funds performing consistently badly will prefer to remain in the dark. This biases the index upward. Depending on which group predominates, the bias is therefore in one direction or the other.

In addition to this self-reporting bias, data vendors often introduce some selection bias by applying specific sampling criteria in their index inclusion process. For example, HFR excludes managed futures and commodity funds, while TASS and MAR include them. In practice, detecting selection bias is not an easy task. The process is further complicated by the fact that most hedge funds choose to report only to one or two databases. Liang (2000) reports, for example, that the HFR database (1162 funds) and the TASS database (1627 funds) have only 465 funds in common.

Backfill bias

Backfill bias arises when a database does not include new hedge funds solely on a going-forward basis, but also includes the funds' historical track record. This will typically overstate the index performance. The reason is that fund managers prefer to wait for a good period of performance before requesting their inclusion in an index. They then truncate their track record adequately and provide only the most recent and more successful part.

Backfill bias is easy to detect by comparing a hedge fund's creation date with the date of its inclusion in a database. If there is a delay, it is a warning sign that the database is subject to backfill bias. Fung and Hsieh (2000b) call this delay an incubation period, and report that the average incubation period for the TASS database is one year. They estimate the resulting bias to be around 1.4% per year. Other databases (e.g. CSFB/Tremont) avoid the backfill bias by only including funds on a going-forward basis.

Double counting bias

Double counting bias occurs when an index includes a hedge fund in more than one category. This is often the case when funds of funds and their underlying hedge funds are considered together in an index. The assets and performance of the underlying funds are then double-counted.

Reporting bias

Reporting bias occurs when an index performance is seen to weaken in the course of the month. For instance, at the beginning of February, an index may have gained 3% for the month of January, while at the end of February the gain reported for January may be 2%. This bias is frequently observed at data providers that update their monthly indices on a daily basis to include the most current data. There are three reasons for this:

- Funds with excellent performance generally rush to report their returns. Therefore, the earliest results for an index tend to include funds that have performed well.

- Funds of funds, which generally have lower returns than some single-manager fund strategies due to diversification, report later in the month than single-manager funds. They have to wait for every subfund report before they can report for themselves.
- Some hedge funds use a variety of derivatives, illiquid strategies or other securities investments that are difficult to price. It sometimes takes several weeks to obtain pricing information for these securities. In the meantime, they communicate an estimate of their net asset value that is typically conservative. Later they provide a better estimate, therefore modifying the past value of the index.

12

Hedge fund performance: beyond NAVs

For the majority of investors, investment performance is ultimately the most important factor in determining which asset to invest in. This is particularly true for assets that are indeed managed portfolios, such as mutual funds and hedge funds, where managers' actions are likely to affect the overall performance.

FROM MUTUAL FUNDS TO HEDGE FUNDS

Investors usually track performance and judge a mutual fund's profitability by following changes in its net asset value (NAV) per share. This is the equivalent of the fund's share price—the value of one share of the fund's stock. It is calculated by dividing the current value of the fund's assets (minus the fund's liabilities, if any) by the number of fund shares outstanding.

$$\text{NAV per share} = \frac{\text{value of the fund's assets} - \text{value of the fund's liabilities}}{\text{number of shares outstanding}}$$

For example, if a mutual fund has securities and other assets worth $100 million and has liabilities of $10 million, its total NAV will be $90 million. If there are 9 million shares outstanding, the NAV of each share will be $9.

Valuation of assets and liabilities is extremely important for open-ended mutual funds, which must redeem and issue their shares to the public at NAV. If the valuation is incorrect, investors will pay or receive too much or too little for their shares. Subscription and redemption orders are usually executed at the closing NAV on the day of each order. This has several implications:

- Mutual funds allowing daily subscription and redemption must calculate and publish their NAV at least once every business day, typically after the exchange close.
- Investors must give their order (purchase or sale) without knowing the exact price of execution. This is called forward-looking pricing. Actually, most funds execute only subscriptions and redemptions received before noon on the day of the execution. Those that arrive later are executed the next day at the corresponding future NAV.

Since subscriptions and redemptions have an equal effect on numerator and denominator, they do not affect the NAV per share. The change in a fund's NAV per share depends only on the fund's performance; for the sake of simplicity, we assume in this chapter that there are no dividend payments. Comparing the performance of NAV per share values therefore enables investors to easily differentiate mutual funds on a relative basis.

Closed-end mutual funds, in contrast, do not provide for regular subscription or redemption of their shares. They sell a fixed number of shares at one time (in the initial public offering), after which the shares typically trade on a secondary market, such as the New York Stock Exchange or the Nasdaq. The price of closed-end fund shares is therefore determined by the market and may be greater or less than the shares' NAV. Consequently, comparing the performance of closed-end funds based on the market price of their shares is not fair. It aggregates two phenomena: the effective attraction of the fund (which will result in a price discount or premium with respect to the NAV) and the performance of the manager (which will affect the NAV and should affect the price equivalently); see Box 12.1. It is therefore more reliable to estimate managers' performance using NAVs and investors' performance using quoted share prices.

Box 12.1   ARBITRAGING BETWEEN NAVS AND QUOTED PRICE: ALTIN AG

Figure 1 shows the performance of Altin AG's shares over the period January 1998 to December 2001. Altin is a Swiss investment company comparable to a closed-end fund investing in other hedge funds. It simultaneously pursues several investment strategies such as merger arbitrage and global macro, combined with investments in various commodity trading advisers. Clearly, the share price shows a significant and persistent discount with respect to the net asset value. Figure 2 shows the same information for CreInvest AG, one of Altin's competitors. Here too we observe a difference between the net asset value and the last quoted price for CreInvest. However, the difference is small and tends to disappear over the years, whereas it seems persistent in the case of Altin.

   The persistence of this situation eventually resulted in an unsolicited bid for Altin by its competitor. On May 14, 2001 CreInvest offered to pay 90% of the value of Altin's holdings, that is, 15% more than Altin's share price at that time. CreInvest's intentions were to merge with Altin, therefore gaining access to a larger and more diversified hedge fund portfolio at a cheap price. In addition, half of Altin's portfolio was made up of stakes in top-tier hedge funds closed to new subscriptions. The merger would have given CreInvest a cheap means of entering into these funds. In

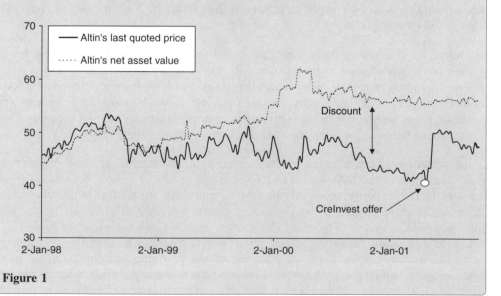

Figure 1

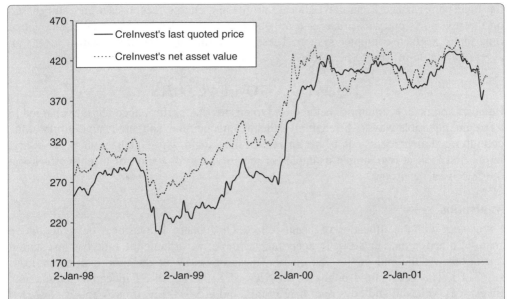

Figure 2

the case of a merger failure, CreInvest announced that it would solicit Altin shares on the open market at 87% of the net asset value.

Following the recommendation of Altin's board, Altin's shareholders rejected the merger offer and accepted a reduction in the nominal value of the shares. It also decided to return cash to shareholders and to appoint Deutsche Bank as an adviser to decrease the discount.

Compared to mutual funds, hedge funds usually have a much smaller number of shareholders. These shareholders are more stable over time and are used to a much lower frequency of NAV calculation and reporting. However, institutional investors tend to require a higher level of periodic reporting than private investors. This may substantially increase the administrator's workload per investor in the forthcoming years. So from the perspective of NAV calculation, these two advantages are small compared to the downsides. For instance:

- Hedge funds usually have some assets but they also have large amounts of liability due to short positions. The corresponding securities are often deposited with several brokers and custodians, so that getting a full list of a fund's assets and liabilities in a reasonable amount of time may be a challenge.
- Several assets in hedge fund portfolios are likely to present pricing challenges. This is the case with non-exchange-traded securities, private placements, illiquid or over-the-counter contracts, distressed debt, or exotic options.

In addition, hedge funds charge several levels of fees. These are usually paid quarterly or at year end, based on the size of the assets managed and/or the performance of the strategy. Since investors can enter and leave the fund at different times, it is essential that administrators ensure a smooth process for the NAV calculation in order to reflect the fund performance accurately; allocate profits and charge fees to each investor, based on the investor's entry/exit date; and be able to report NAVs in a reasonable amount of time using a given computer system. These are conflicting objectives, which means an acceptable trade-off has to be reached.

EQUALIZATION FACTORS

Equalization is an accounting method used to ensure that performance fees are charged in a fair and equitable way to different investors in a hedge fund, so there is no dilution of the continuing shareholders' equity per share. To understand why equalization is necessary, let us first look at two simple examples of inequity: the allocation of incentive fees and the free rider syndrome.

Motivation

Let us start with the allocation of incentive fees. On January 1 investor A buys the unique share of a hedge fund at $100. To keep things simple, we assume the fund has just started operations. At the end of the first quarter, the gross NAV of the fund has increased to say $110. The hedge fund publishes an NAV of $108, net of $2 incentive fee accrual. Investor B comes in and buys one share in the fund at $108. Investors A and B now each own 50% of the fund. Let us say that at the middle of the year the gross NAV of the fund is now $120. The total profit is $32, based on the following:

Investor A invested	$100
Investor B invested	$108
Total invested	$208
Total gross NAV	$240
Gross profit	$32

If the incentive fee is charged semiannually, the corresponding amount would be 20% of $32, i.e. $6.4 in total, or $3.2 per share. The final NAV published by the fund would therefore be $116.8 per share ($120 - 3.2$). Consequently, investor A effectively pays $3.2 on a profit of $20, which equals 16.4% of his profit. Investor B pays the same $3.2, but on a profit of $12, which represents 26.66% of his profit. There is clearly an inequitable allocation of incentive fees.

Our second example is an illustration of the free rider syndrome. On January 1 investor A buys the unique share of a hedge fund at $100. A high water mark clause in the offering memorandum states that the 20% incentive fee can be charged only if the fund manager makes money. At the end of the first quarter, the gross NAV of the fund is now down to say $90. Investor A has lost 10% of his investment. Investor B comes in and buys one share in the fund at $90. Investors A and B now each own 50% of the fund. Then, at the end of the second quarter, the fund manager recovers his $10 loss. The $10 profit is split evenly between the two investors, so the new NAV is $95 for both investors. This means that the rate of return is -5% for investor A and 5.6% for investor B.

Now investor B decides to leave the hedge fund and pays no performance fee, since the fund manager did not make any money according to the high water mark. This gives investor B a free ride on his profits. Moreover, if the fund manager gains $5 in the next quarter, he could start charging a performance fee to investor A, since he has recovered his losses. Investor A would therefore end up with $99 (100 − 10/2 + 5 − 1), i.e. a −1% rate of return, but would have paid $1 (20% of $5) performance fee.

It is precisely to avoid such situations that we need more complex fee calculations. These types of problem do not occur with hedge funds that are structured as limited partnerships. The reason is that limited partnerships are closed structures, so no new investor can come in after the fund has been launched. But the problem is crucial in offshore funds, which are often open-ended—they allow investors to make capital contributions on a regular basis, therefore creating the potential for an inequity between the new investors and the original ones. As soon as investors subscribe at different NAV levels, one shareholder will always be subsidizing another shareholder to some extent. If there is a wide range of different investors who all came into the fund at different times, one can see that the process becomes complex and time-consuming.

Multiple series of shares

A straightforward solution is to issue multiple series of shares. The first series of shares at the fund's creation is called the lead series, and another series is created each time there is a subscription. Consider the case of a new hedge fund that has just started operations. We assume that the fund has a monthly subscription policy and that its manager charges a 20% incentive fee on a quarterly basis, conditional on a 1% quarterly high water mark. Say the performance of the first three months is as follows: 7% in January, 5% in February and −4% in March.

On January 1 investor A buys 1000 Series I shares of the fund at $1000 per share. This series of shares will constitute the lead series. At the end of January, the gross NAV of the lead series of shares has increased to $1070 per share (7%) and the published NAV is $1056, net of $14 incentive fee accrual (20% of the $70 increase). A new series of 1000 shares called Series II is created, with an NAV per share of $1000. Investor B then buys all Series II shares for $1 million.

At the end of February, the gross NAV of the fund's shares is now $1123.50 for the lead series (5%) and $1050 for Series II shares (5%). The hedge fund publishes an NAV of $1098.80 (net of $24.70 incentive fee accrual) for the lead series and an NAV of $1040 (net of $10 incentive fee accrual) for Series II. A new series of 1000 shares called Series III is created, with an NAV per share of $1000. Investor C then buys all Series III shares for $1 million.

At the end of March, the gross NAV of the fund's shares is now $1078.56 for the lead series, $1008 for Series II shares and $960 for Series III shares. The lead series and Series II shares pay their incentive fee ($15.71 and $1.60 per share, respectively). Series III shares are not profitable and do not pay any incentive fee. Table 12.1 summarizes the overall process.

Table 12.1   Evolution of gross and published net asset values

	Jan 1	Jan 31	Feb 28	Mar 31	Apr 1
Performance (%)		7%	5%	−4%	
Series I (lead series)					
Gross NAV ($)	1000	1070	1123.50	1078.56	1062.85
Net NAV, published ($)	1000	1056	1098.80	1062.85	1062.85
Accrual of incentive fee ($)	0	14	24.70	15.71	0
Series II					
Gross NAV ($)		1000	1050	1008.00	1006.40
Net NAV, published ($)		1000	1040	1006.40	1006.40
Accrual of incentive fee ($)		0	10	1.60	0
Series III					
Gross NAV ($)			1000	960	960
Net NAV, published ($)			1000	960	960
Accrual of incentive fee ($)			0	0	960

The major advantage of this procedure is its simplicity. Each series of shares is valued independently of the others and has its own incentive fee accrual. There is no more free rider syndrome. The drawback is that things can easily become cumbersome as the number of series increases. The coexistence of multiple series of shares implies tracking and reporting multiple NAVs (one for each series), which is quite confusing for an investor holding shares in several series. Furthermore, the independence of each series implies that the listing requirements and fees (e.g. on the Irish Stock Exchange) must be applied to each series.

Note that most hedge funds regularly attempt to consolidate series of shares with the lead series in order to reduce the number of series outstanding. The necessary conditions to implement such a consolidation are that (i) the end of an accounting period for the lead series and another series coincide; and (ii) an incentive fee has been paid for both of them. In our previous example, Series II shares could be merged with the lead series on April 1, just after the payment of the incentive fee. Investor B would have to exchange his shares, which are worth $1 006 400, against 946.89 shares of the lead series. This reduces the number of series but introduces fractional shares, which is not much better.

Equalization shares

The simplest equalization approach relies on the distribution of extra fractional shares called equalization shares. Its implementation consists of the following steps. At the end of each accounting period (e.g. at the end of each month), the fund administrator calculates the performance fee and allocates it fairly between all the investors. This results in several NAVs, assuming that investors entered the fund at different levels. The fund simply selects and publishes the lowest of these NAVs as its official one. Shareholders who would have had a higher NAV per share according to the individual calculations are then granted some extra shares (equalization shares) to compensate exactly for the loss resulting from the arbitrary change of NAV.

The advantage of equalization shares is that they preserve the uniqueness of the fund's NAV while remaining relatively simple to implement in terms of calculation. However, the NAV selected by the fund no longer reflects the performance. This confuses most investors, who have great difficulty in understanding that there is no swindle going on.

Equalization factor/depreciation deposit approach

One of the most common methods of equalization is the equalization factor/depreciation deposit approach (EF/DDA). It aims at splitting each new subscription into a net investment amount and an equalization factor amount, so that all investors have the same capital risk per share. At each subscription, the number of shares allotted is obtained by dividing the subscription amount by the gross NAV. The equalization factor is calculated by deducting from the subscription amount the net NAV multiplied by the number of shares allotted.

Let us return to the fund we used in the multiple series example. On January 31 the gross NAV of investor A's shares was $1070 per share (7%) and the published NAV was $1056, net of $14 incentive fee accrual (20% of the $70 increase). Under EF/DDA, investor B would need to deposit $1070 per share to be in exactly the same situation as investor A. This would be split between $1056 invested in the fund and $14 in the equalization amount. The $1056 would appear on the assets side of the hedge fund balance sheet as "investment in funds," and the $14 would also be shown on the assets side but as "other receivables."

What happens with the equalization factor of investor B? The answer depends on the fund's future performance. If the fund performance is good, the equalization factor paid will be refunded in cash or in shares at the end of the incentive fee calculation period. If the fund performance is bad, all or part of the equalization factor will be lost. Investor B will therefore be in exactly the same situation as investor A.

An interesting situation occurs when, at the purchase date, the fund's NAV is already at a discount with respect to the high water mark. This could occur just after a series of losses. In that case the investor has to pay a depreciation deposit. If the fund's performance recovers, the depreciation deposit becomes payable to the adviser as a performance fee. If it keeps on deteriorating, it will be refunded in cash at the end of the incentive fee calculation period. The major disadvantage of EF/DDA is that the assets invested are not necessarily fully invested in the hedge fund.

REDEMPTION POLICY AND PAYMENT SCHEDULES

An important factor that may also significantly affect the usefulness of NAVs to estimate performance from an investor's perspective is the redemption policy and payment schedule offered by hedge funds.

In a traditional mutual fund, the delay between an investor's order and its execution is usually a few business days. A redemption order is usually executed the next business day, and the corresponding amount will be credited to the investor two business days later. In a hedge fund, the same process can take several months, sometimes even more than a year. As an illustration, let us consider the case of the hedge fund Cerberus International Limited, which is active in distressed securities. Its terms of subscription are monthly. Its terms of redemption are quarterly, with a 90-day prior written notice. Its payment schedule is 90% of the redemption proceeds as soon as practicable after the redemption date, with the balance upon completion of the June 30 audit.

Say an investor decides on January 1 that he wishes to redeem his Cerberus shares. He needs to send a notification of his redemption to the fund for the next possible date, which is June 30 (it is already too late for the March 31 redemption date). A few days after June 30, the end-June NAV is published and the investor will receive 90% of the value of his shares. Probably one or two months later, the audit will be completed and the remaining 10% will be paid. In total, the delay between the order and the end of its execution was about 8 months. It could be worse if the investor decides to redeem on July 1. The next possible redemption date is December 31, because it is already too late to announce redemption at the end of September. The first part of the proceeds will be paid at the beginning of January, but the remaining 10% will be available after the completion of next year's audit. In total, the investor will therefore wait about 14 months before final execution (Figure 12.1).

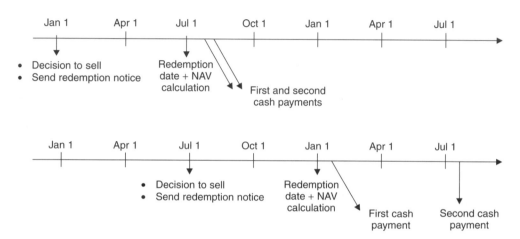

Figure 12.1   Redeeming from a hedge fund: the "good" and "bad" cases

These delays are not specific to Cerberus. They are typical of the hedge fund industry. Consequently, an interesting question is related to the investment of the sale proceeds between the NAV calculation date and the final effective repayment. Since we are potentially talking about several months, it would be reasonable to expect that the corresponding sums be invested in T-bills. Unfortunately, this is often not the case. Beyond the simple performance question, this raises two additional issues:

- *The credit risk of the hedge fund*: the investor is basically depositing some cash in the hedge fund for several months at a rate of 0%. What will happen if the hedge fund defaults?
- *The feasibility and efficiency of a hedge fund switch*: given the subscription and redemption delays, it is virtually impossible to efficiently switch from one hedge fund to another without losing several months in between.

For these reasons, hedge fund NAVs should always be considered cautiously when assessing performance.

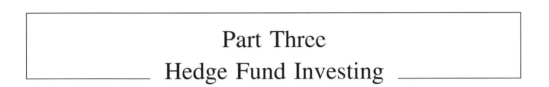

Part Three
Hedge Fund Investing

13

Introduction

This third part of the book covers what is probably one of the most exciting and controversial topics of finance today—the analysis, selection and asset allocation of hedge fund investments.

As of today, the primary form of individual and institutional investments is still composed of traditional assets such as stocks and bonds. However, during the past decade, interest in and financial commitments to alternative investments of all sorts have grown dramatically. Attracted by claims of superior risk-adjusted returns and low correlation to stock and bond markets, institutions and more recently affluent individuals have been allocating a small percentage of their portfolios to alternative investments, and more specifically to hedge funds. In parallel, the bulk of their assets remain invested in stocks, bonds and other traditional securities. Both allocations are usually managed independently on a segregated basis. This gives rise to several interesting questions that we will examine in Chapter 14. First, what are the real benefits, if any, of including hedge funds in a traditional portfolio? Second, what is the optimal proportion of hedge funds in a portfolio? And third, how can one integrate traditional asset management with alternative investments? As we shall see, there are still lots of open questions, no single straightforward answer, and numerous pitfalls that should be avoided.

Indeed, the existing literature shows widespread disagreement regarding the performance and portfolio benefits of hedge funds. This is not really surprising. Different observation periods combined with a wide variety of styles and types of hedge fund lead to different conclusions and make generalizations difficult. Moreover, traditional portfolio selection, portfolio management or performance measurement tools are badly placed to deal with the new risks and challenges posed by hedge funds. This is understandable when one remembers that for most practitioners, and also for many in academic circles, modern portfolio theory—which is now about 45 years old—is still state of the art. Investors are therefore left naked, or even worse, often use inadequate tools when discovering the hedge fund kingdom.

If still convinced that investing in hedge funds may enhance the risk/return trade-off of their portfolios, investors have to identify the correct investment vehicle. Simply stated, there are currently four approaches to participation in hedge funds: investing directly, taking advantage of third-party services (e.g. consultants or hedge funds advisers), using funds of hedge funds, or following the safer road of capital-guaranteed and other structured products.

Direct investments occur when an investor hires a single hedge fund manager or a combination of hedge fund managers on his own. As we shall see, there are significant barriers to this approach. In particular, it involves a complex evaluation process due to the diversity of existing hedge fund strategies as well as the lack of transparency with respect to their portfolios. It also requires a high level of net worth and liquidity. Moreover, the heterogeneity of hedge funds results in the best and the worst coexisting under the same roof, and even the best can fail; remember Long Term Capital Management.

This explains why investors willing to venture along the road of direct investments often hire external advisers and consultants, who are supposed to be experts in the field. For a fee, these intermediaries act as financial matchmakers between investors and appropriate hedge fund managers. As an illustration, even Calpers, the California Public Employees Retirement System, with more than $132 billion in assets and great investment experience, hired Blackstone Group LP, a New York investment firm, to screen the strategy and performance of potential managers, help with due diligence and monitor the $1 billion hedge fund program. However, whether implemented alone or with the help of external specialists, the task remains the same: to seek out from a very large universe the hedge funds that best satisfy the precise requirements of an investor. The various steps of this process are detailed in Chapter 15.

Funds of hedge funds, for their part, are basically prepackaged portfolios of hedge funds usually diversified across many different managers and/or strategies. Their managers perform professional due diligence and have third-party asset allocation expertise. However, since the investors' assets are pooled with those of many other clients, managers of funds of hedge funds cannot offer any alteration to their product in order to accommodate individual needs. Nevertheless, funds of hedge funds are today the preferred hedge fund investment vehicle for many institutional investors. We examine their structure and their investment process in Chapter 16.

Chapter 17 focuses on the latest form of access to hedge funds: principal-protected structured products. Popular essentially in Europe and now gaining adherents in the United States, these new investment vehicles claim to offer hedge-fund-like returns with a guarantee that investors will get back at least the capital they started with if gains do not materialize over a set period. The reality is that they provide security, but at a price. More surprisingly, they rely on portfolio insurance principles that were implemented in the 1980s on traditional equity markets.

Finally, Chapter 18 illustrates, in simple terms, some of the most recent and promising findings of academic research in the domain of hedge funds. Although still at the prototype stage, some of these models will undoubtedly shape the hedge fund landscape of tomorrow.

14
Asset allocation

Diversification and asset allocation are the essential building blocks of portfolio construction and management. Often used in conjunction with each other, they are in fact two distinct investment techniques that rely on the same underlying principles. We first look at the major aspects of each of them, then illustrate their application to portfolios of traditional assets with and without hedge funds. We intentionally avoid complex mathematical developments and aim rather at providing the intuition that lies behind the theory. For those who wish to pursue the subject further, there are excellent textbooks that cover the details of our calculations. I recommend Markowitz (1991).

DIVERSIFICATION AND PORTFOLIO CONSTRUCTION

Diversification consists of spreading investments among different assets or asset classes in order to reduce the overall risk of a portfolio. To most investors, the logic of diversification is obvious and has been intuitively recognized for centuries in the adage: Don't put all your eggs in one basket. However, it was only in the late 1950s that Harry Markowitz, a 25-year-old doctoral student at the University of Chicago, was able to analyze in detail how portfolio diversification worked. Using standard deviation (volatility) to quantify risk, Markowitz developed a new normative theory to demonstrate why and how portfolio diversification works to reduce risk for investors. His ideas were so innovative that at his doctoral dissertation defense, Milton Friedman, winner of the 1976 Nobel prize for economic science, declared that it was "neither economics, mathematics, nor even business administration." Nevertheless, 38 years later, Markowitz shared a Nobel prize with Merton Miller and William Sharpe for what is now regarded as one of the most important analytical tools in twentieth-century finance.

Diversification

To understand the intuition behind diversification, let us simply start with a hypothetical economy where only two companies have listed their shares. The first is an umbrella-making firm and the second produces ice cream. Investors willing to invest in equities must allocate their assets between the stocks of these two companies and have no other choice. Which stock should be selected? There are several possible choices; each is supported by an investment theory. For instance, aggressive investors may take a bet on the weather and prefer the ice cream maker if they forecast a sunny summer or the umbrella maker if they forecast a rainy one.

Chartists will look at the historical prices of both companies and apply some technical indicators to detect trends, support levels, etc., in order to reach their conclusion. Meanwhile, fundamentalists will analyze accounting data, price/earnings ratios or book-to-equity ratios. Momentum investors will prefer the company that has had the best recent historical performance, while contrarian investors will prefer the one that performed badly.

Small-cap enthusiasts will invest in the smallest firm, while blue-chip investors will favor the largest one. We could go on forever, but at the end of the day, who will be right? Hard to say.

Diversification provides a very natural answer to our security selection problem. Only a fool or a prophet would invest exclusively in one of the two stocks. Those who are unable to forecast the weather accurately should diversify risk by investing in both firms. The reasons are twofold. First, stocks have proven to be a superior way to preserve and create wealth for investors adhering to a conservative, long-term, buy and hold investment strategy. By investing in both companies, investors actually capture the higher long-term returns offered by equities as an asset class, but reduce the potential short-term variations. Second, both theory and practice suggest that taking on more company-specific risk does not imply greater potential returns in the long run (and this is actually the best reason for diversifying). In our case, betting on the weather is too much of a gamble. We have more or less one chance in two of being right, so we should expect a zero-sum game before fees on average. After costs, though, weather investing becomes a loser's game by definition. As summarized by John Bogle, chief executive of the Vanguard Group, "The croupier rakes too much out."

By investing in both companies, investors therefore reduce the risk that is unique to a given security (specific risk, such as weather risk in our case) and remain only with the risk that is common to all financial instruments (market risk, or risk of the overall stock market). Graphically, the benefits of diversification are obvious (Figure 14.1). The expected return of the 50/50 allocation between the two stocks is exactly the average of the individual stock returns, while the standard deviation is less than the average of the standard deviations of the two stocks separately, thanks to diversification. This stretches the set of possible allocations to the left of the straight line joining the two securities. That is, for the same expected return, it is possible to incur a lower risk.

The exact shape of the curve of possible allocations between the two securities depends on a statistical coefficient called correlation. Correlation ranges from −1 to +1 and measures how frequently two securities' returns move in the same direction. For instance:

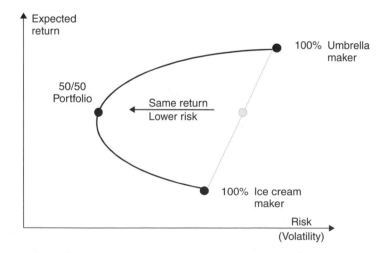

Figure 14.1   The benefits of diversification: creating an all-weather portfolio

- Two securities having a correlation coefficient of $+1$ are perfectly correlated, i.e. they move systematically in the same direction.
- Two securities having a correlation coefficient of -1 are perfectly negatively correlated, i.e. they move systematically in opposite directions (but not necessarily by the same magnitude).
- Two securities having a correlation coefficient of 0 move independently of each other.
- Two securities having a correlation coefficient of say 0.60 are perfectly positively correlated 60% of the time and move independently of each other 40% of the time.[1] Similarly, two securities having a correlation coefficient of say -0.40 are perfectly negatively correlated 40% of the time and move independently of each other 60% of the time.

The smaller the correlation between two securities, the smaller the standard deviation of a portfolio that combines them. The trick is therefore to find assets that offer a worthwhile return while being less than perfectly correlated or even negatively correlated.

Portfolio construction

Once the risks and the benefits of diversification have been quantified, the next logical step is to explain how, under conditions of risk, a risk-averse investor should build a portfolio to optimize market risk against expected returns. This is called mean–variance optimization, because the variance (or its square root, the volatility) is used to measure risk. Markowitz's normative approach allows calculation of the exact expected return and volatility of a portfolio composed of several securities based on four sets of inputs: the percentage of total funds invested in each security, the expected return and volatility associated with each security, and the correlation between these securities.

Markowitz showed that, starting from a limited set of securities, the set of portfolios that one could create by allocating assets among these securities is a region bounded by an upward-sloping curve that he called the efficient frontier (Figure 14.2). Portfolios and securities below this frontier are not efficient in the sense that it is possible to find better risk/return combinations (e.g. a higher return for the same risk or lower risk for the same return). Portfolios and securities above this frontier are not attainable. If they existed, the efficient frontier would be shifted accordingly. The efficient frontier therefore represents the trade-off between risk and expected return faced by an investor when forming his portfolio. There are three things to note:

- A key property of this efficient frontier is that it is curved, not straight. This is essentially due to the benefits of diversification. The curvature increases as the number of assets available increases, and as assets with low or negative correlation are introduced in the investment universe.
- To create an efficient portfolio, it is necessary to combine inefficient assets. As a consequence, the risk of an individual asset should be of little importance to the investor; what matters is its contribution to the portfolio's risk as a whole. This has brought about a revolution in the scrutiny given to portfolios. The entire portfolio should be considered when judging the suitability of investments rather than considering a single investment in isolation.
- It suddenly appears that one does not even need any fundamental information about firms. All necessary information is contained in expected returns, volatility and

correlation statistics. The new difficulty will be to forecast these statistics accurately, which is not necessarily an easier task.

Table 14.1 Diversification can reduce risk and increase returns

Asset class	Annualized return (%)	Annualized volatility (%)	Sharpe ratio
US stocks (S&P 500)	13.2	16.8	0.43
Intl stocks (MSCI EAFE index)	12.5	21.9	0.30
Real estate (NAREIT index)	12.5	17.2	0.38
Commodities (GS commodities index)	12.4	24.9	0.26
Intl stocks + real estate + commodities	13.9	11	0.72

Note: the calculation period is 1972–2000; the risk-free rate for the Sharpe ratio is assumed to be 6%

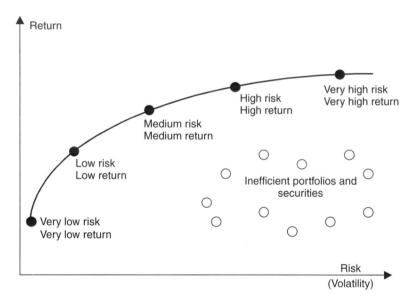

Figure 14.2 The efficient frontier and the trade-off between risk and return

The key result of mean–variance optimization is that one can reduce portfolio risk by diversifying, without necessarily lowering expected returns. Indeed, diversification can even increase returns. As an illustration, consider the following example. Table 14.1 shows the annualized returns and standard deviations of four asset classes over the period 1972–2000. Clearly, the S&P 500 dominates the three other indices, with a lower volatility and a higher return. But if we create an equally weighted portfolio of the three dominating indices, it achieves a higher return and a lower standard deviation than the S&P 500. The reasons for this surprising result reside in the relatively low correlation between these asset classes.

The Sharpe ratio is a key statistic for portfolio construction. For a given asset, it is computed as the excess return over the risk-free rate, divided by the volatility of the asset.

Mathematically,

$$\text{Sharpe ratio} = \frac{\text{return on asset} - \text{risk-free rate}}{\text{volatility of asset}}$$

The Sharpe ratios for the asset classes considered in our previous example are given in Table 14.1. For instance, the Sharpe ratio of 0.43 for US equities can be interpreted as follows: an increase of 1% in the volatility of US stocks is rewarded by an incremental return of 0.43%. This extra return comes in addition to the risk-free rate, which is the reward corresponding to a zero-volatility portfolio. The Sharpe ratio is therefore a clear reward-to-risk ratio.

To understand how this ratio helps in creating a portfolio, consider the diagram of the efficient frontier again, this time with cash drawn in (Figure 14.3). Combining any risky asset with cash results in a portfolio that lies somewhere along the straight line joining the risky asset with the cash. Now we obtain a straight line, not a curve. Cash is risk-free, so there is no possible diversification effect between the cash and the risky asset. To diversify, one needs at least two sources of risk. For a given volatility, since you want the rate of return to be as great as possible, you need to select the risky asset that gives you the line with the greatest possible slope. The slope of this line is equal to the Sharpe ratio of the risky asset.

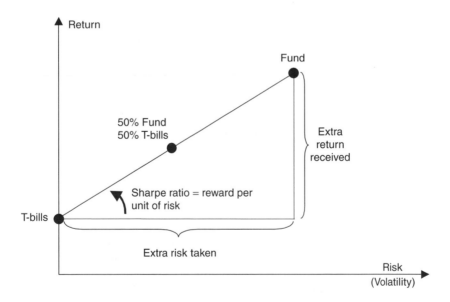

Figure 14.3 Understanding the Sharpe ratio

Putting this all together gives a fast method of building the optimal portfolio from a series of feasible portfolios. First find the portfolio with the highest Sharpe ratio. Next combine this portfolio with cash to obtain the desired value for standard deviation. The result will be the portfolio with the greatest possible rate of return for a given volatility target.

Asset allocation

Asset allocation takes the diversification concept one step further. It does not simply mix several assets, it attempts to combine them optimally. Asset allocation consists in determining a capital allocation in each of the broad categories of assets to maximize overall risk-adjusted performance while ensuring consistency with the investor's goals, risk tolerance, constraints and time horizon.

Mathematically, asset allocation corresponds to a constrained optimization problem. Although the term appears complex, the concept is not. For instance, an investor looking for the optimal portfolio and targeting a 10% annual return would face the following constrained optimization problem:

> Find portfolio weights (i.e. asset allocation). Minimize risk (e.g. volatility). Constraints: no short sales, fully invested, given target return (e.g. 10%).

Equivalently, if the investor now targets a maximum volatility of 7%, he would have to solve the following constrained optimization problem:

> Find portfolio weights (i.e. asset allocation). Maximize expected return. Constraints: no short sales, fully invested, given target risk (e.g. volatility 7%).

The two problems are equivalent and fortunately yield the same solution (Figure 14.4).

Such problems are usually solved at the asset class level rather than for individual securities. There are two reasons for this. First, several necessary parameters (expected returns, volatilities and correlations) are easier to estimate and more stable for asset classes than for individual securities. Second, the number of asset classes is usually much smaller than the number of securities, which reduces the complexity of the problem. There are three things to note:

- A Microsoft Excel spreadsheet with the Solver add-in is sufficient to solve most of the optimization problems that we consider below within a reasonable amount of time.
- Solving this optimization problem is not necessarily an easy task, but it is crucial for successful portfolio management. If the asset allocation is too aggressive, the investor may risk more of his initial investment than he wants. If it is too conservative, he may not achieve the return he seeks. The idea is therefore to find a middle ground that is comfortable, sufficiently productive, and optimal.
- Asset allocation has been shown to be the single greatest determinant of the long-term return on a portfolio. According to Brinson et al. (1986, 1991), more than 90% of the variability of a portfolio's performance over time is due to asset allocation and not to security selection or market timing. Despite this, numerous investors spend sleepless nights worrying about which securities to buy or to sell, but still neglect their overall asset allocation.

ASSET ALLOCATION WITH TRADITIONAL ASSET CLASSES

Asset allocation with traditional asset classes such as stocks and bonds is now a well-known topic in finance. Although it has been perfected over the years, the technique still relies on the same fundamental steps. First, understand and measure the risk and return characteristics of each asset class. Second, understand and measure the interaction

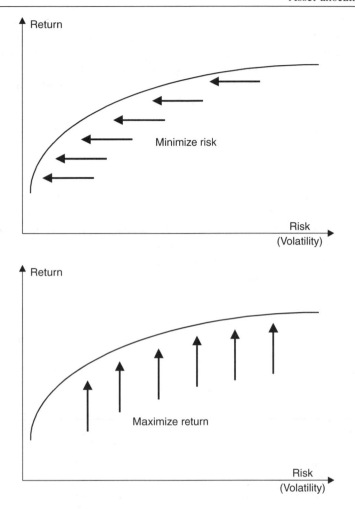

Figure 14.4   Two views of the same optimization problem

between each pair of asset classes. And third, allocate capital to each asset class to optimally diversify overall risk. Since asset allocation is a forward-looking process, the key to success lies in the first two steps. The third step is basically an optimization process—nothing more than solving mathematical equations.

Historical data can be very useful in understanding the returns, risk and interaction between different asset classes. However, what matters for asset allocation is the future returns, risk and interaction, not the historical ones. Investors have long searched for the financial equivalent of the Holy Grail—the magic formula that would forecast movements in financial markets. Indeed, the mathematical techniques and models now used in the forecasting of financial markets have grown ever more sophisticated as traders, analysts and investors seek to gain an edge over their competitors. But there is still a long way to go, and the quest continues.

The following sections adopt a very pragmatic attitude with respect to forecasting techniques—they simply use historical data as a source of forecasts. Since my intention is merely to illustrate a portfolio-building process and its consequences, I do not go into the matter of how the forecasts are built. However, in reality, it is clear that historical data should not be the unique source, since the goal is to build portfolios that will be efficient in the future, not portfolios that would have been efficient in the past.

Table 14.2 shows various statistics for a set of traditional asset class indices over the period from January 1994 to August 2001. Performance differs widely for equity markets, with annual average returns ranging from −5.23% (Pacific ex Japan) to 13.42% (Nordic countries) and annualized volatility ranging from 13.43% (UK) to 23.28% (Nordic countries).

Except for Japan and Pacific markets (ex Japan), most equity markets posted solid returns, but at the expense of a high volatility. This is not really surprising, given that most of the period in question coincided with a strong bull market. The US market dominates the other countries in terms of risk-adjusted returns, closely followed by the Nordic countries, Switzerland and the Netherlands. The Pacific area and Japan are clearly lagging, combining negative returns with high volatility.

Table 14.3 displays the correlation between our various indices. We split the correlation pairs arbitrarily into three groups:

- Correlations above 0.3 are in roman type; these pairs would be poor candidates to improve diversification.
- Correlations between 0 and 0.3 are framed; the corresponding pairs would be reasonable choices for diversification.
- Negative correlations, if any, are displayed in bold; they should provide the most benefit to the portfolio when looking for true diversification.

We observe that correlations between traditional equity markets are all in the first group, except for the Japan/Germany and Nasdaq/Switzerland pairs, which fall into the second group. This confirms the world equity markets trend toward greater global integration. In prior decades, international equity was considered to be an interesting diversification alternative for an investor's domestic equity portfolio. This is no longer the case, consequently the diversification benefits of international equity are somewhat limited. However, correlations between bonds and stocks all fall into the second group, with the exception of the bonds/Swiss equity pair. This constitutes a clue that mixing international bonds and stocks can bring substantial diversification benefits.

The efficient frontier corresponding to optimal mixes of our 12 traditional asset classes is obtained by solving the following optimization problem:

> For all possible target portfolio returns, find portfolio weights (i.e. asset allocation). Minimize portfolio volatility. Constraints: no short sales, fully invested, no hedge funds.

The efficient frontier we obtained is represented in Figure 14.5 as a solid line. Table 14.4 shows the composition of three efficient portfolios (minimum volatility, maximum return and optimal Sharpe ratio). The majority of indices in our sample are below the efficient frontier. The only exceptions are the J.P. Morgan Bond index and the MSCI US, which are almost efficient. Consequently, these two indices will tend to have a large weight in the series of efficient portfolios. The same problem occurs for high-return portfolios, which tend to be biased toward the MSCI Nordic Countries, the highest-return index in

Table 14.2 Returns and risk statistics for traditional asset class indices

	Average return (%)	Volatility (%)	Sharpe ratio	Skewness	Kurtosis	Maximum monthly return		Minimum monthly return		VaR$_{0.95,1M}$ (%)
						Percent	Date	Percent	Date	
World Index (WRD)	7.11	13.85	0.15	−0.57	0.69	9.05	Oct 98	−13.41	Aug 98	−6.10
Europe (EUR)	7.76	14.31	0.19	−0.47	0.59	10.39	Dec 99	−12.94	Aug 98	−5.84
US (US)	12.45	15.38	0.48	−0.61	0.37	9.64	Mar 00	−13.87	Aug 98	−6.17
UK (UK)	5.48	13.49	0.03	−0.26	−0.48	8.27	Sep 97	−9.86	Jan 00	−6.00
France (FR)	8.23	17.83	0.18	−0.01	−0.07	13.21	Mar 95	−11.65	Aug 98	−7.46
Switzerland (SW)	9.35	17.28	0.25	−0.40	1.08	13.16	Oct 98	−16.86	Aug 98	−6.90
Germany (GER)	6.00	18.94	0.05	−0.31	0.82	17.50	Dec 99	−16.88	Aug 98	−8.51
Netherlands (NET)	9.18	16.56	0.25	−0.62	0.42	10.15	Feb 98	−13.17	Jan 00	−7.33
Japan (JAP)	−3.26	20.53	−0.40	0.48	−0.21	16.59	Oct 98	−12.35	Jul 00	−8.30
Australia (AUS)	1.06	17.74	−0.22	−0.15	0.35	13.57	Jun 00	−14.31	Oct 97	−7.12
Pacific ex Japan (PAC)	−5.23	22.60	−0.45	0.05	1.86	20.72	Oct 98	−22.10	Oct 97	−10.43
Nordic countries (NOC)	13.42	23.28	0.36	0.09	1.34	23.86	Dec 99	−19.19	Feb 01	−9.28
Nasdaq (NDQ)	11.63	28.90	0.23	−0.44	0.94	21.96	Dec 99	−22.90	Nov 00	−13.49
JPM Glob. Bonds (JPM)	5.04	5.74	0	0.33	0.43	5.22	Sep 98	−3.34	Feb 99	−2.21

All calculations are based on monthly data between January 1994 and August 2001 and from a US dollar perspective
Data sources are Morgan Stanley Capital Index (MSCI) for stock indices (except for Nasdaq) and J.P. Morgan (JPM) for bonds
Average returns, volatility and Sharpe ratio are annualized, while all other statistics are expressed on a monthly basis
Value at risk is calculated at the 95% confidence interval and using a one-month holding period

Table 14.3 Correlation statistics for traditional asset class indices

	WRD	EUR	US	UK	FR	SW	GER	NET	JAP	AUS	PAC	NOC	NDQ	JPM
World Index (WRD)	1.00													
Europe (EUR)	0.87	1.00												
US (US)	0.92	0.73	1.00											
UK (UK)	0.79	0.86	0.69	1.00										
France (FR)	0.76	0.90	0.61	0.70	1.00									
Switzerland (SW)	0.63	0.72	0.51	0.58	0.58	1.00								
Germany (GER)	0.69	0.84	0.60	0.59	0.75	0.50	1.00							
Netherlands (NET)	0.78	0.90	0.63	0.76	0.77	0.69	0.74	1.00						
Japan (JAP)	0.69	0.46	0.47	0.45	0.40	0.38	0.24	0.45	1.00					
Australia (AUS)	0.70	0.60	0.58	0.58	0.49	0.41	0.46	0.52	0.60	1.00				
Pacific ex Japan (PAC)	0.70	0.60	0.63	0.59	0.51	0.40	0.50	0.56	0.49	0.76	1.00			
Nordic countries (NOC)	0.76	0.82	0.65	0.61	0.73	0.47	0.73	0.68	0.46	0.55	0.50	1.00		
Nasdaq (NDQ)	0.75	0.61	0.76	0.48	0.54	0.24	0.59	0.47	0.44	0.56	0.53	0.69	1.00	
JPM Glob. Bonds (JPM)	0.17	0.22	0.10	0.30	0.18	0.33	0.08	0.29	0.19	0.12	0.16	0.03	0.03	1.00

All calculations are based on monthly data between January 1994 and August 2001 and from a US dollar perspective
Data sources are Morgan Stanley Capital Index (MSCI) for stock indices (except Nasdaq) and J.P. Morgan (JPM) for bonds

the sample. This should not be a matter of great concern, however. When we run the optimization again and constrain each index weight to remain below 25%, we obtain a new constrained efficient frontier, represented in Figure 14.5 as a dotted line. It is not very different to the old efficient frontier, but is made up of portfolios that are much better in terms of diversification. In what follows, we will therefore adopt this constrained efficient frontier as the frontier for traditional assets.

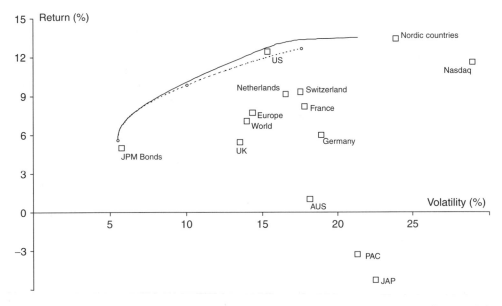

Figure 14.5 Unconstrained (solid) and constrained (dotted) efficient frontiers built by mixing traditional assets. All calculations are based on monthly data between January 1994 and August 2001 and from a US dollar perspective. Data sources are Morgan Stanley Capital Index (MSCI) for stock indices (except Nasdaq) and J.P. Morgan (JPM) for bonds. Note that MSCI World and MSCI Europe are uniquely displayed for information, but are not considered in the optimization process to build the efficient frontier. The constraint is to cap individual equity weights at 25%

HEDGE FUNDS IN THE INVESTMENT UNIVERSE

Motives

There exists a large body of practitioner and academic literature suggesting that alternative assets should be considered at the asset allocation level. The origins can be found in a study on managed accounts and commodity trading advisers made by Harvard University professor John K. Lintner (1983). Lintner observed that "the improvements from holding an efficiently-selected portfolio of managed accounts or funds are so large that the return/risk tradeoffs provided by augmented portfolios clearly dominate the tradeoffs available from a portfolio of stocks alone or from portfolios of stocks and bonds." This was clearly a consequence of the "surprisingly low, sometimes even negative" correlation observed between returns on managed accounts and commodity trading advisers' funds and those on traditional stock and bond portfolios. Lintner's results have since

Table 14.4   Characteristics of some efficient portfolios

	Return (%)	Volatility (%)	Composition
Efficient Unconstrained Portfolios			
Minimum risk portfolio	5.61	5.52	Bonds: 89.18% Equities: 10.82% (6.33% US, 2.75% Germany, 1.64% Australia)
Maximum return portfolio	13.52	21.33	Equities: 100% (74.59% Nordic countries, 17.49% US, 7.86% Nasdaq, 0.06% Australia)
Maximum Sharpe portfolio	11.12	11.91	Bonds: 24.99% Equities: 75.01% (57.44% US, 14.82% Nordic countries, 2.76% Switzerland)
Efficient Constrained Portfolios (Max 25% on Each Equity Weight)			
Minimum risk portfolio	5.52	5.61	Bonds: 89.60% Equities: 10.40% (6.30% US, 2.73% Germany, 1.29% Australia, 0.08% Japan)
Maximum return portfolio	12.67	17.58	Equities: 100% (25% Nordic countries, 25% US, 25% Nasdaq, 25% Switzerland)
Maximum Sharpe portfolio	9.78	9.93	Bonds: 43.12% Equities: 56.88% (25% US, 23.05% Nordic countries, 8.23% Switzerland)

been challenged, because they were based solely on the composite performance of 15 trading advisers or futures funds, with assets allocated efficiently between them, which is clearly not representative of the investment universe. Furthermore, the period examined was rather short, July 1979 through 1982. Nevertheless, as we will see, Lintner's results are quite robust and can easily be extended to other investment styles.

The multiple crises that occurred during the bull market of the 1990s raised awareness that diversification between stocks and bonds was likely to be insufficient in order to withstand the damage inflicted by a significant financial market reversal. Furthermore, increasing valuation concerns for equity markets (particularly in the telecommunications, media and technology sectors), as well as the burst of the internet bubble, spurred the soaring interest in new diversification opportunities. Hedge funds in particular came into consideration for their claimed ability to produce sustainable returns whatever the market conditions; their low correlation with traditional markets; and their double-digit returns over recent years. They are now increasingly viewed as a must-have portfolio building block at the asset allocation level, both for diversifying risks and enhancing performance. Nevertheless, there is still an ongoing debate as to whether hedge funds should be considered as a new asset class or simply as an alternative way to manage traditional asset classes.

One side argues that most sources of hedge fund returns (e.g. market inefficiencies, arbitrage opportunities, or significantly better information than the market) do not differ fundamentally from those of proprietary trading desks. This is not really surprising, since in principle every hedge fund follows its own proprietary strategy driven by the skills of its manager. But as a side effect, the drivers of hedge fund returns differ widely from those of traditional assets such as stocks and bonds. This fully qualifies them as a new asset class, with the potential to become part of any investment process.

The other argument is that hedge funds form an extremely heterogeneous universe. They comprise a wide range of strategies that clearly lack common features, with the exception of the legal structure. Moreover, hedge fund managers may freely change their investment style without notification, so that return patterns from different funds within the same investment style display poor consistency. It is therefore better to consider hedge funds as new active strategies employed over one or more traditional asset classes rather than as a pure new asset class. In that sense, hedge funds simply hold traditional types of assets, but manage them in unconventional ways.

Clearly, both arguments are perfectly valid, and I do not claim to have the definitive answer. I will therefore leave the question open and simply conclude that hedge funds, as an asset class or investment strategy, have a role to play in diversified investment portfolios. They should therefore be considered in asset allocation, be it as a viable source of diversification or as a means of increasing returns.

Naive and planned hedge fund allocation policies

Once convinced of the potential diversification benefits of introducing hedge funds at the asset allocation level, most investors must come to grips with the problem of determining a "neutral" policy allocation. This boils down to deciding what proportion of the overall portfolio should be allocated to hedge funds, and which hedge fund strategies should be preferred, if any. Once again, the answers are quite heterogeneous in the industry.

Many financial institutions do not analyze hedge funds as substitutes or as additions to more traditional assets. Rather, they adopt a very pragmatic attitude and simply recommend allocating an arbitrarily prespecified percentage of portfolios to hedge funds, typically 1%, 2% or even 5%. This particular percentage is usually not justified or really explained, but is just kept small enough to avoid embarrassing questions and large enough to benefit from diversification effects.[2]

A second approach to determining the neutral policy allocation for hedge funds consists of relying on traditional asset allocation techniques, that is, portfolio optimization. We simply determine the importance of hedge funds by looking at how the efficient frontier moves through their inclusion. We therefore repeat our previous optimization exercise, but include in the investment universe the CSFB/Tremont series of hedge fund indices.

Table 14.5 shows the returns and risk characteristics of the CSFB/Tremont index as well as its subindices from January 1994 to August 2001. In comparison with traditional stock and bond investments, it can be seen that on a stand-alone basis, hedge funds are not necessarily riskier. For instance, convertible arbitrage and equity market neutral exhibit impressive risk-adjusted returns—the famous "equity-like returns with bond-like volatility." And at the aggregate level, the CSFB/Tremont index has a much higher return than the MSCI World, but with a significantly lower volatility. However, not all hedge fund strategies were successful: the dedicated short bias and emerging markets funds were definite losers over the period considered.

The dispersion of volatility among the hedge fund strategies is considerable. In particular, arbitrage and equity market neutral strategies display very low levels of

Table 14.5 Returns and risk statistics for hedge fund indices

	Average return (%)	Volatility (%)	Sharpe ratio	Skewness	Kurtosis	Maximum monthly return		Minimum monthly return		VaR$_{0.95,1M}$ (%)
						Percent	Date	Percent	Date	
CSFB/Tremont	11.97	9.59	0.72	0.00	0.87	8.53	Dec 99	−7.55	Aug 98	−3.82
Convertible arbitrage	11.12	4.95	1.23	−1.69	4.54	3.57	Apr 00	−4.68	Oct 98	−1.61
Dedicated short bias	0.18	18.98	−0.26	0.92	2.17	22.71	Aug 98	−8.69	Oct 98	−7.15
Emerging markets	3.99	19.51	−0.06	−0.44	2.69	16.42	Aug 94	−23.03	Aug 98	−7.87
Equity market neutral	11.85	3.31	2.05	−0.02	−0.07	3.26	Jul 97	−1.15	Mar 97	−0.88
Event driven	12.14	6.32	1.12	−3.75	24.86	3.68	Jan 94	−11.77	Aug 98	−0.91
Fixed income arbitrage	6.86	4.20	0.43	−3.42	17.19	2.02	Apr 95	−6.96	Oct 98	−1.52
Global macro	14.03	13.80	0.65	−0.02	0.97	10.60	Aug 95	−11.55	Oct 98	−5.23
Long/short	14.00	12.33	0.73	0.10	2.37	13.01	Dec 99	−11.43	Aug 98	−3.80
Managed futures	5.12	11.38	0.01	0.17	1.30	9.95	Aug 98	−9.35	Sep 95	−4.75

All calculations are based on monthly data between January 1994 and August 2001 and from a US dollar perspective
Average returns, volatility and Sharpe ratio are annualized, while all other statistics are expressed on a monthly basis
Value at risk is calculated at the 95% confidence interval and using a one-month holding period

volatility, about one-quarter those observed in emerging markets. As a rule, all directional-type hedge funds tend to have a higher volatility. This clearly demonstrates the need to adjust returns for risk when analyzing and comparing hedge fund performance, and the necessity of differentiating the various investment styles.

Distribution-related differences are also interesting. While most equity markets do not seem to diverge greatly from normal distributions, some hedge fund strategies (fixed income arbitrage and event driven) display strongly negative skewness and highly positive kurtosis figures. One should therefore be cautious when using volatility as a risk measure for such strategies. Value at risk (VaR) figures also evidence a major downside risk difference between equity markets and hedge fund indices. With the exception of emerging markets and dedicated short bias, which are rather market directional strategies, all hedge funds have a lower value at risk than equity markets.

Table 14.6 displays the correlation between our various indices. Once again, we split the correlation pairs arbitrarily into the same three groups:

- Correlations above 0.3 are in roman type; these pairs would be poor candidates to improve diversification.
- Correlations between 0 and 0.3 are framed; the corresponding pairs would be reasonable choices for diversification.
- Negative correlations, if any, are displayed in bold; they should provide the most benefit to the portfolio when looking for true diversification.

The best opportunities for diversification seem to come from equity market neutral, convertible arbitrage, fixed income arbitrage and managed futures styles. It seems obvious that we can expect to reduce risk and enhance returns by adding hedge funds following these styles to a traditional asset allocation. This is rather intuitive, since most of these arbitragers trade essentially in non-equity-related spreads. In contrast, long/short equity funds have the highest correlation with traditional indices. This implies that their strategies add little value in terms of efficiency improvement, at least in a mean–variance space. In terms of asset class, we also observe that Swiss equities and global bonds are the least correlated with the various hedge fund strategies.

More surprisingly, emerging markets hedge funds also appear to be quite closely correlated with all traditional equity markets, with the exception of Switzerland. This is at odds with the traditional belief that the behavior of emerging markets returns differs sharply from that of developed equity market returns. However, we should remember that most hedge fund managers are influenced consciously or unconsciously by traditional market behavior; and emerging market returns are primarily driven by the dynamics of capital flows from traditional markets. In the end, therefore, it is not so surprising to see the economic fortunes of developing countries becoming more closely aligned with those of the US and Europe.

Finally, it appears that event-driven strategies are indirectly correlated with equity markets, since mergers arbitrage and distressed investing are usually more successful when markets are rising. Note that long/short funds are also correlated with equity markets, which makes sense since they are not fully hedged against market risk (otherwise they would be classified as market neutral). And as expected, dedicated short bias funds produce returns that are highly negatively correlated with all traditional equity markets.

Table 14.6 Correlation between various traditional equity indices (MSCI) and the CSFB/Tremont indices over the period 1994–2001

	WRD	EUR	US	UK	FR	SW	GER	NET	JAP	AUS	PAC	NDQ	JPM
CSFB/Tremont	0.50	0.48	0.51	0.36	0.46	0.20	0.46	0.41	0.15	0.39	0.37	0.44	−0.14
Convertible arbitrage	0.10	0.12	0.10	0.08	0.13	0.07	0.10	0.11	−0.02	0.04	−0.01	0.11	−0.23
Dedicated short bias	−0.76	−0.59	−0.77	−0.53	−0.48	−0.33	−0.46	−0.47	−0.48	−0.62	−0.61	−0.62	0.01
Emerging markets	0.55	0.49	0.49	0.42	0.37	0.30	0.41	0.42	0.36	0.50	0.52	0.52	−0.24
Equity market neutral	0.44	0.32	0.46	0.29	0.33	0.24	0.25	0.33	0.25	0.24	0.37	0.22	0.02
Event driven	0.58	0.54	0.54	0.42	0.43	0.40	0.45	0.47	0.34	0.47	0.43	0.49	−0.16
Fixed income arbitrage	0.08	0.12	0.10	0.13	0.07	0.01	0.08	0.15	−0.10	0.13	0.03	0.19	−0.27
Global macro	0.24	0.26	0.30	0.19	0.28	0.10	0.27	0.25	−0.11	0.15	0.11	0.16	−0.17
Long/short	0.65	0.62	0.62	0.45	0.54	0.27	0.60	0.50	0.34	0.51	0.54	0.67	0.03
Managed futures	−0.03	−0.02	−0.10	0.02	0.08	−0.09	−0.03	0.03	0.03	0.00	0.06	−0.18	0.27

Note: all calculations are based on monthly data between January 1994 and August 2001 and from a US dollar perspective

We now allow investments in both traditional indices and the CSFB/Tremont index, and build the corresponding efficient frontier. This corresponds to the long-only asset allocation problem:

> For all possible target portfolio returns, find: portfolio weights (i.e. asset allocation). Minimize portfolio volatility. Constraints: no short sales, fully invested, CSFB/Tremont index allowed, maximum of 25% on each equity index allocation.

Figure 14.6 summarizes our findings. In all cases, in order to obtain representative results, we imposed a maximum 25% allocation for each equity index. The "no hedge funds" efficient frontier corresponds to the one we obtained previously by investing in traditional assets only. The "max 5% hedge funds" efficient frontier corresponds to the naive approach of imposing an arbitrary 5% cap on the hedge fund allocation. As can be seen, this only provides a limited enhancement with respect to the "no hedge fund" case. Finally, the "no limits on hedge funds" efficient frontier corresponds to the case of an unlimited authorized allocation to hedge funds. This frontier clearly dominates the others. However, most of its constituent portfolios would not be acceptable in terms of diversification (Table 14.7). As an illustration, the minimum risk portfolio contains about 71% bonds and 29% hedge funds. The 29% allocation goes far beyond what a risk-averse investor would tolerate in practice. Moreover, the hedge fund proportion keeps increasing with the portfolio's returns and reaches 78.9% at its peak before decreasing again. For the maximum return portfolio's allocation, we still have a mix of 18% hedge funds and 72% Nordic countries.

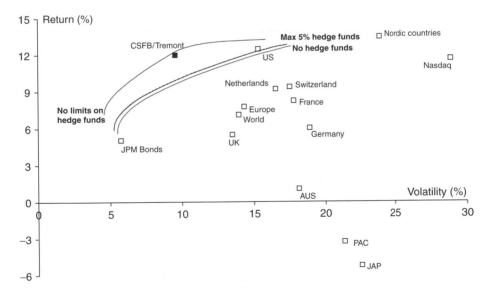

Figure 14.6 Efficient frontiers built by mixing traditional assets and the CSFB/Tremont index. All calculations are based on monthly data between January 1994 and August 2001 and from a US dollar perspective. Data sources are Morgan Stanley Capital Index (MSCI) for stock indices (except Nasdaq) and J.P. Morgan (JPM) for bonds. Note that MSCI World and MSCI Europe are uniquely displayed for information, but are not considered in the optimization process to build the efficient frontier. All equity index weights are capped at 25%

Table 14.7   Characteristics of various efficient portfolios with hedge funds

	Return (%)	Volatility (%)	Composition
Max 25% on Each Equity Weight, No Hedge Funds			
Minimum risk portfolio	5.52	5.61	*Bonds*: 89.60% *Equities*: 10.40% (6.30% US, 2.73% Germany, 1.29% Australia, 0.08% Japan)
Maximum return portfolio	12.67	17.58	*Equities*: 100% (25% Nordic countries, 25% US, 25% Nasdaq, 25% Switzerland)
Maximum Sharpe portfolio	9.78	9.93	*Bonds*: 43.12% *Equities*: 56.88% (25% US, 23.05% Nordic countries, 8.23% Switzerland)
Max 25% on Each Equity Weight and Max 5% in Hedge Funds			
Minimum risk portfolio	5.89	5.27	*Bonds*: 86.53% *Equities*: 8.47% (5.63% US, 1.45% Germany, 1.40% Australia) *Hedge funds*: 5%
Maximum return portfolio	12.81	17.32	*Equities*: 95% (25% US, 25% Nasdaq, 20% Switzerland) *Hedge funds*: 5%
Maximum Sharpe portfolio	9.76	9.23	*Bonds*: 44.14% *Equities*: 50.86% (25% US, 19.72% Nordic countries, 6.15% Switzerland) *Hedge funds*: 5%
Max 25% on Each Equity Weight and No Limits on Hedge Funds			
Minimum risk portfolio	7.17	4.59	*Bonds*: 70.81% *Hedge funds*: 29.19%
Maximum return portfolio	15.83	13.21	*Equities*: 68.03% (25% Nordic countries, 21.77% Nasdaq, 21.26% US) *Hedge funds*: 31.97%
Maximum Sharpe portfolio	10.05	9.67	*Bonds*: 14.33% *Equities*: 14.6% (7.39% US, 4.79% Switzerland, 2.34% Nordic countries, 0.08% Germany) *Hedge funds*: 71.07%

Finally, the last part of our experiment recognizes that the universe of hedge funds is indeed divided into a number of different strategies, each with unique characteristics. We therefore allow investments in the traditional indices as well as in all the CSFB/Tremont individual hedge fund substyles (rather than just the aggregate index):

> For all possible target portfolio returns, find: portfolio weights (i.e. asset allocation). Minimize portfolio volatility. Constraints: no short sales, fully invested, CSFB/Tremont subindices allowed, maximum of 25% on each equity index allocation.

Figure 14.7 summarizes our results. In all cases, in order to obtain representative results, we imposed a maximum 25% allocation for each equity index considered. The "no hedge funds" and "hedge index only" efficient frontiers correspond to the ones we obtained previously. The "all hedge fund styles" efficient frontier corresponds to the case of an unconstrained optimization with respect to all the individual hedge fund styles, while the "constrained hedge fund styles" frontier imposes a 25% cap on each hedge fund style allocation. As we might expect, the former unconstrained efficient frontier dominates the other ones, but results in overconcentrated portfolios[3] (Table 14.8); and the frontiers built using multiple styles dominate the ones restricted to the aggregate index.

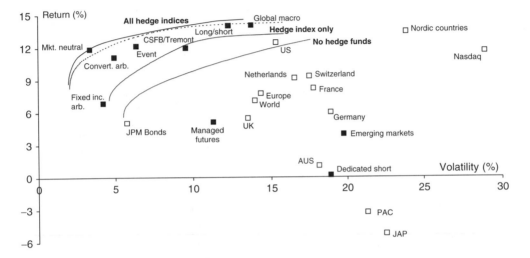

Figure 14.7   Efficient frontiers built using traditional asset classes and all the CSFB/Tremont hedge fund indices. All calculations are based on monthly data between January 1994 and August 2001 and from a US dollar perspective. Data sources are Morgan Stanley Capital Index (MSCI) for stock indices (except Nasdaq) and J.P. Morgan (JPM) for bonds. Note that MSCI World and MSCI Europe are uniquely displayed for information, but are not considered in the optimization process to build the efficient frontier. All equity index weights are capped at 25%

Conclusion

We can summarize our conclusions as follows. Including hedge funds in an asset allocation enhances the risk/return trade-off and shifts the set of efficient portfolios upward. When not constrained, traditional mean–variance portfolio optimization based on historical data suggests portfolios completely dominated by alternative investments. These results are logical, because the "risk-adjusted" returns of hedge funds are superior to those of any other asset class and their correlation with these classes is generally low. Hedge funds therefore come out as the great winners in any asset allocation exercise. So, if hedge funds' supremacy over traditional asset classes is so clear-cut, why not allocate 100% to hedge funds?

Table 14.8   Characteristics of various efficient portfolios with hedge funds

	Return (%)	Volatility (%)	Composition
Max 25% on Each Equity Weight, All Indices Allowed			
Minimum risk portfolio	8.71	1.95	*Bonds*: 15.60% *Equities*: 4.34% (3.2% Nasdaq, 0.77% Australia, 0.32% Japan) *Hedge funds*: 80.06% (40.07% equity market neutral, 20.73% fixed income arbitrage, 10.94% dedicated short bias, 8.02% event driven)
Maximum return portfolio	14.57	13.24	*Equities*: 35.33% (25% Nordic countries, 9.97% Nasdaq) *Hedge funds*: 64.67% (64.39% global macro)
Maximum Sharpe portfolio	10.68	2.31	*Bonds*: 2.12% *Equities*: 3.65% (2.34% Nasdaq, 0.77% Nordic countries, 0.27% US) *Hedge funds*: 94.23% (57.29% equity market neutral, 12.53% dedicated short bias, 10.09% event driven, 9.28% convertible arbitrage, 4.98% long/short)
Max 25% on Each Equity and Hedge Fund Weight, All Indices Allowed			
Minimum risk portfolio	8.31	2.03	*Bonds*: 18.43% *Equities*: 6.90% (3.95% Nasdaq, 1.18% Australia, 0.81% Japan, 0.8% US) *Hedge funds*: 74.64% (24.91% equity market neutral, 18.79% fixed income arbitrage, 12.56% dedicated short bias, 10.13% convertible arbitrage, 7.86% event driven)
Maximum return portfolio	14.26	15.87	*Equities*: 49.80% (25% Nordic countries, 24.38% Nasdaq) *Hedge funds*: 50.20% (25% long/short, 24.98% global macro)
Maximum Sharpe portfolio	10.13	2.37	*Bonds*: 6.66% *Equities*: 7.83% (5.65% US, 1.86% Nasdaq) *Hedge funds*: 85.51% (25% equity market neutral, 15.38% dedicated short bias, 11.34% event driven, 25% convertible arbitrage, 8.71% long/short)

Note: allocations smaller than 0.10% are not reported

THE REALITY BEHIND THE NUMBERS

Why not invest 100% in hedge funds? The first author to ask this provocative question was McFall, in a 1999 article in the *Journal of Investing*. And he concluded, "For more conservative investors, hedge funds should be used in lieu of bonds as a diversification instrument." Most readers will no doubt be shocked by this assertion. But historical market performance and quantitative techniques seem to validate it, leaving us three possible attitudes:

- Blindly accept the conclusion of the quantitative machinery, forgetting about all diversification principles, and allocate a large chunk of our portfolio to hedge funds.
- Treat mean–variance optimization as something of a black box[4] and say that these results illustrate how useless and dangerous quantitative analysis can be. Investors choosing this path generally state that according to personal judgment and experience, an allocation to hedge funds varying between 0 and 5% of the total assets is optimal.
- Go back to the data and methodology in order to understand this new asset allocation puzzle. How come hedge fund allocations are so small in real-life portfolios, given what theory and empirical optimization recommend? Could it be that Nobel prizewinning mean–variance analysis has some pitfalls or is badly implemented?

I prefer the third attitude. Although I remain convinced that mean–variance is a useful tool that has greatly enhanced the portfolio management process and that its conceptual foundations are solid, there are serious limitations and implementation pitfalls that should be considered carefully in a practical setting.

Framework problems: dynamic asset allocation and market efficiency

Traditional approaches to portfolio management assume that we are in a single period model; investors are able to forecast the necessary asset class statistics; and markets are efficient. Let us review the consequences of each of these assumptions.

Dynamic versus static asset allocation

A major issue when comparing traditional portfolios with hedge fund indices is the time dimension. Traditional mean–variance optimization uses a single-period model, with no possible intermediate rebalancing of portfolios. But why should we restrict ourselves to only one period? If we all agree on uncertainty being the central element that influences financial economic behavior, there exists a second important dimension that we have omitted up to now—time. Three time horizons are involved in the portfolio problem:

- *Trading horizon*: the minimum length of time between possible successive transactions
- *Decision horizon*: the length of time between two rebalancing decisions
- *Planning horizon*: the length of time over which the investor considers holding a portfolio

Why should these three time horizons coincide? There exists a body of financial literature on dynamic asset allocation that generalizes the mean–variance approach to allow portfolio revisions and optimization on a continuous basis (e.g. Merton 1969, 1971). A description would go far beyond the scope of this book, but it can be appreciated that taking this new dimension into account affects the optimal composition of efficient portfolios. The new dynamic portfolios are more efficient, because their asset allocation varies over time in the light of new information as it arrives on the market. Consequently, it is quite unfair to compare a static portfolio (such as an MSCI index) with a dynamically rebalanced portfolio (such as a hedge fund). The former is a buy and hold portfolio carved in stone, while the latter varies dynamically with market conditions. Also, portfolios of liquid assets (such as those modeled by MSCI indices) can be rebalanced on a daily basis if needed, while hedge funds lock in the investor for a longer period. Hedge funds therefore capture a long-term liquidity premium that increases their expected return, while traditional and liquid assets—which do not offer this premium—are arbitrarily prevented from being rebalanced, and therefore appear to be losers.

Perfect forecasts

Another potential problem when making portfolio diversification decisions is the quality of the inputs, such as forecasts of expected returns, expected standard deviations and expected correlations across asset classes. If they are free of estimation error, any optimizer is guaranteed to find the optimal or efficient portfolio weights. However, most of the time, the inputs are just statistical estimates and cannot be devoid of errors. Since the outcome portfolio varies according to the inputs, the optimization process may easily become one of "garbage in, garbage out" (Box 14.1).

Box 14.1   ROBUST ESTIMATION

It is now well known in finance that the computation of the efficient frontier can be seriously biased when the data set used contains too many extreme observations, called outliers. These outliers are typically disproportional compared to other returns of the same security. Consequently, they have an infinitesimal probability of having been generated by the same (multivariate) return distribution. The major consequence of their presence in the data is an important bias in the estimated mean return, volatility and correlation values, and therefore an incorrect efficient frontier.

Several authors have recently implemented new techniques to deal with such outliers for portfolio optimization. They have developed robust portfolio optimizers—portfolio optimizers that are less sensitive to incorrectly specified models and/or input data. An interesting review of these techniques as well as an application to commodity trading advisers can be found in Victoria-Feser (2000).

Another key issue is the stability of estimated parameters, such as expected returns, variances and correlation. All but the most naive diversification strategies attempt to make some use of this information, which is assumed to be constant over the period considered for mean–variance optimization. Moreover, these inputs are often derived from historical estimates, with some adjustments. But in reality, it is well known that assuming temporal stability is illusory. For instance, financial time series usually exhibit a characteristic known as volatility clustering, in which large changes tend to follow large changes and small changes tend to follow small changes. In either case, the changes from one period to the next are typically of unpredictable sign so that successive disturbances, although noncorrelated, are nonetheless serially dependent.

Consequently, an allocation that is optimal during normal periods may not be optimal during turbulent periods. As an illustration, Figure 14.8 shows the evolution of the historical three-year correlation between the hedge fund Long/Short Equity Market-Neutral LP and the S&P 500. The average correlation over the whole period is 0.36, but is that really representative? It is obvious that the correlation varies widely over time.

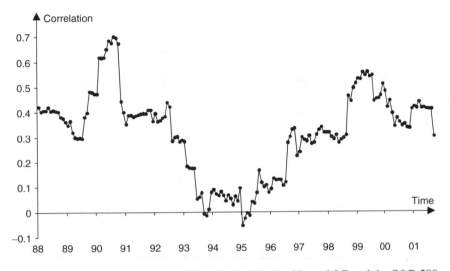

Figure 14.8   Correlation between Long/Short Equity Market Neutral LP and the S&P 500

Table 14.9 displays correlation figures of CSFB/Tremont hedge fund indices with several traditional asset classes over the period 1994–98. For each asset class, we split our sample between up markets and down markets and calculate the correlation figures

Table 14.9   Correlation structures when traditional markets are bearish or bullish

	US equities		European equities		International bonds	
	Up	Down	Up	Down	Up	Down
CSFB/Tremont index	0.18	0.53	0.23	0.31	−0.13	0.13
Convertible arbitrage	0.06	0.33	−0.15	0.29	−0.17	−0.16
Dedicated short bias	−0.51	−0.60	−0.38	−0.44	−0.03	−0.29
Emerging markets	0.17	0.57	0.20	0.45	−0.25	0.17
Equity market neutral	0.38	0.31	0.07	0.29	0.23	−0.16
Event driven	0.20	0.59	0.23	0.52	−0.21	0.17
Fixed income arbitrage	−0.14	0.21	−0.19	0.25	−0.29	−0.04
Global macro	0.07	0.34	0.08	0.11	−0.12	0.02
Long/short	0.34	0.50	0.46	0.40	−0.01	0.32
Managed futures	0.03	−0.33	0.22	−0.28	0.38	−0.11

Based on monthly data from January 1994 to August 2001

in each state. There is clearly an increase of correlation figures during down periods. For instance, consider the CSFB/Tremont Hedge Fund index:

- Its correlation with US equities is 0.18 in up periods (i.e. when US equities are going up), but 0.53 in down periods (i.e. when US equities are going down).
- Its correlation with European equities is 0.23 in up periods (i.e. when European equities are going up), but 0.31 in down periods (i.e. when European equities are going down).
- Its correlation with international bonds is −0.13 in up periods (i.e. when international bonds are going up), but 0.13 in down periods (i.e. when international bonds are going down).

Similar patterns are observed for all indices, with the exception of the dedicated short bias, equity market neutral and managed futures investment styles, where correlation in down periods actually decreases.

One of the thorny problems in asset allocation is therefore to cater for changes in the various statistical parameters that represent asset classes. For instance, at the asset class level, the correlation between hedge funds and traditional bonds and stocks has increased in recent years with the increase in the number of hedge funds that are primarily long stocks and bonds. If correlation between an asset class and an investor's portfolio changes in a predicable way, that information should be useful in determining the optimal allocation to the asset class. Ignoring this information could significantly bias the asset allocation toward officially low-correlation assets, even though the real correlation is likely to be higher. Unfortunately, for the vast majority of assets there is no formula that describes how these changes are likely to occur. So far, with a few exceptions (Box 14.2), most of the existing empirical research has focused primarily on explaining the sources of time-varying parameters rather than on quantifying and modeling them.

Box 14.2   A MODEL WITH CHANGING CORRELATIONS

Spurgin, Martin and Schneeweis (2000) have suggested a simple but interesting econometric model to account for correlation shifts. Their idea is to model the correlation ($Corr_{H,I}$) between a hedge fund return (R_H) and a reference index return (R_I) by a linear function of the index return. Mathematically,

$$Corr_{H,I} = a + bR_I$$

where a and b are coefficients that need to be estimated, for instance on historical data.

The model has obvious defaults. In particular, correlations may become smaller than −1 or larger than +1 and there is an implicit assumption of symmetry between market increases and market decreases. However, it is easy to implement and provides results that are easy to interpret from an economic viewpoint.

Efficient markets

Modern portfolio theory leans heavily on the assumption of efficient markets. By "efficient" we mean that market prices correctly reflect all available information. This explains why the main focus is on portfolio composition rather than individual security analysis. If securities are fairly priced, most of the performance will be explained by asset allocation, not by security selection. In contrast, hedge funds assume inefficient markets. The inefficiency may come from differences in information, liquidity, transaction costs and pricing. Taking advantage of these inefficiencies boosts the possibility of higher returns without necessarily increasing the risk. Mixing hedge funds with traditional asset classes is therefore a clash between two worlds. This explains why the tools of traditional assets may be biased when dealing with hedge funds.

Volatility does not capture all hedge fund risk factors

Hedge funds offer unique risk and return opportunities that are not readily available through traditional investment products. This justifies their classification as a new asset class that expands the set of investment opportunities. The risk factors that drive their returns are indeed different from the market-type factors that drive traditional investments, such as the level of interest rates and the return on equity markets. For instance:

- Distressed securities funds hold illiquid assets and are therefore exposed to liquidity crises in addition to default risk.
- Merger arbitrage funds are exposed to the event risk of a deal failure.
- Emerging market funds are exposed to currency devaluations, nationalizations and regulatory risk.
- Long/short equity funds are exposed to short-squeezes.
- Fixed income arbitrage funds are exposed to spread widening, changes in monetary policy and credit rating migrations.
- Convertible arbitrage funds are subject to volatility risk.
- Market neutral funds are subject to model risk.
- Offshore funds (whatever their strategy) are exposed to regulatory risk.

Each of these risks is rewarded by a risk premium. By bearing some of the risks, a hedge fund manager can capture the corresponding premiums. In ordinary circumstances, this will result in consistently higher average returns and is likely to be identified as superior skills. One would expect a simple mean–variance optimization to result in a disproportionately large allocation to alternative assets. Indeed, this is what occurs. However, in exchange for the premium, the fund manager will also have to sustain very large losses in exceptional circumstances. Most empirical performance measures, including volatility, will not show this if the very large loss has not materialized yet.

Another example of this bias is the mean–variance optimization's overestimation of the capital allocation to nonmarketable instruments such as hedge funds and/or private equity. The reason is that most of the short-term volatility is actually hidden by the lack of liquidity. Typically, if a market index drops in the middle of the month and recovers afterwards, traditional assets will be significantly affected, while hedge funds will simply hide the problem between two monthly net asset value calculations.

The dangers of mean–variance analysis for hedge funds: the skewness effect

Mean–variance analysis provides a powerful framework for asset allocation and portfolio performance assessment. Most investors, consultants and even a few academics feel comfortable applying mean–variance analysis, and therefore Sharpe ratios, to assess the performance of any kind of asset. For instance, Fung and Hsieh (1999b) claim that using a mean–variance criterion to rank hedge funds will produce rankings that are nearly correct. But I disagree. As with any powerful analytical technique, I believe that certain caveats must be respected in applying mean–variance analysis, otherwise erroneous conclusions may ensue.

The concept of variance—and therefore volatility and Sharpe ratios—is based on the idea of a returns distribution that is symmetrical around its mean return. Most of the time investors even have in mind a normal distribution. The bell-shaped curve does indeed have the advantages of offering analytical tractability and well-known statistical properties. However, both theory and empirical research suggest that the normal distribution assumption is not applicable to hedge funds for the following reasons:

- Several hedge fund strategies are based on financial derivatives, whose returns themselves are not normally distributed but exhibit skewness.[5]
- Hedge funds tend to use leverage to magnify returns. This results in frequent price jumps and returns distributions with a higher peak at the mean, a thinner midrange and fatter tails than a normal distribution (i.e. a large number of outliers); statisticians call this leptokurtosis.

As an illustration, consider the histogram of Figure 14.9. It represents the returns distribution observed for the hedge fund III Global Ltd between January 1994 and August 2001. Clearly, the returns distribution is far from a normal. It exhibits skewness (strong asymmetry toward higher returns) and fat tails, particularly at the extreme left.

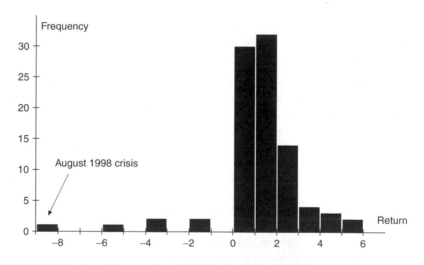

Figure 14.9   Distribution of returns for the hedge fund III Global Ltd

An essential question at this stage is therefore the applicability of the mean–variance framework to hedge funds, or more generally, to assets whose returns move away from the safe haven of a normal distribution. In particular, mean–variance analysis is known to produce difficulties with investments that exhibit highly asymmetric outcomes. The reason is straightforward. By using variance (or volatility) around the mean as a risk measure, one is assuming that investors are indifferent to the direction of risk and have no skewness preference. Upward deviations from the mean are handled exactly the same way as negative deviations. Both are squared in the variance calculation process, so it is impossible to distinguish between positive and negative deviations having the same absolute value. But investors most certainly do have a preference for upside risk and an aversion to downside risk—a preference for positive skewness. Don't you? Well, mean–variance simply ignores this.

These could be regarded as simple statistical details. However, in practice, ignoring these details could easily lead to incorrect conclusions. To illustrate the potential dangers of using the mean–variance framework with option-based portfolios, consider the case of three very simple but popular strategies: investing in an index fund (long the index), selling a covered call (long the index, short a call on the index), and buying a protective put (long the index, long an index put). Can just adding derivatives systematically generate superior performance and add value?

If the market is efficient and the options are fairly priced, the answer is no. The returns and risk reduction derived from the sale or purchase of efficiently priced options when combined with the risk and returns of a diversified market portfolio used as collateral will be offsetting and should yield no excess risk-adjusted portfolio returns. However, in a mean–variance framework this is not the case, and systematically buying or selling fairly valued options does provide "alphas." Alpha measures the excess performance that is attributable to a manager's actions. Consequently, covered call selling dominates the long index, which itself dominates the protective put. Let us illustrate why.

Figure 14.10 shows the expected return, volatility and Sharpe ratio for the three strategies as a function of the option's exercise price. As might be expected, for very low exercise prices, the covered call strategy behaves like a risk-free bond, while it is almost a stock for very high exercise prices. Therefore, increasing the exercise price should increase expected returns and expected volatility. At a very low exercise price, the protective put strategy is almost a naked stock, while it behaves like a risk-free bond for very high exercise prices. Therefore, increasing the exercise price should decrease expected returns and expected volatility.

What is more surprising is the way the Sharpe ratio changes. We are moving from a pure stock to a pure bond when the exercise price of a protective put position increases. The Sharpe ratio therefore decreases from that of a pure stock position to zero. We are moving from a pure bond to a pure stock when the exercise price of a covered call position increases. Therefore, the Sharpe ratio increases from zero to that of a pure stock position. So far so good, but the Sharpe ratio of covered calls exceeds the Sharpe ratio of the long stock position for a set of exercise prices that are higher than the at-the-money position, while protective puts have a Sharpe ratio that is always below the long stock position ratio. Consequently, covered call strategies will form a dominating efficient frontier in the mean–variance space (i.e. have a positive alpha), while protective put strategies will be dominated (i.e. have a negative alpha). These findings are based on theoretical option premiums, so they do not result from options mispricing. Nor

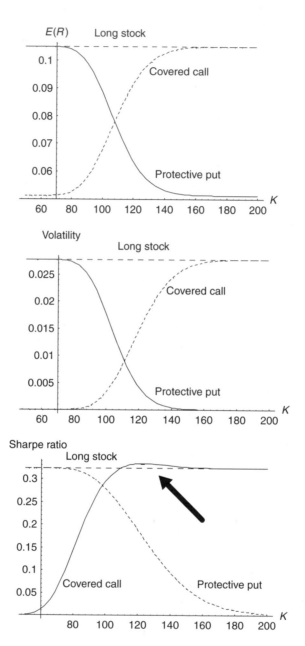

Figure 14.10 Expected return, volatility and Sharpe ratios for the three strategies as a function of the moneyness. All options are one-year to maturity. Option premiums were calculated using a Black–Scholes pricing model and assuming no dividend. Volatility was set at 15%. Moneyness (K) is expressed as a percentage of the underlying asset price

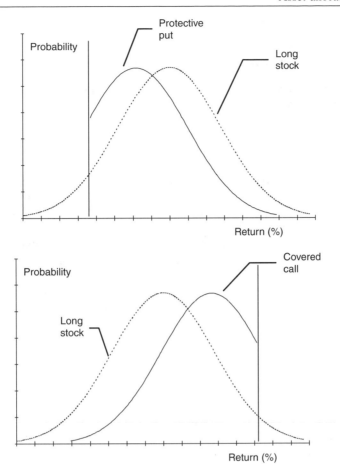

Figure 14.11   Returns distribution for the three strategies

do they depend on market expectations. They have also been observed using effective market prices in various market conditions (Lhabitant 1998, 1999, 2000). Moreover, they are in line with most institutions' perceptions that covered call writing is a means of augmenting portfolio returns and protective put buying is a solution to avoid downside risk.

So did we find the new winning solution to the portfolio optimization problem? Is it now possible to beat an efficient market without any stock-picking or timing ability? Not really. This is just a statistical illusion. When looking at the mean and variance of our distributions (or at the Sharpe ratios), we overlook the fact that the risk variation is not symmetrical, so that volatility does not present the whole picture. As illustrated in Figure 14.11, covered call writing has three impacts on the returns distribution:

- It increases the expected return because we cash in a premium, which is desirable.
- It reduces risk by truncating a tail of the distribution, which is desirable in the mean–variance framework.

- It generates negative skewness because it truncates the right-hand side of a distribution, and this is not desirable.

Similarly, protective put buying also has three impacts on the returns distribution:

- It decreases the expected return because we cash out a premium, which is undesirable.
- It reduces risk by truncating a tail of the distribution, which is desirable in the mean–variance framework.
- It generates positive skewness because it truncates the left-hand side of a distribution, and this is desirable.

It is thus natural that the compensation varies between the two strategies, as there must be a reward for holding a portfolio with a skewed returns distribution. Indeed, the call writing has reduced the upside potential (undesirable) while protective put buying has reduced downside risk (desirable).

Mean–variance analysis is myopic to aspects of the returns distribution beyond mean and variance. Similarly to the skewness bias, a kurtosis bias (or extreme event bias) can be identified in the mean–variance framework; see Lhabitant (1997) or Spurgin (1998) for a review. Since mean–variance analysis ignores asymmetry, it will identify some dominance, but this is simply a statistical illusion. The conclusion is that managers who have relatively high (but negative) skewness are likely to perform better than their counterparts.

Out of this come three points that are relevant to hedge funds. First, hedge funds often use options in their portfolios and this affects their returns distribution. Hedge fund managers might be tempted to accept negatively skewed returns in exchange for improving the mean or the variance of their portfolio. Out-of-the-money call writing is a typical "portfolio enhancer" in that respect. If they are lucky, hedge fund managers implementing this strategy may survive for years, boast superior Sharpe ratios (as the premiums flow directly in the bottom line with no apparent increase in the volatility), attract several investors and cash in hefty performance fees before being seriously hit once. In fact, out-of-the-money option writing has already been the source of several disasters in the hedge fund industry (Box 14.3). This is not surprising considering that option writers are essentially taking an almost unlimited future risk in exchange for what is usually a rather small immediate gain (the premium).

Box 14.3   BEWARE OF THE SKEWNESS EFFECT

As an illustration of the dangers of skewness, we should mention Victor Niederhoffer and his three funds (Global Systems, Friends, and Diversified). Among other things, Niederhoffer's strategy consisted in selling short out of the money put options on the S&P 500. This led to steady gains from the end of 1993 to the end of 1996. The three funds had a compound annual return of approximately 40% and a Sharpe ratio close to 3. This ranked as one of the best ever performances for directional commodity trading advisers over a three-year period. However, things deteriorated in 1997. The three funds had to file for bankruptcy following the crash that occurred on October 27, because they were unable to face the exercise of the previously sold put options.

The second point was only recently established by academic research, when several authors pointed out the option-like nature of hedge fund returns:

- Fung and Hsieh (1997a) were the first to suggest that trend-following funds had a return profile similar to a straddle (i.e. long a put and a call) on US equities and that the global macro style behaved like a straddle on the US dollar.
- Mitchell and Pulvino (2000) pointed out that merger arbitrage strategies exhibit a payoff similar to writing an uncovered put option on the market index. Consequently, the two authors have created a risk arbitrage index that investors can trade. The index is now managed by AQR Capital Management.
- Agarwal and Naik (2001) observed that the returns of relative value arbitrage funds are significantly related to the returns of call options on the Lehman High Yield index, deep out-of-the-money call options on the Russell 3000 index, and at-the-money put options on the MSCI Emerging Markets index.
- Fung and Hsieh (2001a) benchmarked trend-following hedge funds by using lookback straddles,[6] which deliver the performance of a perfect foresight trend follower.
- Amin and Kat (2001) developed a new performance measurement approach that is based on combining S&P 500 options to approximate hedge fund returns distributions.

This does not necessarily mean that hedge funds are actually using options, but more generally that the payoffs they offer can be replicated by passive strategies that involve options on standard asset classes.

Finally, the third relationship is linked to hedge fund managers' remuneration contracts, which often involve a performance-related fee. This is equivalent to the investor writing and granting some free call options on the fund's assets to the manager. For instance, if the incentive fee is 20% of profits, then the investor is short one-fifth of a call option. The exercise price of the option depends on the hurdle rate and high water mark provisions, if any. The expiration of the option corresponds to the end of the period used to calculate the incentive fee. As a consequence of this option-like nature of performance fees, even if the prefee returns do not exhibit option-like characteristics, the postfee returns will.

Hedge funds and options are clearly not dissociable. For that reason, I believe that caution should be the watchword in using mean–variance analysis with hedge funds. The free lunch it seems to offer may just be a statistical mirage rather than a first-class meal. In particular, when considering the various levels of skewness and kurtosis we observed in Figure 14.5, there is a high probability that some of the strategies depart sufficiently from normality to negate the overall conclusions. Then overreliance on Sharpe ratios might skew allocations toward suboptimal long-term strategies.

Correlation solely captures linear covariations

Correlation analysis is the most ubiquitous concept in portfolio optimization and asset allocation, but it is probably also one of the most misunderstood. What does correlation really measure? Statistically, correlation is a measure of the *linear* dependence between two random variables. In the case of perfect linear dependence (which does not necessarily imply perfect equality), correlation should be equal to one. In the case of totally independent variables, correlation should be equal to zero. In the case of perfect linear dependence opposite in sign, correlation should be equal to minus one.

As soon as the relationship between two variables is not linear, correlation will provide inaccurate results. Consider for instance a convertible bond. What should be its correlation with a traditional equity market index and with a bond index? It varies depending on the underlying price with respect to the conversion price (Figure 14.12):

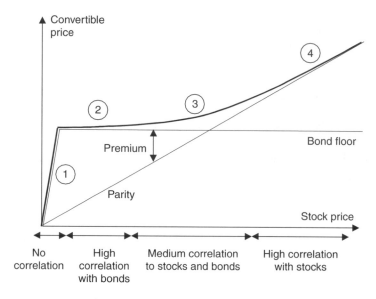

Figure 14.12   The four stages in a convertible bond and correlation analysis

- In area 1 the convertible bond is distressed and should not be correlated with stock or bond markets.
- In area 2 the convertible bond behaves like a traditional bond; it should therefore have a very low correlation with the stock index and a high correlation with the bond index.
- In area 3 the convertible bond is a hybrid asset; it should see its correlation with the stock increase and its correlation with the bond index decrease.
- In area 4 the convertible bond behaves like a pure stock; it should therefore have a high correlation with the stock index and a low correlation with the bond index.

This is great, but correlation needs to be a single number. We therefore see the limits of the model. A single number will average all the possible states, but will fail to capture the true *nonlinear dependences* between the convertible bond, the equity market and the bond market. One should therefore be cautious when considering a correlation figure, as it may hide several nonlinear phenomena.

Hedge fund indices are not hedge funds

The last criticism we will address in this chapter relates to the use of hedge fund indices rather than true hedge funds at the asset allocation level. By construction, hedge fund indices are summary statistics for a large universe. They tend to aggregate the performance of several hedge fund managers, and therefore internally diversify risks. They are also subject to well-know return biases (e.g. survivorship bias, selection bias, stale pricing[7]). Consequently, hedge fund indices exhibit considerably lower risks and higher returns than individual hedge funds. This is particularly problematic when considering equally weighted indices based on a large number of funds. These are useful indicators of the industry's average behavior, but are not investable in practice. First, rebalancing is impossible due to lockup periods and fees; second, the minimum investment requirements preclude any individual from holding a portfolio of several hundred hedge funds.

FINAL THOUGHTS

There have been several ad hoc attempts to solve the above biases of mean–variance optimization and obtain a more robust framework for asset allocation and performance analysis. A first attitude consists in measuring explicitly the bias of traditional measures. If a meter reading is systematically 20% high, the meter can still be used by applying the necessary correction. This was the approach pioneered by Leland (1999), who suggested a skewness adjustment, and Lhabitant (1998), who explicitly computed the Sharpe ratio bias. However, relying on biased tools is not very satisfactory.

Several practitioners prefer replacing variance by another risk measure in the optimization process. In particular, professional investment consultants recommend using the Sortino ratio, which is defined as the incremental return over a minimum acceptable return (MAR), divided by the downside deviation below the MAR; deviations are only based on return occurrences with value below the MAR. In my opinion, a better alternative is to use a drawdown—a statistic that captures the deepest loss a portfolio has experienced over some historical period. Drawdown measures considerably change the perception of risk, as well as the usefulness of correlation. In the return/volatility approach of Markowitz, diversification results from the linear correlation between traditional portfolios and alternatives. In the return/drawdown approach, diversification comes from the low correlation during the downside movements.

More recently, several academics have suggested using value at risk as a risk measure. Since value at risk is the maximum loss over a given interval in "normal" market conditions, optimizing according to expected return and value at risk is equivalent to increasing the return while limiting the risk of a major loss, which is in line with investors' preoccupations. I highly recommend Favre and Galleano (2000) to the interested reader.

Nevertheless, most of these studies tend to confirm that there is a compelling argument for the inclusion of hedge funds in traditional investment portfolios. Though highly stylized, the analysis of efficient frontiers in a risk/return environment—not necessarily a volatility/return environment—provides a good foundation for assessing the corresponding value added. However, the benefits may not be as great as expected. For instance, Favre and Galleano (2000) observe that (i) the diversification effect claimed by hedge fund managers is not true for the extreme negative market returns; and (ii) investing in a diversified portfolio of 53 large hedge funds increases the value at risk (which accounts for skewness and kurtosis) by 13% to 27%. It is therefore rather illusory to quest after a systematic target optimal proportion of hedge funds in asset allocation. The benefits will vary greatly, depending on the nature of the traditional portfolio already held; the type of hedge fund strategy considered; and the risk measure selected.

Consequently, the pros and cons of adding hedge funds to traditional assets should be assessed on a case-by-case basis and using the necessary information and tools. The talisman of most investors and advisers is still too often a high Sharpe ratio—high returns per unit of risk taken. This is a shortsighted attitude; in addition to the traditional risks inherent in stocks and bonds which will show up in the variance of returns, hedge fund investing does have specific risks which should not be overlooked. Clearly, the difficulties associated with estimating their risks and returns make hedge funds poor candidates for strategic asset allocation optimization, but not necessarily poor candidates for asset allocation.

Last but not least, investors should remember that, with hedge funds, they are investing in a strategy and not an asset class, which means that their investments depend on the ability of the manager and the constancy of the investment strategy. Researching and evaluating hedge funds therefore presents a host of challenges to even the most sophisticated investor. These topics are covered in the next few chapters.

NOTES

1. Although this does not exactly correspond to the statistical interpretation, it helps in understanding the overall concept.
2. It is amusing to recall that a similar argument was applied to gold for centuries. Not so long ago, prudence dictated a proportion of between 5% and 10% of gold in a portfolio in order to diversify and balance risks. Gold was then perceived as a perfect hedge against inflation and as an ideal insurance in times of war, financial turbulence, serious recession or simply falling stock markets. It was only after several years of heavy losses on these gold positions that investors started selling them to move into more lucrative asset classes such as equities.
3. When unconstrained, the portfolio allocation is still predominantly in hedge funds, more specifically in equity market neutral funds (40.7% of the minimum risk portfolio, 81.6% at its peak, and not present in the maximum return portfolio) and macro funds (not present in low-risk portfolios, but 58.3% of the maximum return portfolio).
4. Of course, the box could be opened, but many investors would consider its contents to be a mass of impenetrable statistics.
5. Imagine buying a call or a put option. The maximum loss is capped at the initial premium paid, while the gain is virtually unlimited. This obviates [reduces] the chance of ending up with a nice-looking symmetrical normal distribution.
6. A lookback call option grants its owner the right to buy the underlying asset at the lowest price reached over the life of the option. A lookback put option grants its owner the right to sell the underlying asset at the highest price reached over the life of the option. The combination of a lookback call and a lookback put creates a lookback straddle.

7. Stale pricing occurs when a fund holding illiquid, exotic, privately placed or hard-to-price securities estimates the new value of such assets from the last known valuation. This introduces serial correlation in prices, lowers volatility and decreases correlation! According to Morgan Stanley Dean Witter (2000), the resulting downward bias in volatility can be as much as 100%.

15

Hedge fund selection

Once the investor has decided the percentage of his portfolio to be allocated to hedge funds, the fund selection process can start. Simply stated, the role of the hedge fund selection process is to screen the industry for exceptional talents. Gaining access to one of the very few quality managers was for long the most difficult element of investing in hedge funds. Historically, hedge funds were only available through the "whisper network" of large institutional and very wealthy individual investors. There was no question of selection. The question was rather one of being invited to invest in a fund.

The strong economy and raging bull market of the 1990s have expanded the pool of vehicles, and the problem is now exactly the opposite: choosing a particular hedge fund in a universe of about 6000 funds can be one of the most daunting challenges an investor has to face, even though it need not be. The lack of publicly available information and the limited transparency of hedge funds do not facilitate the selection process. In addition, the consequences of being wrong are weighty. Even in a small peer group, the dispersion of risk and returns among hedge funds can be quite large, particularly on the downside, since no common benchmark or tracking error federates the asset allocation.

That being said, it is possible to avoid a large number of pitfalls by setting emotion aside and applying the appropriate analytical principles to the decision. In a sense, the process of selecting a particular hedge fund should be very similar to selecting a stock—systematic, disciplined, well structured and rational. Research and common sense are the keys to good decisions. If you are not an expert, hire one but first ensure that he is a truly independent expert. And remember that in reality most so-called experts who claim to use proprietary techniques to select hedge funds, based on their personal relationships, years of experience, or quantitative models, simply follow the steps of the hedge fund selection process that we will now describe (Figure 15.1).

STATING OBJECTIVES

Before beginning the search for a hedge fund or a hedge fund manager, we need to state precisely what an investor wants to achieve. What type of hedge fund are we looking for? The answer should take the form of a coherent set of fund characteristics that are mandatory or desirable for this investor. Anything that may affect the final choice should be mentioned:

- Should the fund be restricted and/or avoid a particular strategy or market or a specific investment style?
- For tax efficiency, should the fund have its domicile or be registered in a particular country?
- Should the fund have a minimum size of assets under management? A minimum length of identifiable track record? A minimum level of disclosure and/or reporting? These

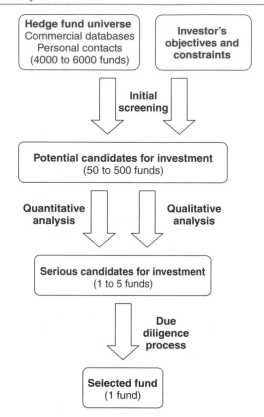

Figure 15.1   A typical hedge fund selection process

last two objectives are often conflicting: younger managers have less experience, but they are often more willing to open their funds to scrutiny.
- Should the fund have a specific redemption policy, e.g. monthly or quarterly?
- Should the fund be willing to accept a given investment, whether large or small?
- Should the fund's returns be hedged against a specific currency?

Stating these objectives constitutes the foundation of the hedge fund selection process. Specifying them loosely will extract hedge funds that will not satisfy their investors. It is therefore essential to take the time needed to define one's needs precisely. Unfortunately, most investors who are new to alternative investments have only a vague idea of what their objectives are. How many requests have been made for funds that "add value" or hold "noncorrelated assets"? These are neither clearly defined terms nor investment goals. And, by the way, noncorrelated to what?

FILTERING THE UNIVERSE

Once the hedge fund's desired characteristics have been clearly stated, an efficient and effective elimination process can begin. It is usually implemented on a computer database containing information on several thousand hedge funds. By applying the necessary filters to this database, one can effectively eliminate a large number of funds that do not fulfill the mandatory criteria, and grade the remaining funds according to their adequacy. The top funds will go forward to the next step— perhaps between 50 and 500, depending on the selectivity of the search criteria.

The key to filtering is gaining access to information. For several years, hedge fund databases were proprietary and investors looking to invest in hedge funds did not have access to performance data. Only those who were in the know and had committed capital for several years managed to obtain "behind the scenes" information. Fortunately, since the mid 1990s, the situation has changed. A number of hedge funds databases have become publicly available (e.g. the databases of Van Hedge, Tuna, MAR/Hedge, Hedge Fund Research, Altvest and TASS). Some of them even now offer online access and search capabilities, with some analytics and portfolio risk monitoring. Investors can therefore leverage these powerful tools to make hedge fund investing easier and base their strategic decisions on comprehensive information.

However, no official database is complete. Since hedge fund managers are not required, and in many cases not allowed, to advertise or report performance data to any central authority, information is reported only on a voluntary basis. Consequently, many of the top hedge fund managers are not listed in commercially available databases. Therefore, hedge fund consultants and investment advisers often build their own database by subscribing to public databases, but also by adding in the managers they know through their network of professional contacts and with whom they feel comfortable investing. Funds closed to new money for the foreseeable future and funds where the management group refuses to disclose a sufficient amount of information should be systematically eliminated from these databases.

Keep in mind that very large databases are not necessarily ideal. It is true that they increase the likelihood of finding suitable managers but they also include several funds that are not truly hedge funds, are not suitable for investment, or are totally unknown in the industry. I remember visiting an asset manager who proudly exhibited a database of more than 60 000 funds. After a few checks, it transpired that most of these funds were long-only funds, and the same fund appeared many times under different codes, once for each place where it was authorized for distribution, once for each class of shares, etc. This clearly demonstrates the advantage of working with a prefiltered set of funds that fulfill minimum initial requirements.

Once the database is ready, it is subjected to a preliminary refinement based on quantitative criteria such as performance, volatility and correlation to traditional markets, assets under management, the experience of the fund manager, the track record length, the investment style, the selected financial instruments and leveraging. This first selection is made on the basis of marketing research, management meetings and short visits to the fund managers.

Once the filtering process is terminated, the investor is left with a short series of hedge funds—the short list. All meet the stated requirements and are therefore potential candidates for investing, at least from an external viewpoint. The next step is to look behind the screens, get a clearer picture of what these hedge funds are really doing and narrow the choice down from several hundred funds to a manageable pool of a few tens. The tools to perform this task are quantitative analysis and qualitative analysis.

QUANTITATIVE ANALYSIS

Hedge funds managers like to point to their long-term track record, if any, as an evidence of their ability to weather different market conditions successfully. However, although desirable, a good track record is no guarantee of future performance, nor is it a reliable indicator of historical performance. One needs to look behind the numbers and extract the relevant information content from the time series. This is the role of quantitative analysis.

Quantitative analysis focuses on the statistical evaluation of the past performance of a hedge fund over different periods of time. It typically uses ratios and other statistical measures to compare absolute and relative performance, performance in rising and falling markets, and risk-adjusted performance with that of managers and benchmarks with similar investment styles and risk levels. Ideally, it should focus on three aspects: manager returns, strategy returns and portfolio contribution. Knowing the effective primary drivers behind a manager's returns and a strategy's returns is particularly important to:

- Assess the consistency and validity of the track record, volatility patterns and correlations with major indices.
- Quantify the size and stability of the fund's exposures over time and compare them with the strategy's exposures.
- Understand the systematic and specific risks involved, at least on a historical basis.
- Analyze the risk premium received as well as the excess return (alpha) over time.
- Validate a manager's specific implementation and/or trades

If the selected fund needs to be incorporated in an existing portfolio (of other hedge funds, traditional assets, or a mix of these), it is also necessary to estimate the overall portfolio systematic and specific risk exposures as well as the fund's marginal contribution to risk.

Because it relies essentially on historical time series of net asset values, quantitative analysis has the advantage of low cost and easy access. However, it is often criticized as being a backward-looking process. As we all should know, past performance is of questionable relevance when looking forward, because history may not repeat itself. It is therefore illusory to select hedge funds solely on the basis of their historical performance. However, the past may provide prudent guidance for the future. For instance, track records in stressful periods often tell something about how a manager behaves under pressure. Does the performance make sense, given the announced strategy and the underlying market conditions? Comparing managers to themselves at earlier periods can be quite revealing about their real-world style and risk appetite. Ideally, this type of quantitative analysis should be performed over a historical period of at least 3–5 years to allow a hedge fund to move through a full market cycle with both bull and bear markets. However, most hedge funds have a shorter time record, so shorter periods are not uncommon.

QUALITATIVE ANALYSIS

Qualitative analysis is the logical complement to quantitative analysis. Its primary aim should be to gain a clearer picture of the general strategy and investment philosophy followed by a given hedge fund, and in particular to understand where the performance (the alpha) comes from and why the fund should be able to extract it. It also raises awareness of the returns and risks that are plausible. When correctly implemented, qualitative analysis provides a means of differentiating between two apparently identical statistical hedge fund profiles. It is often useful in eliminating an additional series of hedge funds that are not compatible with the investor's wishes.

The sources of qualitative analysis are usually to be found in the private placement memorandum. This is a document available only to qualified investors that describes a hedge fund's objectives, the backgrounds of its principals, the fees charged, the minimum contribution accepted, etc. Hedge fund databases, simple evaluation questionnaires sent to fund managers, and any audited financials may also be used to obtain the necessary qualitative information that is not disclosed in the private placement memorandum.

DUE DILIGENCE

Once the quantitative and qualitative analyses have yielded their conclusions, only a few funds should remain as suitable candidates for investment. Before committing any equity capital, it is necessary to analyze the candidates in detail, not from an external perspective (past returns, offering memorandum, etc.), but from an internal viewpoint (investment process and philosophy, style, approach, risk controls, performance record against appropriate index, in various markets and against peers, depth and quality of internal organization, manager background, investment references, etc.). This is called due diligence.

In a sense, due diligence is a form of more comprehensive and more thorough qualitative analysis. It is usually conducted by a team of experienced professionals through due diligence questionnaires combined with visits to the fund's offices and face-to-face interviews with each fund's senior management and portfolio manager. Each aspect investigated usually has a scoring system, which allows funds to be graded and compared on a similar basis. Hedge funds were long perceived as something of a black box, with managers unwilling to provide any significant information regarding their strategies or their portfolios. However, the situation has gradually changed with the competition resulting from the emergence of new managers and the increased interest of institutional investors. Most managers now employ some staff dedicated to answering due diligence questionnaires sent by serious potential investors.

We look at five key areas that should be analyzed in any due diligence process: the strategy, the fund itself, the management team, the infrastructure and the investment process.

The strategy

What is the hedge fund doing exactly? At this stage of the analysis, that may seem a silly question. With traditional investments, figuring out the strategy of a fund manager is easy. One just needs to look at the fund's benchmark, which is often very similar to the fund's asset allocation. However, with hedge funds and other absolute return performers, this is no longer the case. The idea of a benchmark is indeed the very antithesis of absolute performance. Most hedge funds do not use benchmarks, or just rely on some "increment to cash returns" approach.

Of course, most hedge funds disclose the general type of strategy they intend to follow, and data providers often rely on this information to classify funds in a series of predefined categories. Unfortunately, managers' definitions are highly subjective, so that even within a particular investment strategy, one can find a mixture of four-star chefs and burger flippers. In my experience, the best way to understand a hedge fund strategy is to request the manager to provide examples of a few trades and then go over them line by line. It is essential that these trades include successful ones, but also ones that failed. This will allow the investor to be aware of the risks associated with the strategy and what is done about them. And remember that a manager that claims to have no losing trades is untruthful or, even worse, overconfident.

Once the current investment strategy is understood, the focus should turn to understanding historical changes with respect to this strategy, as well as the potential consequences in the future. For instance:

- Has the fund manager changed his strategy over time? Strategies are not carved in stone, and it is common for managers to change their initial positioning. If they have done so, it is important to know why.
- Is the current manager responsible for the fund's long-term performance or did he inherit it from another departed manager?
- Did the fund manager run the strategy prior to the inception of the fund? If so, were there any structural advantages or disadvantages?
- What are the prospects for the strategy? Are there limits to the amount the fund can manage effectively without sacrificing performance? If so, at what level will the fund's assets be capped?
- Are audited statements available? Are the returns consistent with the strategy?
- What is the average leverage? Is leverage necessary or just speculative?
- How concentrated are the positions? How liquid are they?

Finally, an important issue is that of competition. No one is better placed than the manager of the fund to describe its major competitors, their size, their differences, etc. This is extremely useful information to understand the value added by the manager and to be able to build a peer group to benchmark a fund.

The fund itself

Once a comfort level has been established with the strategy, the next step is the analysis of the fund itself. Well before committing to any investment, special attention should be paid to understanding the terms of the fund and its structures as well as the quality of the various parties involved. In particular, the following questions should be asked:

- Where is the fund's domicile? Why? What are the rights of investors under the jurisdiction of the country of domicile?
- What is the legal structure of the fund? What are the rights and duties involved?
- Is the management firm regulated? If so, by whom? If it is not regulated, what exemptions are relied upon?
- What is the subscription and redemption policy? Is it likely to change? Has it been changing already?
- What are the fees and expenses charged to the fund and to the investor?
- Who are the fund's service providers (custodian, administrator, etc.)? How were they selected? How is their performance monitored? Have there been any recent changes?
- Where are the assets of the fund held? Who can transfer the assets into the accounts of the fund and what process must be followed to do so? Are there liabilities or assets used as collateral?

- What is the process undertaken to value investments? Have there been any material problems in pricing, calculation of net asset values or remittance of proceeds?
- Is there an independent board of directors made up of people with the necessary background, experience and independence to fulfill their responsibilities?
- How many other investors are in the fund? How large is the largest investor or the five largest investors? How much of the equity capital was committed by the manager?
- Is there any other available means of investing in the same strategy with the same manager (e.g. onshore and offshore funds, managed accounts, different types of shares)? What are their differences?
- Do any other investors in the fund have preferential terms (fees, liquidity, transparency)? It is often the case that closed funds reopen with worse terms for the new investors (longer initial lockups, higher fees, etc.).

The due diligence team may also require a review of the other agreements that are part of an offshore fund, i.e. investment advisory or administration agreements.

The management team

Once the first two stages have been completed, the next step is to appraise the people involved in managing the fund. This is an important step, because a hedge fund's success is largely dependent on its managers' ability to navigate through different market conditions and business cycles. Here are some essentials:

- *The key individuals in the fund*. Who are they? What are their backgrounds and reputation within the industry? How experienced are they? What does their experience give them? When and why did they leave their previous employer? Some investors may be reluctant to ask such personal questions, but he should remember that a significant portion of his wealth would be at these people's discretion. If desired, third parties could perform the necessary checks. The secretive nature of hedge funds makes them enticing vehicles for charlatans, but also for crooks.[1]
- *Any actual or threatened legal action*. The answers should be checked with different regulatory agencies that maintain sanctions and enforcement databases (the Securities and Futures Authority, the Commodity Futures Trading Commission, etc.).
- *The nature and coherence of the management team*. Does the senior manager really delegate, or is he more like a star surrounded by executants? How long have members of the team worked together? Do they share the same vision and strategy? Have there been any recent departures, or disciplinary or regulatory problems with any members of the staff or the firm as a whole? How vulnerable is the organization to the departure of a specific fund manager?
- *The motivation of the management team*. Is management sufficiently motivated? Did managers commit their own capital? If a hedge fund manager is not willing to risk much of his own money, why should you? If he does, what is the sum involved? How many employees are also rewarded according to performance? How are the staff paid?
- *The potential conflicts of interest*. Are there incentives for trades to be executed via any particular channel? Are managers dedicated to a single hedge fund, or do they manage several hedge funds simultaneously?

The infrastructure

Analyzing the current and expected future infrastructure of a hedge fund in terms of software, hardware and office space is necessary but not easy. The reason is that there is no infrastructure that can be defined a priori as "right," but several valid competing ones that need to be in line with the fund's overall activity. It pays to build for success. Several funds end up being constrained in their business development opportunities because of inadequate infrastructure. Here are some key issues to monitor:

- The software used in the front-office analytics, the mid-office risk systems and the back-office accounting and execution systems.
- How these systems communicate and are reconciled with one another.
- The automated backup processes and facilities for disaster recovery, as well as insurance policies, if any.
- The existence of a website and how it is used to inform existing customers of developments at the fund.

The process

The last step of the due diligence should focus on understanding and validating the investment process of the hedge fund. Here are some critical questions:

- What are the processes for taking investment decisions? Is there an investment committee or are the final decisions taken by one single individual? How do new ideas enter the portfolio construction?
- Who is allowed to trade? What assets can be traded? How are trades executed, reported and entered into the systems? What are the safeguards to prevent any unauthorized trading or to prevent tickets from being hidden?
- Is there an independent risk management unit? What are the risk management limits at trade and portfolio level? How are these limits imposed? Is there a risk committee? How is compliance with the risk limits monitored?
- How does the reconciliation process operate, internally and with respect to the prime brokers and the administrator? Have there been any material issues and how were they resolved?

Another important issue is the amount of cash balances held by the fund. Frequently, due diligence questionnaires request the average cash percentage of the fund over a year, as well as an explanation for any significant deviation from this average over the past five years or since the fund's inception.

ONGOING MONITORING

The final outcome of the selection process is a formal report that should fully document the "hire" or "do not hire" decision. It sometimes contains recommendations relative to the maximum size of the allocation, or if the fund is not retained, indications for the future. For instance, a fund may be temporarily excluded for a minor reason but still monitored for future use.

However, once an investment has been made, things do not end there. Selected managers should be subject to a rigorous ongoing monitoring and oversight process to ensure they adhere to their stated investment strategy and their performance on a risk-adjusted basis compares favorably with their peers'. Funds that fail to achieve their stated goals or that deviate from their stated philosophy should be subject to replacement.

This thoughtful and thorough monitoring program should be structured as an ongoing analysis and due diligence. It focuses on the same issues (the people in the fund, the investment process, the nature of the portfolio and the resulting performance, etc.) and is at least as time-consuming, but it reaches different conclusions. Once the investor has committed some capital to a hedge fund, there are three possible choices: leaving things unchanged (default), committing more capital, or redeeming assets in whole or part. The role of monitoring should therefore be to support this type of decision making based on regular contacts with managers, site visits, conference calls, discussions with other industry participants, and internal quantitative and qualitative analysis.[2] Any information received as a shareholder in the fund (regular shareholder newsletters, nonaudited monthly statements of positions and audited financial statements) should therefore be circulated for review within the due diligence team.

MISTAKES TO AVOID

Focusing on immaterial issues

Attention should only focus on (the numerous) issues that might affect the final selection decision. As one of my former colleagues used to say, "Focus on coconuts, not on peanuts!"

Reliance on emotions

To be efficient, the selection process should eschew any emotional considerations. An excellent manager may be disagreeable, unfriendly or even arrogant, while a crook will often be extremely likable and pleasant. What matters is not how one interacts emotionally with the manager, but the quality of the management process. However, in some cases, much like when hiring a manager or a doctor, the question of personal attitude may also weigh in the final decision. For instance, a manager who seems unfocused and disinterested or even unaware of his latest deals gives a strong signal that something is wrong in a hedge fund's organization.

Overreliance on qualitative aspects

This bias is unfortunately still too frequent. Several analysts do not feel very comfortable with quantitative measures, and tend to neglect them on the grounds that they rely solely on the past and are not good indicators of the future. They prefer to rely on qualitative analysis and due diligence, and solely use quantitative analysis to screen large databases of hedge funds, to rank them according to a particular choice of performance measures and to show the corresponding results with eye-catching graphics. As a result, they tend to produce thick quantitative reports, with several dozen pages filled with statistics, net asset values and other numbers, but without value added to these numbers or any real analysis. This is clearly a dangerous attitude, given the low transparency and loose regulation of hedge funds activities. I believe quantitative analysis has a useful role to play per se, but also as a complement to qualitative analysis. In particular, it is the only historical trace of what has effectively been done by a manager. Therefore, the key to success lies in combining historical guideposts with current and ongoing personal knowledge of the hedge fund and its manager.

Waste of information

Any information collected during the selection process and the ongoing monitoring should be recorded in a predetermined information management system. This helps to avoid oversights and throws light on the evolution of the fund manager and his strategy over time. It also provides for easy transfer of knowledge if someone else is designated to take care of the selection process in the future.

NOTES

1. For instance, Michael Smirlock, a former Goldman Sachs mortgage trader raised $700 million to start three hedge funds just after the SEC had suspended him in 1993. Would you have followed him? Well, in 2000, the SEC sued him again for hiding $70 million in losses from his investors.
2. An interesting question here is the availability of managers. Investors like to receive updates on performance, investment approach and/or outlook directly from the manager; but on the other hand, the role of the manager should be to focus on asset management, not on investor relations. It is therefore important to find a mutually acceptable communication arrangement.

16
Funds of funds and metadiversification

As we saw in the previous chapter, although hedge funds may offer some specific benefits, it is quite difficult and time-consuming for an investor to just go out and hire a single hedge fund manager on his own. Significant barriers, such as the complexity of the evaluation process and the experience that is necessary to perform effective ongoing monitoring of the selected funds, will discourage most investors. Furthermore, given the high minimum investment requirements of individual hedge funds, direct investments have every chance of turning into concentrated portfolios (i.e. one to three managers), which are inherently poorly diversified and often highly illiquid. This explains why investors with time constraints, little experience, or limited capital often prefer to gain access to alternative investments through funds of hedge funds to reach a proper diversification.

WHAT ARE FUNDS OF FUNDS?

Funds of hedge funds, hereafter funds of funds, do exactly what their name suggests—they allocate capital to several hedge funds. Investors buying shares in a fund of funds are not investing in a specific hedge fund, but rather gaining exposure to many different managers and strategies. Indeed, they acquire a proportionate share of ownership in a collective portfolio of typically 15–30 hedge funds.

Although funds of funds may appear innovative for most investors, it is not really a new concept. Rothschild Capital Management started up the hedge fund Leveraged Capital Holdings in November 1969, which was from the beginning a fund of hedge funds. Its assets have since grown to over $1 billion and it is now closed to new investors.

However, it is only recently that funds of funds have really begun to win significant business. In particular, they are now the preferred access path to hedge funds for many pension funds, endowments, insurance companies, private banks, high net worth families and individuals. Zurich Capital Markets' database (formerly MAR/Hedge) lists 197 funds of funds, out of which only 9 started operations before 1990. According to recent estimations by New York consultants of the Hennessee Group, funds of funds now represent 20–25% of the whole hedge fund universe in terms of assets under management, and they will undoubtedly be an important catalyst in the evolution of the hedge fund industry. As an illustration, Europe's biggest pension plan, the Netherlands' Algemeen Burgerlijk Pensioenfonds, announced that it would invest up to €2 billion over the next three years in funds of funds. That is nearly twice the amount that Calpers, the biggest US pension fund, has committed to hedge funds.

ADVANTAGES OF FUNDS OF FUNDS

In theory, well-designed and well-managed funds of funds can deliver a number of valuable benefits. We review and comment on the contributions that funds of funds commonly claim to offer: risk diversification, affordability, accessibility, professional management, and built-in asset allocation.

Efficient risk diversification

Meaningful diversification benefits are the key argument advanced by promoters of funds of funds. Prudent investors would not sink all their money into a single stock, but rather lower the risk of loss by buying shares in a number of companies. They may not earn the stellar returns of the best-performing stock, but they will not lose as much as they would if that single stock were to collapse in price. As with stocks, so with hedge funds. Investment returns, volatility, and risk vary enormously among the different hedge fund strategies. By selecting managers rather than assets, funds of funds aim to provide investors with an extra level of diversification and allow them to smooth out the potential return inconsistencies of having all assets invested in a single hedge fund.

Risk diversification within a fund of funds can be achieved by two means. The generalist approach consists simply in using several hedge funds that cover a wide array of strategies, managers, markets and risk factors. It is often implemented by mixing hedge funds following different investment styles that have displayed historically low correlation. In practice it yields the biggest risk reduction, because the selected funds are likely to hold fewer stocks in common. By opposition, the specialist approach is to invest in a large number of hedge funds following the same strategy. It aims at avoiding the risk of poor manager selection, while still remaining exposed to an investment style.

There are, however, different opinions about the optimal number of hedge funds in a fund of funds. Some managers (e.g. Global Asset Management) take a bold view and prefer to run concentrated portfolios of 15–20 funds with larger single allocations, while others (e.g. Glenwood) run a highly diversified portfolio of about 50 funds.

The following simple experiment will reveal the corresponding benefits of funds of funds. I selected a sample of 21 hedge funds active over the period January 1994 to August 2001.[1] All of them appear regularly as core holdings in funds of funds quarterly reports and cover a wide spectrum of strategies: convertible arbitrage, distressed securities, emerging markets, fixed income arbitrage, global macro, long/short equity, merger arbitrage, short bias and trading.

Table 16.1 shows the risk and return of each of these funds over the period 1994–2001. For comparison I have also included the three largest funds of funds over the same period[2] as well as two indices (the J.P. Morgan Global Bonds index and the S&P 500). Given the variety of strategies, it is not surprising to observe that hedge funds' annualized returns range from 0.67% to 25.90%, and annualized volatilities range from 2.36% to 45%. Looking at the correlation matrix of these 17 funds (not displayed here because of its size) also reveals some interesting facts. The average correlation is surprisingly low at 0.16, with individual correlations ranging from −0.46 to 0.90. Some correlations between hedge funds following the same investment style are also extremely low. This gives a clue that the diversification benefits to be derived from mixing these hedge funds in a portfolio should be considerable.

If we were to manage a fund of funds, a naive strategy to capture the benefits of diversification would be to allocate assets equally between our 21 hedge funds. The corresponding portfolio has an expected return of 14.84% and a volatility of 8.80%. This is more than remarkable, bearing in mind particularly that the performance of a few hedge

Table 16.1 Risk and return of a sample of hedge funds (1994–2000)

	Average return (%)	Volatility (%)	Sharpe ratio	Skewness	Kurtosis	Maximum monthly return		Minimum monthly return		VaR$_{0.95,1M}$ (%)
						Percent	Date	Percent	Date	
Cerberus Partners LP	13.08	3.22	2.50	−0.62	1.85	3.70	Mar 93	−2.30	Aug 98	−0.39
GAM Arbitrage	10.27	2.76	1.90	−0.20	−0.07	2.75	Sep 97	−1.24	Oct 94	−0.54
GAM Japan	6.60	17.05	0.09	0.27	−0.12	13.94	Jun 97	−10.93	Jul 00	−6.60
GAM Trading USD	13.58	6.24	1.37	0.45	1.98	7.24	Dec 00	−4.87	Feb 94	−1.30
GAM US	13.35	13.58	0.61	−0.49	1.20	9.35	Oct 99	−13.78	Aug 98	−4.79
GAMut	20.12	12.29	1.23	0.25	0.47	11.99	Jul 99	−7.01	Jan 01	−3.03
III Global Ltd	12.35	9.78	0.75	−3.81	20.12	5.77	Jan 99	−16.20	Oct 98	−2.26
JMG Capital Partners LP	21.16	3.78	4.26	−0.26	3.31	5.50	Jan 01	−1.87	Aug 98	−0.08
Kingate Euro Fund Ltd	12.86	3.01	2.59	0.45	−0.48	3.30	Jan 97	−0.77	Nov 94	−0.09
Latinvest Fund Ltd	2.40	39.19	−0.07	0.05	2.24	39.01	Mar 99	−38.47	Aug 98	−15.79
Manchester Institutional Fund	11.20	9.17	0.67	0.50	0.56	8.58	Jan 96	−4.55	Jan 99	−3.27
Nestor Partners	9.37	16.51	0.26	0.14	0.74	14.90	Mar 95	−12.04	Oct 98	−6.78
P.A.W. Partners LP	19.29	8.95	1.59	0.74	2.21	10.90	Feb 00	−6.30	Aug 98	−1.91
Pactual Infinity Fund	0.67	42.59	−0.10	0.14	1.48	36.37	Mar 99	−42.33	Aug 98	−15.92
Permal Essex Media & Techno. Ltd	7.21	45.15	0.05	0.42	2.29	49.55	Feb 00	−34.06	Apr 00	−20.81
Perry Partners LP	17.00	6.72	1.78	−0.78	3.12	7.24	Mar 98	−6.31	Aug 98	−1.47
Raptor Global Fund LP	25.90	14.92	1.40	0.87	2.32	17.90	Dec 99	−9.88	Apr 00	−3.52
Spinner Global Technology Fund (Class A)	28.21	20.06	1.16	0.57	1.76	22.35	Feb 00	−11.72	Aug 98	−6.38
TQA Arbitrage Fund LP	9.29	2.36	1.80	−1.07	3.40	2.28	Jul 97	−2.27	Apr 94	−0.48
UBS Currency Portfolio Ltd	9.26	11.09	0.38	0.72	1.86	11.98	Jun 04	−5.12	Aug 94	−4.59

(*continued*)

Table 16.1 *Continued*

	Average return (%)	Volatility (%)	Sharpe ratio	Skewness	Kurtosis	Maximum monthly return		Minimum monthly return		$VaR_{0.95, 1M}$ (%)
						Percent	Date	Percent	Date	
Zweig DiMenna.	16.09	22.31	0.50	-0.27	2.66	19.10	Dec 99	-22.87	Aug 98	-7.91
GAM Diversity	11.67	10.23	0.65	0.16	1.85	10.13	Dec 99	-7.92	Aug 98	-4.00
Haussmann Holdings	10.55	11.30	0.49	-0.12	1.02	9.52	Dec 99	-9.00	Apr 00	-3.82
Leveraged Capital Holdings	11.46	13.04	0.49	-0.36	1.77	13.00	Dec 99	-11.40	Aug 98	-4.88
S&P 500	12.28	15.08	0.48	-0.68	0.76	9.67	Mar 00	-14.58	Aug 98	-6.04
J.P. Morgan Bond Index	5.04	5.74	0.00	0.33	0.43	5.22	Sep 98	-3.34	Feb 99	-2.21

All calculations are based on monthly data between January 1994 and August 2001 and from a US dollar perspective
Average returns, volatility and Sharpe ratio are annualized; all other statistics are expressed on a monthly basis
Value at risk is calculated at the 95% confidence interval and using a one-month holding period

funds in the portfolio during that period was catastrophic. The naively managed fund of funds displays a better risk-adjusted performance with respect to the equity indices, but has more risk (and offers more return) than the bond index.

How does our naive portfolio compare with its professionally managed peers? Their risk-adjusted performance is clearly worse than our naive strategy, despite the fact that they had access to a much larger number of funds and they were able to structure and rebalance their portfolio as often as they wanted to. However, we should remember that our fund of funds did not charge any fee, and this may actually explain its superiority. Furthermore, our naive portfolio is clearly advantaged by survivorship bias.

Now, if we are able to do better than professionally managed funds of funds by investing directly, one may wonder what is the advantage of using them? Indeed, if markets were perfect, there would be no advantage in using funds of funds just for diversification purposes. One could invest diversely but naively in a series of hedge funds at no extra cost. However, in reality, things are quite different. To achieve these benefits by himself, an investor would need to commit capital with at least 10–15 individual hedge funds. Each of these funds would have to go through the complete selection process and pass all the due diligence tests. Then the investor would have to deal with the different investment and redemption policies, and monitor the selected funds on an ongoing basis, which would need additional resources. A fund of funds is therefore a more efficient vehicle, because a single trade can offer immediate access to diversification.

Affordability and accessibility

Another major advantage of funds of funds over individual hedge funds is their affordability and ease of access. Minimum requirements of $1 million and above are the rule at the individual hedge fund level. An investor willing to allocate 5% of his total assets to hedge funds would therefore need a $15 million commitment—a total portfolio value of $300 million. Anything less will subject his capital to inadequate diversification. By comparison, a fund of funds pools the resources of several individuals and commonly offers the same diversified portfolio with a minimum investment of around $20 000 or less. This makes hedge fund diversification affordable even for the smallest investors.

Furthermore, several European funds of funds are listed on an exchange (e.g. Dublin, Frankfurt, London, Zurich) and are members of a clearing system (e.g. Euroclear, Cedel). This facilitates investment and settlement procedures, because it is usually easier to invest in a listed share using familiar trading and settlement mechanisms than it is to purchase a basket of unregulated offshore funds domiciled in the Cayman Islands and Bermuda.

Professional management and built-in asset allocation

Through funds of funds, investors should be able to leverage the expertise and resources of professional managers who have an extensive background in the investment or banking industry and/or experience in evaluating the very complex strategies employed by the funds they select. Most of the time, they are also very well connected to people who leave banks and brokerage houses to set up their own hedge funds. This gives them a competitive advantage to access a selection of tomorrow's best hedge fund managers, sometimes even before the news becomes public.

These managers can also add value by optimizing the mix of hedge funds in the fund's portfolio to target specific goals. The two extreme choices are to maximize the portfolio's expected return and to minimize some risk indicator, such as the portfolio volatility or value at risk (VaR), but there are a whole range of intermediate targets.

Given their privileged position, professional managers are likely to estimate individual hedge funds' risk, returns, correlations, etc., more accurately than individual investors, and should therefore end up building more "efficient" portfolios. Value added can come from fund picking (selecting the best hedge funds), fund timing (identifying market cycles and investing in and out of hedge funds accordingly[3]), or simply strategic allocation (finding the best mix of funds to achieve a specified goal).

Access to closed funds

Several of the top-tier hedge funds are closed to small investors, but also to new money from any source. Their managers often have a capacity constraint and do not want to harm their existing investors by sharing some of their large but limited profits with newcomers. What funds of funds are said to bring to the table is their ability to tap long-standing relationships with these prominent fund managers in order to provide access to their hedge funds, even though these are closed to new investments. If this were true, it would constitute a strong value proposition.

Unfortunately, reality is often somehow disappointing. It is true that hedge funds do not treat their clients equally; some funds are effectively closed to any new investors (hard close), whereas others may officially be closed but unofficially accept long-term investors with high commitments (soft close). However, there are so many funds of funds and the size of the requested commitment is so large that they cannot all have access to the "best of breed" hedge funds.

How about successful fund picking? A manager of a fund of funds who claims to have some picking ability should already be invested in these highly desired closed funds. The reason is that he should have identified their talented managers when they needed money, not when they started closing their funds. Therefore, a fund of funds containing closed funds will be able to put a performance case deserving of scrutiny. In such a situation, any new investor in the fund of funds will indeed gain access to the desired single-manager hedge funds. But this will be at the expense of existing investors, who will see their initial allocation in these funds progressively diluted and replaced by cash.[4]

Open access is therefore a good way to participate, but it will also harm new investors once they are in. Of course, the process is reversed when investors redeem their fund of funds shares, but the number of redemptions will usually be small compared to the number of subscriptions, particularly if the performance is good. This explains why several funds of funds themselves have started closing their doors. For instance, GAM Trading II became closed to new subscriptions in June 2001 because a number of its core underlying funds closed. New subscribers will have to wait until the launch of GAM Trading III.

Better internal and external transparency

The hedge fund industry is known to be inefficient and opaque, at least in terms of information flow. This is the "black box" syndrome. Retail investors often have no access or at best delayed access to information about individual hedge funds positions and strategies.

In reality, information is available but it is costly. Only long-term commitments and large investments will open the doors of hedge fund portfolios. According to Ineichen (2001), "We are all in a dark room; however, the one who has been in the room for some time has an advantage over someone who just entered."

Fund of funds managers should therefore have an advantage over individual investors. In some cases the size of their assets allows them to gain some additional transparency through confidentiality agreements with fund managers, and even to be granted privileged access to an individual fund's positions (Box 16.1). This is precisely what institutional investors like in funds of funds—the ability to off-load much of their fiduciary responsibilities to fund of funds managers.

Box 16.1   INNOVATIONS TOWARDS TRANSPARENCY

An innovative way for funds of funds to monitor closely the positions of their underlying hedge funds consists in using a separate managed account for each of them. This is the investment approach selected by the National Bank of Canada's Multi-Strategy Program. Created in July 1996, this fund of funds is in reality a fund of managed accounts, which are managed by hedge fund managers in parallel to their hedge fund vehicles.

The National Bank of Canada acts as a custodian for the managed accounts. This ultimate transparency allows the fund of funds risk manager to see the actual positions marked to market daily, and to immediately identify events that may cause concern, such as sharp drawdown, trading in nonapproved markets or assets, or the use of nonauthorized leverage. Stress tests are easy to implement and can be performed on a daily basis. Furthermore, in an emergency, any of the managed accounts can be closed in 24 hours. The only drawback is that some hedge funds do not want to offer managed accounts. However, given the large size of the investment universe, it is not really a major problem to avoid its darkest alleys.

Asset Alliance Corporation, a New York investment management holding company with $3.2 billion under management, prefers an alternative path to obtain transparency. Asset Alliance considers hedge funds as being close to private equity investments. Both actually share similar organizational structures and have a low correlation with traditional stock and bond markets. Consequently, Asset Alliance seeds promising young hedge fund managers and purchases stakes in established ones. The funds of funds managed by Asset Alliance are invested in the funds where it has privileged relationships. Being shareholders of their management company allows easier access to the underlying funds' portfolios, full transparency on every trade and better control over style drift. It also protects the company against talent shortage in the hedge fund industry.

On the other side, fund managers also enjoy significant benefits when selling their company to Asset Alliance. They receive a large amount of cash that they can invest in their own fund or in one of Asset Alliance's funds. They are freed from distribution and marketing aspects, and can focus solely on investments.

So far, Asset Alliance has acquired stakes in eleven hedge funds, including two in London, and owns an offshore fund administrator located in the British Virgin

Islands. It also advises several funds of funds, including San Paolo IMI, Italy's largest money manager, and the private banking arm of the Bank of Ireland Group. Major US hedge funds acquisitions of Asset Alliance include Beacon Hill Asset Management, Bricoleur Capital Management, JMG Capital Management, Liberty Corner Asset Management, Milestone Global Advisors, Pacific Assets Management, P/E Investments, Silverado Capital Management, and Trust Advisors. In addition, the firm holds an equity interest in Hedge Fund Services (BVI) Ltd, an offshore fund administrator, and has recently acquired stakes in Wessex Asset Management and Zola Capital Management, two London-based hedge funds.

In addition, fund of funds managers offer a greater transparency with respect to their portfolios than individual funds with respect to their positions. In particular, funds that are listed on an exchange must comply with some minimum regulatory requirements on reporting and documentation. Some even post on their website a monthly listing of their underlying funds, as well as manager comments on their strategy and risk profile. This is often reassuring for the retail or less sophisticated investors.

THE DARK SIDE

Yet another layer of fees

The major drawback with fund of funds structures is the cost of their services, which are not cheap. Indeed, funds of funds can charge several types of fees. The most visible ones are management fees, usually set at 1% of the total assets under management, and performance fees, usually 10% of the performance of the fund of funds. A few funds of funds also have a hurdle rate of some sort in place, varying from 0% (no loss) to the S&P 500 returns.

In addition to this, funds of funds also benefit from less rarely announced streams of income. These include retrocession, which is a fee-sharing agreement whereby a portion of the fees charged by the underlying hedge fund is returned to the fund of funds or its manager, and kickbacks, which are fees paid by a clearing broker to the fund of funds for forcing the underlying fund to use its clearing services. Some funds of funds also receive a trailing fee, which is a percentage of the assets that remain invested in a hedge fund after the lock-in period.

A few funds of funds credit these fees back to their clients, but most do not even mention them. Even if they do, the double fee structure remains and may significantly affect performance, at least from the investor's viewpoint. Consider, for example, a fund of funds charging 1% of its assets as a management fee plus 10% of any upside. This goes on top of the fees of the underlying fund managers, typically 2% of assets plus 20% of the upside. In total, this represents a potential of 3% per year, plus 30% of the performance. If the underlying funds yield on average and before fees 20% per year, the investor is left with a mere 11.8% annual return.

Even more dreadful, suppose the fund of funds simply diversifies by equally allocating assets between two managers. One makes 50% and the other loses 50%. Do you break even? Not really. Before incentive fees (and not counting the management fees), you are breaking even. After incentive fees, you lose 10%.

Given the impact of this second level of charges, potential investors should naturally wonder whether the fund of funds concept really does provide added value, or whether it's just another device cleverly designed to extract fees from their credulity. Naturally, managers of funds of funds argue that the extra layer of skills justifies an extra layer of fees. They insist that they do provide a valuable service by monitoring the performance of hundreds or even thousands of funds in order to assemble the optimal selection of managers. Opponents, on the other hand, consider funds of funds as parasites, at best on the greatness of others and at worse on the artlessness of investors. They judiciously observe that several of these funds of funds profess a sophisticated quantitative process to identify and select managers, while they simply choose the top-performing managers from newspaper rankings.

Finally, another threat on the fees side is the increasing competition from hedge fund consultants. Overall, funds of funds are typically more expensive than appointing several managers directly through the traditional consulting model. For investors that do not face the minimum investment requirements, hiring consultants might be a less costly solution.

Extra liquidity

Liquidity is often a double-edged sword in the kingdom of hedge funds. By liquidity, we mean the conditions that must be fulfilled for an investor to be allowed to enter in the fund and/or redeem his shares.

In theory, funds of funds should not offer greater liquidity than their components. In practice they do. In particular, funds of funds' redemption policies tend to be much more flexible than those of the underlying funds. About 80% of the funds of funds accept contributions and redemptions on a monthly or quarterly basis. At first glance, this may appear to be a positive feature. Unfortunately, it also has important repercussions on asset allocation and therefore on performance.

Fund of funds managers must ensure that their portfolios will not experience difficulties if investors start redeeming their assets. In that respect, their task is similar to asset liability management in a bank, where customers are allowed to come to the cashier and redeem their assets. However, it is unlikely that all customers would wish to redeem their shares at the same time.[5] By playing with expected redemptions and probabilities, most fund of funds managers are able to balance the liquidity desired by investors against the lengthy lockup periods and infrequent redemption dates requested by individual fund managers.

However, to be able to cope with potential redemptions, fund of funds managers have four possibilities. Clearly, a balance has to be found. Liquidity is a desirable feature, but it comes at a cost:

- They can rely on the cash from new contributions to pay for redemptions. This is quite hazardous: it may work well for a time, but in periods of poor performance, the fund will have to face important redemptions and will be short of new contributions. The only advantage is that new investors face lockup periods, so liquidity may not be a problem in the short run.
- They can hold a liquidity buffer. However, the return on this buffer is usually extremely low compared to the expected return on the underlying hedge funds; and investors may not be willing to pay two layers of fees to end up not being fully invested.

- They can invest in hedge funds with easier redemption policies. However, these funds are essentially directional players and their performance is more volatile. In addition, they are often correlated with each other because they are active on the same markets. Consequently, the fund of funds will not have access to star managers, who tend to focus on very profitable inefficiencies in smaller, less liquid and less efficient markets, but frequently impose long lockup periods.
- They can get listed on a regulated secondary marketplace (Box 16.2).

Box 16.2   REGULATED SECONDARY MARKETPLACES INCREASE LIQUIDITY

The increased interest in hedge funds raised awareness that (i) most of the best-performing non-US-domiciled funds are closed or have restricted subscription and redemption clauses, and (ii) little independently verified valuation and risk information is available on hedge funds and their portfolios. Consequently, low liquidity can rapidly become a problem for sellers as well as access for buyers.

A solution may go through the development of internet-based regulated secondary marketplaces dedicated to hedge funds. These offer several advantages, including increasing liquidity for investors, avoiding liquidations of assets to face redemptions for fund managers, and providing information on hedge fund exposures and risks. Several of these marketplaces were created in the last two years, and here are some of them. So far, the hedge fund industry has been quite hostile to these new trading platform initiatives, and none of them has really made its mark to date.

- *HedgeTrust Exchange* is an electronic communications network (ECN) launched in February 2000. It offers accredited investors secure online trading facilities for existing non-US-domiciled hedge funds that are closed or that have restrictive subscription or redemption periods. It has a strategic partnership with the Bermuda Stock Exchange and offers integrated online access to the TASS database of funds.
- *PlusFunds.com* is a New York web platform founded by J.P. Morgan, Chase, Credit Suisse First Boston, and Merrill Lynch. It publishes independently verified net asset values of 18 hedge fund shares on a real-time basis, as well as risk assessment reports containing value at risk, historical stress tests and risk concentration analysis on a daily basis. It also has a strategic partnership with the Bermuda Stock Exchange and manages a secondary market in their shares. It aims at becoming a strong secondary trading market in the near future.
- *Hedgebay.com* is the latest in the list. Modeled after E-bay.com, the online auction site, it allows registered users to bid on and offer shares in well-known hedge funds. The clearing takes place through the Bermuda Stock Exchange or directly between buyers and sellers.

Lack of control, overdiversification and duplication

Another drawback with funds of funds from the investor's perspective is the lack of control. The investor does not have as much control over a fund of funds as he does over a portfolio of individual funds. For example, an investor who does not approve the presence of a certain type of strategy in a fund of funds is powerless to change that allocation, short of bailing out of the fund altogether.

Moreover, fund of funds managers themselves have little control over what the underlying managers are doing. As an illustration, in a recent Capital Market Risk Advisors survey, several funds of funds disclaimed knowledge of what their underlying funds were doing regarding pricing issues and net asset values calculations. There are also anecdotal reports on managers allocating money in other "hot" funds without performing any serious due diligence, under threat of imminent fund closure. Here are some other typical problems:

- *Cancellation of trades*: fund A might sell short a share while fund B might buy it long. If both hedge funds are part of the same fund of funds portfolio, the two transactions will simply cancel each other in terms of risk exposure, but will generate ample commissions for brokers, as well as performance fees for one of the two funds.
- *Duplication of positions within underlying hedge funds*: this is particularly true when bubbles and hot sectors drive most of the allocation. In 1999, for example, most of the long/short equity funds were heavily invested in technology or internet-related stocks. They all collapsed when the bubble burst. And so did the funds of funds that relied on them to diversify.
- *Duplication of positions within funds of funds*: assuming their popularity continues, the increasing number of funds of funds will eventually lead to a duplication of each other's holdings as a result of the sheer lack of available managers. This also applies to risk management. Since individual hedge funds should primarily be concerned about risk control, the gathering of several hedge funds in a basket may only duplicate and not necessarily enhance the risk-control effort.

Finally, many also level the criticism that funds of funds are overdiversified; beyond a certain number of managers, adding new ones is unlikely to produce major improvement on risk or return. Although there is no consensus on the exact threshold value, common sense argues that portfolios of 15–25 hedge funds should be sufficient.

SELECTING A FUND OF FUNDS

It used to be hard to select stocks. It was harder to select traditional managers. As we have just seen, it is even harder to select hedge fund managers. How about selecting a fund of funds?

The major difficulty comes from the low barriers of entry to the fund of funds business. In this surreal world of investment advice, anyone can claim to be an expert and get paid for it. Since the key talent is actually in the underlying hedge funds, funds of funds have proliferated, particularly in Europe, where almost every bank, insurance company and asset management firm has launched its own. Thanks to the marketing power of their founding group, these funds of funds have no problem attracting money, essentially from unsophisticated retail investors. However, the quality of some funds of funds management teams approaches borderline incompetence.

Recognizing talent still takes talent in its own right and being a good fund of funds manager requires several skills that are far beyond the simple analysis of past hedge fund performance. Among other things, we should mention an understanding of the hedge fund business, an experience of several market cycles, good connections in the industry and strong negotiation skills. In addition, a good fund of funds manager should be willing to identify hedge funds that develop mismatches between claimed strategy and effective actions, and replace them with new and more promising funds. Even if the hedge fund that has to leave the portfolio is an in-house fund or pays a higher amount of retrocession.

Consequently, an investor selecting a fund of funds should, in a sense, act as if he were selecting an individual hedge fund. Initially, it is essential to assess the manager's talent, search and identification capabilities; validate his due diligence process; understand his business model, including his asset allocation policy and investment goals; and verify the quality and consistency of his track record, if any. Later comes a rigorous ongoing monitoring of the underlying managers and the fund of funds portfolio as a whole.

Once again, there are numerous consultants that provide advice, but their independence and competence should be carefully verified. Some of them tend to favor managers who would rebate to the fund of funds part of their underlying manager's fee, others solely look at track record and past performance, and a minority of them even manage funds of funds. Finally, other types of intermediary have emerged to help with due diligence and monitoring, such as PlusFunds.com and Global Fund Trader Plus.

FUND ALLOCATION: INSIDE THE BLACK BOX

The composition of a fund of funds portfolio is the result of two separate actions: the selection of a series of hedge funds as potential candidates for investment, and the effective allocation of assets among these funds. I regard the selection activity as a particular case of the approach in Chapter 15.[6] We will therefore not elaborate on the topic, but rather focus on the second aspect. A fund of funds allocation process is usually as opaque as the investment process of its underlying hedge funds. Most of the time, the manager only discloses marketing verbiage, e.g. experience, proprietary database, contacts, privileged access, track record. In reality, what do things look like inside the black box? It all depends. Once again, qualitative approaches contrast with quantitative.

Qualitative approaches

Qualitative approaches usually allocate assets using a balance between naive diversification and intuition. Managers relying on naive diversification simply invest in a number of different hedge funds and hope that the overall portfolio risk will be lowered. The most extreme version of this approach consists in allocating an equal amount of money to every manager in the portfolio and periodically rebalancing the portfolio to ensure it remains well diversified. This is known as the $1/N$ rule, where N is the number of managers and $1/N$ is the weight assigned to each of them. This rule has a long history in asset allocation; it was already recommended in the Talmud in the fourth century, when the Rabbi Isaac bar Aha used to say, "A man should always place his money, a third into land, a third into merchandise, and keep a third at hand" (Talmud Bavli, Baba Metzia 42a). Later on, even Harry Markowitz, the founder of modern portfolio theory and portfolio optimization, is reported to have used the rule for himself (Zweig 1998).

The $1/N$ heuristic is not very sophisticated but is it necessarily bad? The answer varies. When systematically applied, the $1/N$ rule conveys some risks. For instance, if one investment style predominates in the group of candidates resulting from the selection process, that style will also predominate in the fund of funds portfolio if the $1/N$ rule is applied. In addition, effective risk is not necessarily linearly related to asset allocation. For example, a 30% allocation to a truly market neutral fund may represent as much risk contribution as a 5% allocation to an emerging market hedge fund. It is therefore judicious to place ceilings on the amount of risk involved in each hedge fund allocation rather than on the weight itself.

Nevertheless, as we will see later on, in practice the $1/N$ rule often gives good results, sometimes even better than several more sophisticated asset allocation models. But no fund of funds manager will ever admit to relying on it. There are two reasons for this. First, it is virtually impossible to charge a management fee for such a naive asset allocation service. Second, most managers are still persuaded—and so are their clients—that they can add value by relying on their "experience" and "feeling of the markets." They therefore tend to adjust the weights of their portfolio according to their own forecasts of future market and economic conditions. This approach does not aim at maintaining a constant allocation profile but rather at undertaking opportune short-term tilts in the hedge fund mix of a portfolio in response to the changing patterns of returns available in the capital markets. Typically, exposure periodically shifts away from hedge funds showing exceptional near-term vulnerability toward those showing the likelihood of an exceptional return.

Quantitative approaches

Quantitative approaches are just the opposite of qualitative ones. Rather than acting on subjective perceptions and intuition, they rely exclusively on predefined mathematical models. Their goal is usually quite ambitious—to find the best proportions to be invested among the set of hedge funds considered.

Most quantitative managers take a two-stage approach when allocating money among hedge funds. First, expected returns and risk parameters for each hedge fund in question are estimated—often from some sort of factor model—and are input into an optimizer. Then money is allocated among them based on the optimizer's recommended allocation. Factor models assume that the return on any individual hedge fund can be expressed as a function of one or more factors plus an error term that is independent of the factors and of the errors on all other investments. Rather than focusing on funds, analysts can therefore focus on factors' returns, risks and correlations.

The most common optimization problem for funds of funds consists in finding the portfolio weights that minimize the risk, given some allocation constraints. What is used to measure the risk is left to the appreciation of the investor, but it commonly includes volatility, value at risk, semivariance, drawdown, etc. So our optimization program is:

> Find the hedge fund weights (i.e. asset allocation) under some allocation constraints while minimizing risk.

This problem may be set up in a single-period context or a multiple-period context. In the single-period context, the fund weights are set up initially and there is no portfolio rebalancing. In the multiple-period context, the fund weights are regularly rebalanced, so the final outcome consists in finding both the initial optimal weights and the dynamic rebalancing trading strategy.

There is rarely just one solution to the optimization problem, so an investor will have to be more precise when setting his constraints. For instance, he may have to specify his target return. The optimization program then becomes:

> Find the hedge fund weights (i.e. asset allocation) under some allocation constraints, while minimizing risk and given a target return.

Such problems may or may not have a solution, depending on how "aggressive" is the target return with respect to all constraints. Constraints can take several forms:

- A maximum or a minimum allocation to a hedge fund
- A maximum or minimum allocation to a particular investment style or custodian
- A target portfolio return
- A maximum or minimum number of hedge funds
- A given risk factor exposure constraint, absolute or benchmark relative (e.g. a maximum sensitivity to a market index or to interest rate variations)
- A maximum turnover and limits on the number of assets traded or held in the rebalanced portfolio

An investment committee comprised of the team's asset allocation managers usually discusses the result of the optimization. The committee analyzes and back-tests the model's output, discusses current market conditions, develops a market outlook and validates the appropriate allocation to each asset class. Back-testing is the process of examining the implications of the suggested asset allocation on a historical basis.

An example of fund of funds optimization

Let us now illustrate a practical example of fund of funds optimization. Our investment universe will be limited to the group of 21 hedge funds that we used previously. To simplify things, we will base our optimization on historical data (risk, return and correlation) rather than on forecasts. Naturally, when building real fund of funds portfolios, it is absolutely crucial to be predictive and look forward rather than backward, since it is useless to identify yesterday's winners. But in this illustration, historical data will be sufficient.

Given the historical risk, return and correlation of our funds (Table 16.1), we can expect to obtain interesting diversification benefits. To illustrate this point, we first use mean–variance optimization. Our optimization program is therefore:

> For all possible target portfolio returns, find the hedge fund weights (i.e. asset allocation) that minimize the variance of the overall portfolio. Constraints: no short sales, fully invested.

I realize this approach is subject to severe criticism, since it is known that volatility does not accurately capture risk when returns distributions are not symmetrical, which is often the case for hedge funds. However, since most fund of funds managers use mean–variance optimizers, let us look at the results they would get.

Figure 16.1 shows our set of hedge funds, as well as the efficient frontier that they form. The only constraint set for this first efficient frontier is that portfolio weights need to be positive (no short selling of hedge fund shares). As one might rationally expect, the efficient frontier dominates all the hedge funds in our sample. However, the corresponding portfolios are concentrated in a few funds (Table 16.2). Most funds of funds would not be willing to hold the majority of these efficient portfolios, due to their high concentration. In order to allow for this, we run the same optimization program with an additional constraint

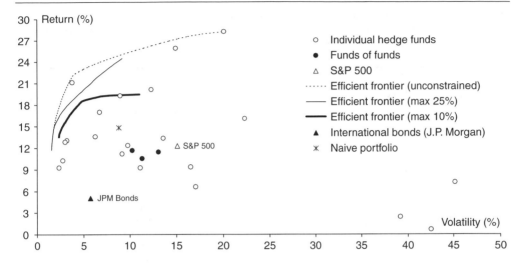

Figure 16.1 Efficient frontiers built using individual hedge funds. All calculations are based on monthly data between January 1994 and August 2001 and from a US dollar perspective. Note that S&P 500 and JPM Bonds are uniquely displayed for information, but are not considered in the optimization process to build the efficient frontier

relative to the maximum relative weight of each fund in the portfolio. Figure 16.1 shows the new efficient frontiers we obtain (dotted lines) for maximum weight set at 25% and 10% respectively.

Clearly, the asset allocation constraints have a significant impact on performance. The lower the maximum allocation for a hedge fund, the more diversified the portfolio, but also the lower the efficient frontier. In particular, we observe that the best hedge funds suddenly appear as being superefficient (i.e. above the efficient frontier). The reason is that they cannot make up more than 10% of the fund of funds portfolio, so the set of achievable returns is effectively capped.

Another interesting aspect is the position of the professionally managed funds of funds that we have in our sample. All of them tend to be distinctly inefficient and far away from the efficient frontiers (constrained or unconstrained). Of course, they still perform pretty well when compared to stock market indices, such as the S&P 500 or the Nasdaq, but one may wonder whether these are really adequate benchmarks for funds of funds.

To test the robustness of our results, we repeat the experiment but use a different risk definition. This time we define risk as the value at risk at 95% confidence over one month; that is, the maximum loss that one could incur over one month, excluding the 5% worst cases. Our new maximization program is:

> For all possible target portfolio returns, find the hedge fund weights (i.e. asset allo-
> cation) that minimize the portfolio value at risk (one-month holding period, 95%
> confidence). Constraints: no short sales, fully invested.

Figure 16.2 shows our set of hedge funds as well as the new efficient frontier that they form in the mean–VaR space. There are two points to note:

Table 16.2 Characteristics of some efficient hedge funds portfolios

	Return (%)	Volatility (%)	Composition
Efficient Unconstrained Portfolios (Major Allocations >10%)			
Minimum risk portfolio	11.41	1.54	TQA Arbitrage Fund (33.79%), Kingate Euro Fund Ltd (25.56%), GAM Arbitrage (21.59%)
Maximum return portfolio	28.19	20.01	Spinner Global Technology Fund (99.57%)
Maximum Sharpe portfolio	19.22	2.77	JMG Capital Partners LP (64.90%), Kingate Euro Fund Ltd (24.16%)
Efficient Constrained Portfolios (Max 25% on Each Hedge Fund)			
Minimum risk portfolio	11.74	1.55	TQA Arbitrage Fund (25%), Kingate Euro Fund Ltd (25%), GAM Arbitrage (22.19%), Cerberus Partners LP (14.10%)
Maximum return portfolio	24.45	9.14	Spinner Global Technology Fund (25%), Raptor Global Fund LP (25%), JMG Capital Partners LP (24.93%), GAMut (24.93%
Maximum Sharpe portfolio	14.54	1.75	Cerberus Partners LP (25%), JMG Capital Partners LP (25%), Kingate Euro Fund Ltd (25%)
Efficient Constrained Portfolios (Max 10% on Each Hedge Fund)			
Minimum risk portfolio	13.45	2.34	Below 10% by construction
Maximum return portfolio	19.46	11.01	Below 10% by construction
Maximum Sharpe portfolio	16.87	3.66	Below 10% by construction

• Based on the set of data that we used, the minimum risk portfolio has a VaR equal to 0.24%. This means that under normal market conditions, its worst-case return would have been 0.24% per year (i.e. no loss).
• Since the goal is to minimize the VaR and not the volatility, the resulting portfolios may be completely different from the portfolio obtained using mean–variance optimization. In particular, mean–variance portfolios are usually not efficient from a mean–VaR perspective, and mean–VaR portfolios are not efficient from the mean–variance viewpoint. It is therefore essential to define one's objectives clearly before starting an optimization.

THE FUTURE

Funds of funds tie together many of the positive elements of building a hedge fund portfolio, while removing a number of the negatives. They offer an interesting investment vehicle for institutional and private investors who seek to access hedge funds without having to search for investment opportunities themselves. Fund of funds managers can help to add value as experienced pathfinders on this daunting unmapped terrain. In a sense, they are the panaceas for discerning investors.

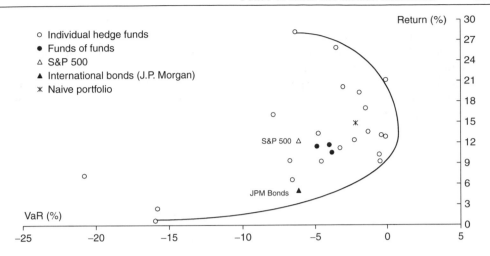

Figure 16.2 The VaR efficient frontier

However, there are valid fears that the proliferation of funds of funds may increase quantity at the expense of quality. In particular, due to capacity constraints and if they haven't already done so, funds of funds should soon face a greater challenge in finding consistent performers among hedge funds. This could result in two possible consequences:

- Systemic risks that have the potential to hurt the entire industry could build up. The reason is that a definite talent shortage has developed among funds of funds. Consequently, a large number of less able and neophyte managers are entering the fund of funds business. This results in a lack of proper due diligence, poorly constructed portfolios, overconcentration in a few well-known hedge funds, and insufficient information disclosed to clients.
- There could be a wave of consolidation in the fund of funds industry, with a few winners managing much larger amounts and closing their funds to new subscribers. These megafunds of funds would then find themselves in the position of gatekeepers to one of the world's fastest-growing and most dynamic marketplaces.

NOTES

1. The funds selected were Cerberus Partners LP, GAM Arbitrage, GAM Japan, GAM Trading USD, GAM US, GAMut, III Global Ltd, JMG Capital Partners LP, Kingate Euro Fund Ltd, Latinvest Fund Ltd, Manchester Institutional Fund, Nestor Partners, P.A.W. Partners LP, Pactual Infinity Fund Ltd, Permal Essex Media & Technology Ltd, Perry Partners LP, Raptor Global Fund LP (Class A), Spinner Global Technology Fund, TQA Arbitrage Fund LP, UBS Currency Portfolio Ltd and Zweig DiMenna. This list should not be considered as an investment recommendation.
2. According to Fothergill and Coke (2000), the three largest funds of funds are GAM Diversity, Haussmann Holdings NV and Leveraged Capital Holdings. This list should not be considered as an investment recommendation.
3. But this assumes the fund of funds manager is able to forecast the next phase of the cycle and which funds will benefit during each phase.

4. New shareholders solely bring cash but immediately gain access and enjoy the benefits of the so desired closed funds shares.
5. Except if there is a lack of liquidity and a flight to safe assets, as was the case in the summer of 1998, for example.
6. The only difference with respect to an individual investor is that a fund of funds manager usually has a clearer idea about the desired characteristics and properties of the hedge funds he seeks.

17

Capital-guaranteed products

Many investors are attracted to hedge funds by the promise of diversification benefits and superior performance, but they still feel nervous and uncomfortable once they actually have to commit capital. Several reasons justify their sentiments. First, hedge funds are still perceived as extremely risky and carry a significant downside, particularly after the torrent of negative publicity that accompanied Long Term Capital Management's debacle. Second, regulated entities such as pension funds and other institutional investors are often restricted by their supervisors from investing in loosely regulated and/or unlisted securities such as hedge funds without some kind of insurance. Third, many individuals are still discouraged by the relatively high minimum amounts required to invest in hedge funds.

To bridge the gap between supply and demand, a growing number of financial intermediaries have responded to these problems by proposing structured products linked to hedge funds, and more particularly capital-protected notes. These new products combine an upside participation in hedge fund performance with the guarantee that investors will get back at least a specified portion of the capital they initially invested.

THE PACKAGE

Capital-protected notes usually take the form of medium-term notes (3–5 years) with a final repayment linked to the performance of a specified hedge fund. They typically display the following characteristics:

- *Capital protection*: a bona fide structured investment should provide some explicit form of guarantee on the principal amount invested. The level of this guarantee depends upon the risk profile of targeted investors, but it is usually between 90% and 100%. It is applied irrespective of the performance of the underlying hedge fund.
- *Guaranteed minimum return*: this may be capitalized into the investment and form part of the total terminal value paid out at maturity, or distributed at intervals during the investment term as coupon payments. This feature may be required for instance by investors that cannot invest in zero-coupons.
- *Upside market participation*: this is usually expressed as a percentage of the upside hedge fund moves.

In its plain vanilla form, a typical capital-guaranteed note will have a redemption price calculated with a formula of the following form:

$$100\% + (\text{participation rate} \times \text{underlying fund's performance})$$

The participation rate is also called "gearing." Its level depends on the other characteristics, such as the maturity of the structured note and the characteristics of the underlying hedge fund. The principal protection is usually bought at the expense of some of the hedge fund's profit potential. This explains why the participation rate is usually not equal to 100%, or the maximum gain may be capped.

Capital-guaranteed notes linked to hedge funds offer several advantages:

- They allow risk-averse investors to learn the basics about hedge funds without exposing themselves to the downside risk.
- They overcome the regulatory hurdles, because the capital guarantee meets the regulators' concerns for investor protection.
- In most countries, the notes may be treated as an interest rate security for tax, accounting and administration purposes. This allows
  — institutional investors to invest in hedge funds when they may otherwise be restricted
  — offshore hedge funds to be indirectly distributed in several markets without needing to be registered with local authorities

FINANCIAL ENGINEERING

An interesting question for most investors is the functioning of the engineering process behind these products. In particular, many investors do not understand how financial intermediaries such as banks and insurance companies dare providing guarantees on unpredictable products such as hedge funds. Some even believe that these intermediaries are taking large risks to provide these guarantees, or that they accept to share the risk with their clients.

Reality is somewhat different. When a bank issues a capital-guaranteed product linked to the performance of a hedge fund, it is in fact selling a guarantee to the investor. This is equivalent to a short put option position, where the underlying asset of the option would be the hedge fund. As a rule, the bank would immediately hedge such a position by trading on the market, or transfer the corresponding risk to another market participant. Some insurance companies may agree to bear such a risk against the payment of a premium. One should not forget that this is exactly their business. Indeed, the goal of the issuing bank is not to profit from the variations in the underlying hedge fund's net asset value, but rather to gain a series of commissions and fees:

- The various fees and commissions charged to issue and sell the notes
- The bid/ask spread on the secondary market, where the issuing bank often acts as a market maker
- The management and performance fees on the underlying fund, which is often directly or indirectly related to the issuing bank

The ability to hedge the transaction or to find another financial intermediary willing to bear the risk is central to the completion and cost of the note. This explains why it is common to see capital-protected notes linked to a hedge fund issued by a bank in association with an insurance company. The bank handles the financial aspects and the insurance company provides the insurance. Let us now briefly review the three major generations of capital-protected products linked to hedge funds and describe the way they were engineered by their issuers.

First generation: the naive approach

The creation of capital-guaranteed notes linked to hedge funds dates back to the 1980s. The basic mechanism underlying the first series of products was indeed extremely simple. Issuers simply allocated the initial capital between high-quality zero-coupon bonds maturing at the same time as the note and shares of the underlying hedge fund. The zero-coupon allocation provided the principal protection, while the hedge fund investment ensured participation in the fund's return.

As an illustration, consider the case of an investor purchasing $100 000 of a 3-year capital-guaranteed note on a hedge fund (Figure 17.1). The 3-year interest rate is 5% per year, so a 3-year zero-coupon with $1000 face value is worth approximately $863.84. The issuer of the note receives $100 000 from the investor and invests $86 384 in the zero-coupon and $13 616 in the hedge fund. Three years later, the zero-coupon bonds mature and pay back $100 000. This provides the capital guarantee. Suppose the hedge fund gained 50% over the period, then the fund investment would be worth $20 424, and the total repayment to the investor would be $120 424. If the hedge fund lost 50% over the period, the fund investment would be worth $6808, and the total repayment to the investor would be $106 808.

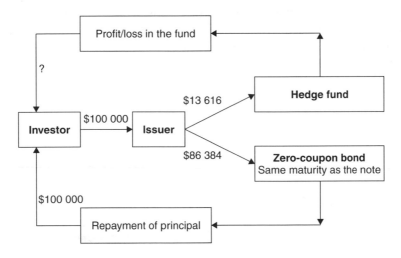

Figure 17.1   First generation of hedge fund capital-guaranteed notes

The major problem with this approach is that the total return on the guaranteed note is extremely limited, due to the relatively small fraction of the initial capital exposed to the hedge fund. In our previous example, even when the hedge fund gained 50%, the investor's performance was 20.42%—a mere 40.84% participation in the upside. And this calculation was done in a perfect world, where the issuer did not charge any fees. As one might expect, in the real world, investors realized rapidly that such products did not have any real added value, and they were able to replicate the structure directly without the costly help of investment banks. Creative issuers therefore started working on a means of increasing participation rates.

Second generation: the option-based approach

The second generation of capital-guaranteed notes linked to hedge funds adopted a different approach, relying on option-based methodologies similar to those used in notes linked to equity indices or individual equities. They basically allocated the initial capital between high-quality zero-coupon bonds and at-the-money call options on the underlying hedge fund. Both instruments needed to mature at the same time as the note. The zero-coupon bonds provided the principal protection. The call options granted their holders the right to buy hedge fund shares if the fund's value appreciated; that is, they provided part-icipation in the hedge fund's performance. Since an option is a leveraged instrument (the premium paid is small with respect to the underlying fund's investment), using options rather than direct investment in shares allowed for much better participation rates than with the first generation of products.

As an illustration, consider the case of our investor purchasing $100 000 of a 3-year capital-guaranteed note on a hedge fund (Figure 17.2). The 3-year interest rate is 5% per year, so a 3-year zero-coupon with $1000 face value is worth approximately $863.84. The issuer of the note receives $100 000 from the investor; he then invests $86 384 in the zero-coupon bond and keeps $13 616 to purchase call options. Let us say that the price of an at-the-money 3-year option on the hedge fund is 20%.[1] That is, to ensure $1000 invested in the hedge fund, the premium to be paid is $200. With $13 616 available, the issuer can purchase options on $68 080 worth of the hedge fund—a participation rate of 68.08%.[2] The buyer of the structured note therefore knows from the beginning what his participation rate will be.

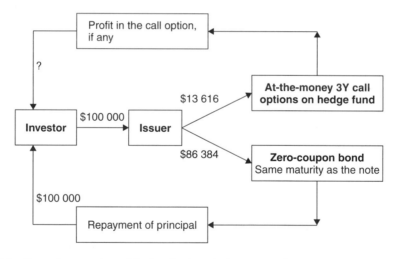

Figure 17.2   Second generation of hedge fund capital-guaranteed notes

Three years later, the zero-coupon bonds mature and pays back $100 000. This provides the capital guarantee. Suppose the hedge fund gained 50% over the period, the options would be worth the difference between the strike price ($68 080) and the new value of the fund shares ($102 120)—a gain of $34 040. The total repayment to the investor would then be $134 040. If the hedge fund lost 50% over the period, the options would be worth nothing, and the total repayment to the investor would be $100 000.

Note that an alternative to the "bond plus call" structure is investing directly in the fund and protecting the investment by put options on the same fund. This gives exactly the same results in terms of participation rate, because of the put/call parity. This relationship, which is well known to option traders, states that

$$\text{Bond} + \text{call} = \text{underlying asset} + \text{put}$$

where the call and the put options have the same maturity date, exercise price and underlying asset. It explains why the two strategies yield the same results. Box 17.1 explains how to lower the price using an Asian tail.

Box 17.1   AN ASIAN TAIL TO LOWER THE PRICE

It is quite frequent to observe capital-guaranteed notes with an "Asian tail." This refers to a payoff at expiration that is based on the average of several successive net asset values (e.g. the average over the last six months) rather than on the net asset value at expiration of the note. There are two reasons for using this Asian tail. Firstly, using an average value rather than a single value protects the investor against sudden downward movements in the underlying fund's shares prior to maturity. Secondly, options on an average price are known to be less expensive than options on a single price. The reason is that the average smooths the variations and reduces the volatility, which is a key determinant of an option premium. Lower option premium means a larger number of options for the same price, and therefore a higher participation rate (or the ability to charge higher fees).

Of course, options on hedge funds do not trade on organized markets. The issuer therefore needs to create them synthetically, for instance through a dynamic trading strategy, or purchase them on an over-the-counter (OTC) market, for instance from an insurance company or reinsurance company. In synthetic strategy, the issuer of a fund-linked structure would delta hedge its exposure as though it had sold any other option-based structure—by investing in and out of the underlying hedge fund. In that respect, a call option on a hedge fund is akin to a call on a basket of stocks. However, delta hedging requires vigilance and liquid markets, since the corresponding portfolio must be rebalanced regularly. As a counter to this, the most popular hedge funds restrict their investors to monthly or quarterly adjustments, impose long lockup periods and are unlisted. This explains why most of these second-generation structures restrict themselves to funds that offer access through managed accounts and/or future funds with daily liquidity.[3]

However, even with these funds, there is still the risk of a precipitous meltdown. If the market suddenly crashes and liquidity dries, as occurred on September 11, 2001, there may be no time for the issuer to adjust its hedge position before the decline. That is why many issuers prefer to delegate the hedging problem and purchase their options on an OTC market, essentially in the form of an insurance policy. Several reinsurance companies such as Swiss-Re and Zurich-Re have created dedicated subsidiaries that are specialized in issuing these types of product. They pool the risk of the underlying alternative assets with the risks of their traditional insurance portfolios. In case of loss, the insurance company can draw on its premium income and accumulated reserves as necessary.

Third generation: the dynamic trading approach

The third generation of capital-guaranteed products on hedge funds rely essentially on dynamic trading principles. The basic mechanism is quite simple. The proceeds of the note sales are invested in a portfolio composed of zero-coupon bonds and shares of the underlying hedge fund. Then capital is shifted dynamically between the two investments according to a prespecified asset allocation rule. The two most popular variants of these strategies are contingent immunization and constant proportion portfolio insurance.

With contingent immunization, the issuer constantly compares the value of his portfolio against the amount of capital that would have to be invested in zero-coupon bonds to guarantee the capital at maturity. As long as the portfolio value is higher, the entire capital remains invested in the hedge fund. However, if the hedge fund investment does not perform well and the portfolio value drops close to this minimum amount, the issuer withdraws entirely from the hedge fund to allocate capital to the zero-coupon bonds. The main disadvantage for investors entering into such arrangements is the automatic deleveraging of the amount actively managed. A sharp drawdown in the fund's net asset value may lead to the capital being entirely invested in zero-coupon bonds. If the drawdown is followed by a rally, it is not possible to switch back to the hedge fund portfolio. In this case investors will only receive the cash return and must wait until maturity of the structure to recover their initial capital.

Constant proportion portfolio insurance (CPPI) is a dynamic asset allocation strategy that was initially introduced by Black and Jones (1987) and later formalized by Black and Perold (1992). It recently reappeared in several hedge fund structured products. The basic mechanism of CPPI is to allocate the capital dynamically between the zero-coupon bonds and the shares of the underlying hedge fund. If the value of the hedge fund shares rises, more capital is invested in the hedge fund. If the hedge fund does poorly, more money is shifted into bonds. In a sense, CPPI is a form of feedback-driven investment strategy, where one sells risky assets in proportion to their price decline and buys them in proportion as prices rise. The aim is to ensure that at maturity the product will be worth at least as much as the amount invested at inception (plus fees).

The major advantage of CPPI is that it is simple to explain and easy to implement. Initially it just requires the definition of three parameters:

- A *floor* is the amount of money that would have to be invested in zero-coupon bonds to guarantee the capital at maturity. Because of the time value of money, as one gets closer to maturity, the floor value increases.
- A *multiplier* determines the aggressiveness of the strategy. A multiplier equal to 1 would be considered as nonaggressive, a multiplier higher than 1 may imply leverage.
- A *rebalancing policy*, e.g. at the end of every month.

At each rebalancing date, one computes a quantity called the *cushion*, which is defined as the difference between the value of the portfolio and the current value of the floor. Then an amount equal to the multiplier times the cushion is allocated in the hedge fund and the remaining part of the portfolio is invested into zero-coupon bonds. As an illustration, say a CPPI strategy is implemented on a portfolio with a floor at $10 million and a multiplier equal to 1.2. The portfolio value is currently $13 million. The cushion is therefore equal to $3 million. The CPPI reallocation rule would say that $3.6 million (i.e. $3 million times 1.2) should go into the hedge fund and $9.4 million should go into the zero-coupon

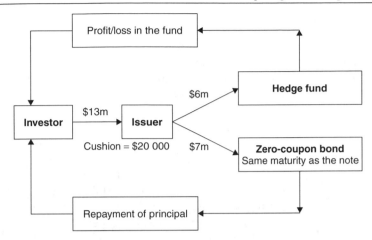

Figure 17.3 Third generation of hedge fund capital-guaranteed notes. Example of a CPPI strategy with a floor at $10 million and a multiplier of 2

bonds. If the multiplier were equal to 2, then $6 million would go into the hedge fund and $7 million should go into the zero-coupon bonds (Figure 17.3). Later on, of course, the portfolio would be rebalanced whenever needed.

Another advantage of CPPI is that the up-front costs of implementing the strategy are not linked to the distribution (and in particular the volatility) of the underlying hedge fund. By contrast, a capital guarantee implemented with options may not be able to provide sufficient upside participation if the volatility of the underlying fund is high and therefore increases the premium paid for the options. CPPI may therefore provide better participation rates in such environments. Box 17.2 looks at financial engineering and hedge funds.

Box 17.2   FINANCIAL ENGINEERING AND HEDGE FUNDS

A good illustration of the recent financial innovations for hedge funds is the launch of several capital-protected full-participation notes. These new instruments attempt to provide the best of both worlds: full upside participation and full downside protection. As an example, consider the following SGA note, which was a recent private placement.

Issuer	SGA, Société Générale Acceptance NV
Guarantor	Société Générale (Moody's Aa3, Standard & Poor's AA−)
Type	Euro-Bond
Underlying fund	SCS Alternative Fund
Issue date	07/17/2001
Maturity	5 years
Currency	USD
Issue size	Up to 20 000 000 USD

Nominal	10 000 USD per note
Issue price	100% of the nominal
Capital guarantee	100% of the nominal
Participation	100% of the positive performance of the underlying fund
Redemption	On the maturity date, the noteholder will be entitled to receive the highest of the following two amounts:

(a)   Nominal $\times$ 100%

(b)   Nominal $\times \left[100\% + 100\% \times \dfrac{\text{FNAV}-\text{INAV}}{\text{INAV}} \right]$

FNAV = net asset value actually settled by the fund for a redemption order sent on the 10th business day preceding the maturity date

INAV = initial net asset value per unit of the fund (set at 100 US dollars)

Settlement	Clearstream/Euroclear
Listing	Luxembourg Stock Exchange
Secondary market	SG quotes a weekly secondary market in the notes until the maturity date, with a maximum bid/offer spread of 1% under normal market conditions

SCS Alternative Fund, the fund underlying the note, is a dedicated unit trust domiciled in Jersey, one of the Channel Islands. It uniquely serves as an underlying to the note and is not accessible to external investors. Its investment policy is to seek capital appreciation by allocating capital to a selection of trading advisers. The initial allocation was as follows: 70% in long/short European equities managers (Gartmore, Thames River, Park Place and Sabre, 17.5% each), 15% to commodity trading advisers (Beach Discretionary, Campbell and PE Investments, 5% each) and 15% in arbitragers (Forest, Third Point and Highland, 5% each).

These trading advisers will implement their investment strategies through clearing and prime broker accounts (managed accounts) held in trust by the fund. The manager of the fund is Lyxor Asset Management, a 100% subsidiary of Société Générale. It charges 1.4% of the assets as an annual management fee and 1.4% of the assets as a risk management fee. The investment adviser is SCS Alliance. It is entitled to 0.5% per year on the fund's net assets. In addition, an administrative management fee of 0.40% per year is charged on the fund's assets to cover the auditing and accounting fees.

Let us now examine the fund's allocation policy. To neutralize the cost of the capital guarantee and capture, as far as possible, 100% of the performance of the underlying trading advisers, the fund managers implement an active leverage policy independent of any leverage employed by underlying advisers. Their technique consists of dynamically allocating capital between trading advisers and short-term deposits.

First, a "reference level" is calculated as follows: it starts at $75 and increases linearly day after day to end at $100 five years later (the note is a five-year product). Then the proportion of the fund's net assets invested in the managed accounts (called trading level) is defined as four times the distance between the net asset value (NAV) and the reference level. For instance:

- At launch, the net asset value of the fund is set at $100, so the distance between the NAV and the initial reference level is $25. The initial trading level is thus equal to $4 \times 25/100 = 100\%$. That is, all the fund's assets are invested in the managed accounts.
- Six months after inception, say the net asset value is $109. The new reference level is 77.5. The distance between the NAV and the initial reference level is $31.5. The trading level is thus equal to $4 \times 31.5/100 = 126\%$. That is, the fund must borrow 26% of its net assets (i.e. 26% of $109) and invests 126% of its net assets (i.e. 126% of $109) in the managed accounts.
- One year after inception, say the net asset value is $75. The new reference level is 80. The distance between the NAV and the initial reference level is −$5. The trading level is thus equal to $4 \times (-5)/100 = -20\%$. That is, the fund must invest 20% of its remaining net assets (i.e. 20% of $75) in the short-term deposits and the rest (i.e. 80% of $75) in the managed accounts.

This policy allows a progressive increase or decrease of the capital allocated to the fund according to market conditions. In good times, the leverage provides larger gains, which compensate for the capital guarantee cost. In bad times, the capital is progressively withdrawn and invested in short-term notes. To avoid extreme situations, the minimum trading level was 10% (no stop-loss), whereas its maximum was set at 150%.

WELCOME TO THE DARK SIDE

The concept of investing in hedge funds with a guaranteed return of principal after a certain number of years is quite appealing. However, there is no free lunch in finance, and before investing, one should also consider some of the less publicized aspects of these products.

Lack of liquidity

Capital-guaranteed notes linked to hedge funds are not very liquid products. This is easy to understand when one remembers that any change prior to maturity implies a rebalancing of the underlying hedging portfolio. For instance, if an investor redeems his notes, the issuer needs to sell some of the zero-coupon bonds as well as some of the hedge fund shares. Liquidity is therefore limited by the redemption policy of the underlying fund.

Nevertheless, most issuers usually make a monthly secondary market to buy the product back from investors who want to get out before maturity. Some issuers even offer weekly liquidity, but solely on a best effort basis. An important problem in both cases is the estimation of the net asset value of the underlying hedge fund.[4] Issuers usually conclude special arrangements with the underlying hedge fund in order to get frequent estimates of the net asset value in addition to the official ones. However, when they do not know exactly the true value of the underlying fund, they may not always quote the best price and bid/ask spreads may be large. In addition, they often charge an early redemption fee.

Guarantee? At maturity!

The capital guarantee only applies to investors who remain invested for the full term of the bond. Investors should be aware that they might receive less than the guaranteed investment if they redeem midway through the term of a capital-guaranteed structure. Early redemption values depend on prevailing interest rates, market volatility and the time to maturity as well as the performance of the underlying fund and redemption flows. In particular, the note value may fall below the initial purchase price if interest rates rise, volatility decreases and/or the hedge fund performs badly. Investors redeeming their notes in such conditions—if they can—will usually suffer some loss on their initial investment.

Fees for what?

Most principal-protected notes are linked to the performance of funds of hedge funds rather than to individual hedge funds. The reason is simple—funds of funds already offer a form of risk reduction by spreading their assets among a variety of investment strategies. They are therefore less volatile on average than individual hedge funds. Since option premiums increase as the volatility of the underlying asset increases, a call option on a fund of hedge funds will be less costly than a call option on an individual hedge fund. Since the cash available to purchase call options is limited, cheaper call options means more options; that is, a substantially higher participation rate for the investor. This is often perceived as good news by investors. However, low volatility is also synonymous with less chance of outperforming, which is the only thing that should matter here since the capital is already protected by a zero-coupon. The investor is therefore paying fees to participate in a nonperforming hedge fund.

Following the same line of thought, several notes have specific clauses that force the underlying fund of funds to rebalance its portfolio if the volatility of its net asset value per share passes a threshold number. The rebalancing usually reallocates assets in hedge funds that have exhibited low volatility, or even worse, it reallocates into cash and other short-term interest rate instruments. The investor then takes the risk of having a long-term call option on a T-bill portfolio.

Hedge fund, or what?

Due to the large part invested in zero-coupon bonds, capital-guaranteed notes are exposed to interest rate hikes and typically display a positive correlation with the short- to medium-term domestic bond market. This may reduce the diversification benefits of investors already owning fixed income assets in their portfolios.

Watch the fees!

Hefty fees are usually levied on capital-guaranteed products. This is particularly true if the underlying fund is a fund of hedge funds. Annually the individual hedge fund managers take 2% of the assets and 20% of the profits. Next the fund of funds manager takes 1% of the assets and 10% of the profits. On top of that, the note issuer takes a 1–2% fee at note issuance, and guarantee fees can range from 0.5% to 3% annually, depending on the size of the issue; the liquidity and volatility of the underlying investments; guarantee and participation levels; and the nature of the structure. In addition, there may be some sort of distribution fee.

THE FUTURE

What is the future for capital-guaranteed products? There are currently two contradicting opinions. On the one hand, a few investors have rejected capital protection as an unnecessary expense. Their arguments are twofold. First, they consider that when the hedge fund underlying the capital-guaranteed product is in fact a fund of hedge funds, it is likely that most of the risk has already been diversified. Consequently, buying a capital guarantee means paying a lot of money to offset a very low level of risk. Second, given the superior returns and low volatility offered by hedge funds in the last few years, they consider that capital guarantees are rather unnecessary.

On the other hand, more conservative or risk-averse investors consider guaranteed structures as being an excellent choice to gain exposure to hedge funds while enjoying some form of downside protection. They believe that when it is set at a fair level, the cost of the guarantee does not necessarily lead to underperformance, particularly when markets are volatile. On the contrary, the guarantee provides them an excellent means of avoiding anxious waits for the end-of-the-month net asset value.

Given the current economic climate of low interest rates and uncertainty on global markets, I think the second group's opinion should dominate in the near future. Today capital-guaranteed products on hedge funds are already extremely popular in Switzerland and Germany, where small and medium-sized banks package them and sell them to their private banking clients. But they are also now gaining adherents in the United States, particularly in the retail market, as well as in other European countries with regulatory regimes that are not favorable to making direct investments in offshore fund structures.

The problem lies in choosing the appropriate products. Since capital-guaranteed products were not all created equal, consultants (once again) may add substantial value by helping clients evaluate the trade-offs among initial participation levels, guaranteed coupon levels, and characteristics of the underlying fund of funds portfolio.

NOTES

1. To value and/or hedge options on hedge funds, banks that offer them have developed proprietary pricing models, whose mathematical complexity is far beyond the scope of this book. The interested reader can consult, for instance, Henderson (1999).
2. Note that the participation rate can easily be calculated by dividing the relative amount left for the options (13.616%) by the relative option premium (20%).
3. Note that since hedging a put requires short selling hedge fund shares, or equivalently, short selling the underlying hedge fund's portfolio, put-writing banks need to obtain complete disclosure of the positions held by the fund, sometimes even before the positions are actually taken. Hedge funds are reluctant to accept such agreements and this explains the preference for "bond plus call" structures.
4. The problem is particularly likely to occur with notes indexed on funds of hedge funds, because it may take administrators several weeks to collect the net asset values of each hedge fund comprising the fund of funds.

18

Advanced topics: inside the black box

Comparing investments solely on the basis of their mean return and volatility can be quite misleading. Two very different investments can display very similar statistics, while the drivers of these statistics may indeed be completely unrelated. For example, the fixed income arbitrage style is exposed to mortgage spread and credit spreads while the merger arbitrage style has some exposure to the S&P 500, especially in down markets. So even if their standard deviations look similar, the risks are quite different. Just looking at numbers may therefore be misleading.

This problem is particularly virulent with hedge funds, where the transparency with respect to the underlying portfolio, if any, is very limited; and the freedom granted to the manager with respect to his investment strategy is quite large. Investors and consultants alike are therefore often left in the position of having to base their assessment of a hedge fund's performance or behavior on a few statistics provided by the manager. This is a typical illustration of the "black box" syndrome. Fortunately, there exist a few quantitative techniques that throw some light into the black box. In this chapter we review some of them in greater detail.

MULTIFACTOR MODELS

Multifactor models are useful tools to describe the behavior of any investment fund and break down its returns and risks into identified component sources. Techniques based on multifactor models attempt to determine the link that may exist between the returns on a fund and a series of predefined factors. If such a link exists, the multifactor model will also yield an estimate of the sensitivity of the fund's returns to the particular factor. These sensitivities—one for each factor—are often denoted by the Greek letter beta (β).

Since the fund's returns are usually not perfectly explained by the preselected factors, there remains an unexplained component, which is specific to the fund (Figure 18.1). If the factors are carefully selected, this unexplained component should be small. If the factors are unrelated to what the fund is really doing, the unexplained component will become large and the model will not really be useful. A key statistic to assess the quality of the model is therefore the proportion of the fund's variations that are captured by the model. This is called R^2 or R-square. It varies between 0 (no explanatory power, the factors selected are unrelated to the fund's behavior) and 100% (the fund's behavior is fully explained by the factors selected).

Of course, there are an indefinitely large number of possible multifactor models. So to believe in multifactor models in general still leaves unanswered the question of which particular model one should use. In particular, the major difficulty in implementing multifactor models is the identification of common and relevant factors. The multifactor methodology gives no guidance as to which factors should be considered, but the usefulness of a factor model depends absolutely on the factors chosen for its implementation.

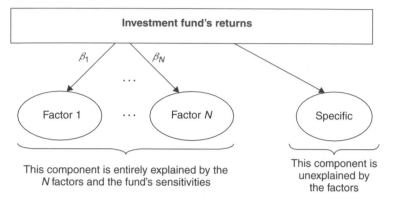

Figure 18.1   The multifactor view of a hedge fund

It is therefore crucial to select good factors to explain return dynamics, i.e. factors that have a good explanatory power.

Two techniques compete for this task. The first one consists in deriving endogenously a set of implicit factors using principal component analysis (Box 18.1). This ensures an optimal fitting of the model, but the difficulty then lies in the economic interpretation of the implied factors. The second technique consists in specifying exogenously a set of factors that we believe or know to be relevant. The economic interpretation is then straightforward, which makes it the preferred method for investment analysis. The factors are often selected from one of the following categories:

- Factors pertaining to particular observable stock (firm) characteristics, such as a market index, sector index, amount of sales, price/earnings ratio, market capitalization, leverage, dividend yield, and trading volume. An important aspect to remember is that the corresponding factor should affect all assets under consideration; see for instance Fama and McBeth (1973).

Box 18.1   PRINCIPAL COMPONENT ANALYSIS

Principal component analysis (PCA) is a complicated mathematical technique that extracts the best "hidden" components in a series of data. The intuition behind PCA is quite simple and can be illustrated through the following example.

Say several hedge fund managers are using the same trading strategy on the same security. The returns of their funds will then be partly determined by a common component. This component's influence will be hidden in the historical returns data of each fund but mixed with other influences from other components. PCA can detect this common component without anyone explicitly mentioning its existence. The process should be repeated for as many components as desired.

However, the output of the PCA is nothing other than time series of returns, one for each component. These time series remain to be identified, and this is the harder part of the process. By comparing these time series with several possible candidates, PCA users may be able to identify the corresponding factors.

- Macroeconomic factors, such as the shape or level of the term structure of interest rates, foreign exchange rates, industrial production, and GDP growth; see for instance Blake *et al.* (1995).
- Returns on relevant portfolios, which themselves capture the broader influences on the assets considered. Examples are small-cap versus large-cap portfolios and high book-to-market versus low book-to-market portfolios; see for instance Fama and French (1992).

Popular examples of factor models include the single-factor capital asset pricing model and the generic Roll-Ross APT model, as well as fixed income models relying on duration and convexity and all derivative models relying on sensitivities (delta, gamma, etc.). On the practical side, numerous implementations are now available, such as the series of BARRA models, the twenty-factor APT model from Advanced Portfolio Technologies Inc. (APT), the six-factor model developed by Quantec Systems Ltd, or the Salomon Brothers risk attribution measurement (RAM) model. In the domain of hedge funds and commodity trading advisers, we should also mention the works of Schneeweis and Spurgin (1998c), who have pioneered the field with a certain amount of success.

STYLE ANALYSIS

Sharpe's methodology

An interesting application of multifactor models is the returns-based style analysis initially suggested by Sharpe (1988). Returns-based style analysis is basically a multifactor model with three additional constraints: (i) the factors are returns on asset classes;[1] (ii) the fund's sensitivity must be positive; and (ii) the sum of all the fund's sensitivities must be equal to one.

Imposing these constraints on a factor model makes sense if we start thinking in terms of asset allocation. Say one wants to create a portfolio of indices whose returns replicate as far as possible the considered fund returns. A standard multifactor model could provide us the fund's sensitivities to the various indices, but these may be hard to interpret in terms of portfolio allocation, particularly if they are negative or do not sum to 100%. Imposing the above constraints therefore allows for a direct and intuitive interpretation of the sensitivities as weights in the replicating portfolio. The "sum to one" constraint therefore reflects a fully invested requirement, while "no negative exposure" can be seen as an interdiction of short sales (Box 18.2).

Box 18.2   QUANTITATIVE CORNER

Mathematically, for a given fund, the style analysis problem can be stated as the following econometric model:

$$R_t = \alpha + \sum_{i=1}^{N} \beta_i R_{i,t} + \varepsilon_t \tag{1}$$

where R_t denotes the return on the fund at time t, $R_{i,t}$ is the return on index i at time t, β_i is a factor loading that expresses the sensitivity of the fund's returns to index i returns, and ε_t represents the portion of the fund's return not related to the

N factors (idiosyncratic noise). So that they can be interpreted as portfolio weights within an asset allocation framework, the factor loadings must add up to one:

$$\sum_{i=1}^{N} \beta_i = 1 \tag{2}$$

Each factor loading must also be positive in order to meet the short selling constraint that most fund managers are subject to:

$$\beta_i \geqslant 0 \quad i = 1 \ldots N \tag{3}$$

The model in equation (1) subject to the constraints of equations (2) and (3) can easily be estimated by quadratic programming to provide point estimates for the β_i; under some conditions, it is also possible to derive the asymptotic distribution for them. Confidence intervals can thus be inferred and statistical significance tests carried out. However, because of the constraints imposed by equations (2) and (3) on the estimated coefficients, this is not a straightforward exercise. See for instance Gouriéroux et al. (1982).

For an investor or a sponsor, returns-based style analysis offers major advantages. Knowing the replicating portfolio of asset classes, makes the following tasks much easier:

- Analyze the effective investment style of a fund, if necessary even before obtaining end-of-year official figures.[2] This can be performed on a static basis at one point in time by just looking at the replicating portfolio's composition, or from a dynamic perspective by monitoring the evolution of the replicating portfolio.
- Create style benchmarks for assessing performance. The return obtained by the fund in each month can be compared with the return on the replicating portfolio, which has by definition the same investment style. This portfolio is a viable and identifiable alternative that can easily be replicated, and is therefore an adequate benchmark. The difference between the fund's returns and its benchmark's returns is therefore the net contribution from the manager, accounting for his investment style.
- Measure the complementarities or similarities between various investment funds, at a much more detailed level than provided by a correlation coefficient. In a sense, correlation simply measures the link between two funds, whereas style analysis explains the parameters that create this link.

A drawback of returns-based style analysis is that it assumes style consistency over time, at least over the period of returns measurement. A time series of data is used to perform a single constrained regression, providing a single style for the entire period. It is therefore common practice to use moving window regressions to incorporate new information and evaluate how a manager's style shifts with time.

Application to hedge funds

Style analysis works remarkably well for investment funds and traditional portfolios; see for instance the extraordinary results obtained by Sharpe (1992). However, it performs poorly with hedge funds. The major reason is that the factors underlying hedge fund returns have not yet been fully identified. Indeed, hedge fund managers have investment styles and market opportunities that are different to those of traditional stock and bond fund managers. Stock and bond fund managers are usually strictly regulated and must hold primarily long positions in the underlying assets; hedge fund managers have broad mandates, can take long and short positions, and can use varying degrees of leverage in varying market conditions. This results in nonlinear returns that can flaw the (linear) returns-based style analysis. As an illustration, let us recall the major results reported by Fung and Hsieh (1998a, 1998b).

Applying principal component analysis to a large sample of US mutual funds in the Morningstar database, Fung and Hsieh find there are 39 dominant investment styles in their sample. Most are subsets or mixes of nine broadly defined asset classes.[3] Given that mutual funds do not change their asset allocation frequently, Fung and Hsieh observe that style analysis has a large explanatory power with respect to mutual funds' variations. About 73% of the funds considered have R^2 higher than 0.80 and 56% have R^2 higher than 0.90.

Applying the same methodology to a sample of 409 hedge funds and CTAs, Fung and Hsieh arrive at dramatically different results. They identify five dominant styles, two being linked to traditional asset classes (US equity and high yield). The remaining three are dynamic trading strategies, i.e. nonlinear functions of the traditional asset class returns. Even worse, hedge funds often follow aggressive tactical asset allocations between these classes, hence the style analysis model has a very low explanatory power, and therefore reduced usefulness.

To apply style analysis in a meaningful way, it is therefore necessary to determine factors specific to hedge funds, and in particular the factors that are nonlinear combinations of existing asset classes. Several approaches have been suggested in the literature.

Capturing nonlinearity: the option-based approach

Fung and Hsieh (1998a, 1998b) suggest that hedge fund returns are the result of three factors:

- *Location factors* determine where a hedge fund invests on a long-term basis (e.g. domestic bonds, foreign stocks). They are typically linearly related to conventional asset classes.
- *Trading strategy factors* are the result of the hedge fund manager's active decisions and short-term trades. They are typically nonlinearly related to location factors and harder to identify.
- *Leverage decisions* may differ between individual location and trading strategy factors, so that identifying leverage decisions precisely may be quite difficult.

Fung and Hsieh's approach does not result in a very reliable model, but it simply motivates the use of both linear and nonlinear indices in style analysis. Fung and Hsieh suggest using a broad set of traditional market indices as location factors. To determine adequate trading factors remains a harder task.

Fung and Hsieh develop a new form of nonparametric regression to identify the types of dynamic trading strategies used by hedge funds. From an intuitive perspective, their approach is equivalent to splitting the underlying market returns into several categories, and observing how the hedge fund performs in each category. Applying this technique to their sample, Fung and Hsieh conclude that a twelve-factor model—nine asset classes and three trading strategies—provides better results, and could be used to assess the performance of hedge funds.

Agarwal and Naik (2001) extend the framework of Fung and Hsieh to simplify the determination of trading factors. Looking at historical hedge fund returns, they first observe that a number of nondirectional hedge fund strategies actually produce return patterns similar to those of various option positions. They therefore suggest using returns on simple option-based strategies as a proxy for trading factors.

Agarwal and Naik tested their model on a sample of 584 funds over the period January 1990 to October 1998. They used the returns on 12 market indices as location factors[4] and the returns on 30 simple one-month option strategies as trading factors.[5] Their analysis reveals that a significant percentage of the time series variation of hedge fund returns can be explained by their set of location and trading factors. However, the quality of the explanation varies greatly among strategies (Table 18.1). Agarwal and Naik also provide the average alpha for each category, after controlling for location and trading indices. Clearly, the evidence is mixed. Some hedge fund styles seem to add value, whereas others exhibit negative alphas.

Table 18.1   Assessing the quality of Agarwal and Naik's model

Strategy	Mean total R^2 (%)	Mean location R^2 (%)	Mean trading R^2 (%)	Mean alpha
Long	74	17	57	−0.21
Short	70	61	9	0.8
Hedge (long bias)	65	32	33	1.31
Fixed income arbitrage	61	15	47	−1.07
Restructuring	57	10	47	−0.26
Equity hedge	55	27	28	1.2
Event driven	53	20	33	1.03
Macro	48	17	31	0.72
Capital structure arbitrage	45	15	30	0.68
Event arbitrage	37	7	30	0.24

Although extremely interesting, these results are subject to caution. In particular:

- Since the number of factors (42 in total) is becoming extremely large, Agarwal and Naik use a particular statistical technique called stepwise regression[6] to decide which of the factors should be considered for each hedge fund. Although appealing, this technique is known to bias all R^2 upward, because factors will be selected only on the basis of their ability to increase the R^2.
- Many of the 42 factors will tend to behave similarly (statisticians call this collinearity). In the regression it is therefore extremely difficult to identify which of the similar indices really contributes to the hedge fund behavior.

Nevertheless, Agarwal and Naik's technique opens new doors to hedge fund analysis and provides some evidence regarding the sources and amounts of value added by hedge fund managers.

Capturing nonlinearity: the hedge fund index approach

Although I entirely support the approaches pioneered by Fung and Hsieh (1998a, 1998b) and Agarwal and Naik (2001), recent academic research provides evidence that additional factors such as convenience yields, market momentum, and other institutional features result in potential arbitrage opportunities for hedge fund managers (e.g. Chan et al. 1996; Blake et al. 1999). Accounting for these factors—as well as factors yet to be discovered—within the above approaches creates several estimation problems. In particular, the number of factors may rapidly become larger than the number of funds, and since the data usually consists of monthly net asset values, we may run into an overspecified problem.

Fortunately, new elements have come to light and may provide a solution to these problems. In 1999 Credit Suisse First Boston and Tremont combined their resources to create new benchmarks of hedge fund performance. Based on the TASS+ database, which tracks over 2600 hedge funds, the CSFB/Tremont Hedge Fund indices offer several advantages over their competitors:

- They are transparent (both in their calculation and in their composition) and constructed in a disciplined and objective manner.
- They are computed on a monthly basis and asset-weighted, which makes them representative of the various styles.
- They do not include funds of funds and separate accounts. Therefore, each subindex is mutually exclusive, which should avoid most of the multicollinearity problems.

Lhabitant (2001a, 2001b) therefore suggests adapting the Sharpe (1988) returns-based style analysis model by using the nine CSFB/Tremont subindices as asset class proxies. Since each index is built from individual hedge funds, the nonlinearity with respect to traditional asset classes previously observed should therefore be contained in the indices. The model preserves the analytical tractability and ease of interpretation of Sharpe's model. Rather than referring to traditional asset classes, it just uses alternative classes. Therefore, for a given hedge fund, the beta coefficients can be seen as exposures to the different CSFB/Tremont styles. The alpha coefficient is the excess return generated by the hedge fund manager, taking into account his investment style.

As an illustration, Figure 18.2 represents graphically the nine betas obtained for two existing hedge funds. The shapes of these graphs—we call them hedge funds radars—allow for an immediate style classification. The first fund is a pure convertible arbitrage hedge fund ($\beta_1 = 0.41$ all other betas below 0.04). The second fund is a fund of hedge funds that appears to be diversified across styles. Its highest exposures are in the convertible arbitrage ($\beta_1 = 0.22$), market neutral ($\beta_8 = 0.22$) and global macro styles ($\beta_4 = 0.19$), and moderate exposures in long/short equity ($\beta_5 = 0.15$), emerging markets ($\beta_6 = 0.13$) and event driven ($\beta_3 = 0.07$ all other betas below 0.01).

Thus, using hedge fund radars, it suddenly becomes easy to monitor what managers actually do regardless of what they claim to be doing. It also helps in identifying hedge funds with a "pure" investment style and hedge funds with a diversified style approach.

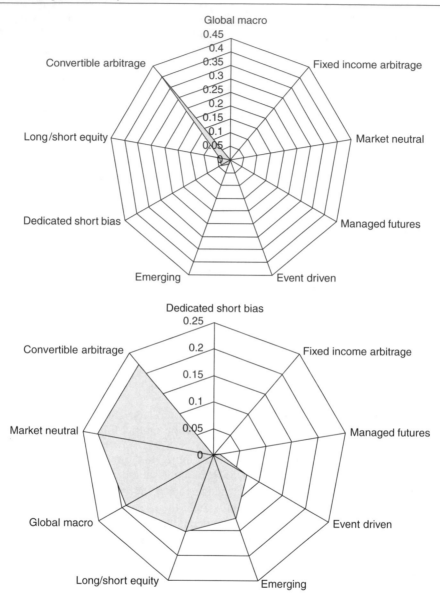

Figure 18.2   Hedge fund radars and style exposures
Reprinted, with permission, from Lhabitant (2001b)

This is specifically useful for funds of hedge funds and multimanager portfolios, which offer investors an efficient way of diversifying risks across a number of managers and strategies. Are they effectively diversified across styles? A single fund radar will easily help answer this question.

   Fund radars only provide a static picture of a hedge fund's behavior, but the model also allows for a dynamic assessment of a hedge fund's behavior. By using a rolling observation period, it is possible to build up a series of radars that represent the evolution of the fund's exposures over time. These can also easily be represented graphically, allowing us to verify the stability of the fund's behavior.

As an illustration, Figure 18.3 shows the dynamic behavior of the style allocation (betas) for the two funds considered previously. For our first fund, the exposure to convertible arbitrage appears only since the first quarter 1999. Before this, the fund was clearly exposed to the long/short equity, event driven and market neutral styles. This evidences that the track record of this fund will not be the track record of a pure convertible arbitrage

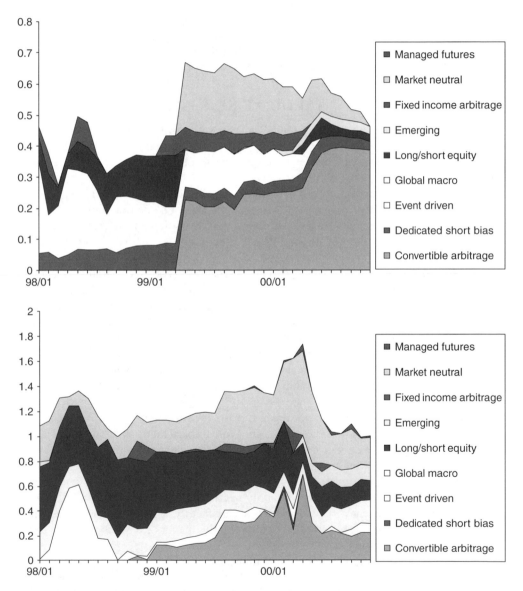

Figure 18.3   A dynamic view of style drift
Reprinted, with permission, from Lhabitant (2001b)

fund, although the fund is now almost only exposed to this style. By contrast, the fund of hedge funds appears diversified since it was created.

Clearly, the application of returns-based style analysis has proven to be beneficial, and not only for investors. From the manager's viewpoint, style analysis may be helpful if it provides a better understanding of how his own portfolio and competing portfolios are positioned. It may also be helpful for fund of funds managers if different styles can be expected to perform well or badly over particular time scales (in which case the manager should tilt towards the style most likely to outperform over the period in question). However, the results of style analysis must be carefully interpreted. It is often stated that the weights in the replication portfolio correspond to the effective allocation of the fund's portfolio among the asset classes. This is incorrect. In actuality, the most one can say is that the fund behaves "as if" it was invested using these weights. It is therefore more a behavioral model rather than a pure asset allocation model.

VALUE AT RISK

From a functional perspective, hedge funds' investment activities are not really different from market making and/or proprietary trading, two domains long confined to large financial institutions' trading rooms. However, despite the similarity, trading rooms and hedge funds have adopted somewhat opposing views on risk management.

Risk management in trading rooms is entirely quantitative and mandatory. Spurred by the increasing complexity of financial instruments, the size of some trading books and the large losses sustained by several major institutions, market participants have acknowledged the need for a unified method of measuring risk that could be useful for both regulatory reporting and internal risk management purposes. As a result of important developments in financial risk modeling, value at risk (VaR) and scenario analysis have gradually become best practices for measuring, controlling and reporting on a regular basis the market risk exposures of institutions and their proprietary trading desks. They are now being used within leading financial institutions and corporations and are supported by regulators, including the Basle Committee on Banking Supervision, the Group of Thirty, the Bank for International Settlements, and the European Union.

On the other hand, asset managers in general and hedge fund managers in particular have adopted VaR less readily than trading rooms. While most asset managers are particularly proficient at measuring returns and constructing benchmarks to evaluate performance, they argue that this expertise does not extend to the measurement of risk. Indeed, asset managers view risk management in general, and VaR in particular, as being inherently at odds with their primary business mandate—taking risks. Therefore, they are still reluctant to disclose their VaR figures or anything about their positions or strategies. They claim to focus on absolute returns and ignore risk-adjusted performance. The most that is available is still too often a nonaudited monthly net asset value provided by a hedge fund performance-reporting agency. This is clearly unsatisfactory. Consequently, hedge funds advisers and investors still rely essentially on qualitative factors to assess risk, due to the lack of available information and/or competent staff.

In the medium term, there is no doubt that transparency will improve in the hedge fund kingdom, particularly if managers want to attract institutional investors. In the meantime, however, given the complexities involved in hedge fund strategies, qualitative approaches to risk and performance evaluation are not sufficient. There is a need to introduce new quantitative tools to assist investors in assessing the investment characteristics and the risks of hedge funds.

In April 1999, in response to the collapse of Long Term Capital Management, the President's Working Group on Financial Markets[7] issued a report calling for a group of hedge funds to draft and publish sound practices for their risk management and internal controls. The answer[8] was the *Sound Practices for Hedge Fund Managers* report issued in February 2000, which made some innovative recommendations, at least for the hedge fund industry. In particular, it suggested that hedge fund managers should employ a VaR model for measuring and communicating the risk of loss for their portfolios.

Let us recall that VaR aims to measure the magnitude of the likely maximum loss that a portfolio could experience over a finite time horizon at some specific confidence level. The time horizon typically corresponds to a holding period hypothesis, which should reflect the features of the portfolio on which the risk is being measured. The confidence level indicates the frequency of the maximum loss. The user sets the confidence level according to the purpose at hand (risk management, regulatory reporting, etc.) and within the limits of what are considered as "normal" market conditions.[9]

VaR collapses the entire distribution of a portfolio's returns into a single number. It aims to do what virtually no other financial tool has ever attempted—provide a unified framework for a meaningful and easily interpretable aggregate measure of risks for portfolios composed of complex instruments with various market sensitivities, maturities and pricing mechanisms. While the definition of VaR is broad and encompasses, at least in theory, all sources of market risk for a portfolio, estimating VaR can be challenging in practice. Once the confidence level and holding period have been decided, the next two steps consist of forecasting large future movements of underlying markets and assessing the sensitivity of the portfolio to these movements. Various methods may be used, including parametric methods, extreme value estimates, or historical or Monte Carlo simulations. Each methodology has its own strengths and weaknesses (Jorion 1997; Dowd 1998). Most of them need the composition of the underlying portfolio and are therefore inapplicable to hedge funds.

I have suggested a straightforward extension of my style analysis approach to compute the value at risk of a hedge fund, based solely on its net asset values (Lhabitant 2001b). Intuitively, my model consists of calculating a VaR for each factor then aggregating the VaRs at the hedge fund level, accounting for risk factor exposures as well as for the correlation between risk factors (Figure 18.4). The nice feature of my model is its analytical tractability, as well as its ability to run stress scenarios.

How trustworthy is this approach? I back-tested my VaR model on a sample of 2934 hedge funds from January 1994 to October 2000. Using a three-year observation period, I computed fund exposures, the market parameters, and the fund VaRs (one month, 99% confidence level). Then I compared the VaR of each fund with its profit and loss of the following month. If the loss was greater than the VaR figure, this was recorded as an exception. Out of a total of 96 549 three-year observation periods, 1026 exceptions were observed. This gives an exception rate slightly higher than expected (1.06% versus 1%). However, things have to be taken with caution, since 614 of these exceptions occurred in August 1998 immediately after the LTCM crisis, which can be qualified as an abnormal market situation. If one excludes this month from the sample, the exception rate falls to 0.43%, a rather conservative figure (Table 18.2).

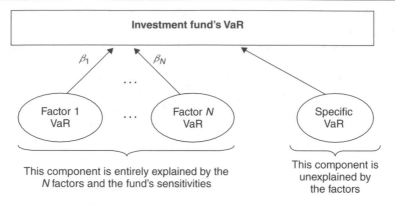

Figure 18.4   Computing the value at risk for a hedge fund

Table 18.2   Back-testing the VaR and exception rate: as a percentage of the number of tested funds

	Exception rate (%)							
	1997	1998	1999	2000	All	1998*	All*	Aug 98
Convertible arb.	0.11	3.43	0.12	0.31	1.10	1.36	0.49	23.64
Emerging	1.96	3.70	0.00	0.00	0.67	0.00	0.27	60.00
Event driven	0.63	4.46	0.25	0.15	1.47	0.56	0.39	41.49
Long/short equity	0.10	2.75	0.03	0.38	0.79	0.19	0.16	36.73
Managed futures	0.00	0.28	0.17	0.10	0.16	0.30	0.16	0.00
Market neutral	0.59	3.20	0.13	0.22	0.68	0.59	0.29	33.33
Multistrategy	0.46	2.69	0.11	0.63	1.00	0.58	0.43	26.24
Fixed income arb.	0.78	5.40	0.03	0.65	1.84	2.19	0.92	36.60
Global macro	0.00	2.50	0.00	0.53	0.62	1.37	0.38	14.29
Dedicated short	0.00	0.61	2.13	0.00	0.83	0.68	0.85	0.00
All sample	0.45	3.34	0.13	0.39	1.06	0.86	0.43	30.13

*Excluding August 1998
Source: Lhabitant (2001a)

The above VaR methodology has since been adopted by several institutions as well as consulting groups. However, despite this success, it is important to recognize that value at risk is not perfect and also has limitations. It should be seen as a quantitative tool used to complement, but not replace, human judgment and market experience. Long Term Capital Management itself had a fairly sophisticated VaR system based on historical data to try to limit potential losses. However, the combination of the exceptional market conditions at the end of 1998 (spreads moving many standard deviations) with excessive leverage led to a disaster.

NOTES

1.   Following Sharpe's recommendations, they should be mutually exclusive, exhaustive with respect to the investment universe, and have returns that differ. If some indices are too closely correlated or not mutually exclusive, the model will yield unstable or

oscillating results from period to period. Likewise, if the set of indices does not span the investment universe, the methodology will fail in identifying a benchmark that consistently explains the fund's behavior.

2. Although a fund's prospectus should obviously provide this information, recent research by DiBartolomeo and Witkowski (1997), Brown and Goetzmann (1997) and Kim *et al.* (1999) presents evidence of serious misclassifications when self-reported investment objectives are compared with actual investment styles.

3. These are MSCI US, MSCI non-US, and IFC Emerging Market for equities; JP Morgan US Government Bonds, J.P. Morgan non-US government bonds, and Merrill Lynch High Yield Corporate Bond index for fixed income; one-month eurodollar rate for cash; gold for commodities; and the Federal Reserve Bank Trade Weighted Dollar index for currencies.

4. These are the Russell 3000 index, the MSCI World excluding USA index, the MSCI Emerging Markets index, the Salomon Brothers Government and Corporate Bond index, the Salomon Brothers World Government Bond index, the Lehman High Yield index, the Federal Reserve Bank Trade Weighted Dollar index, and the Goldman Sachs Commodity index. They also include three zero investment strategies to capture popular investment strategies: the Fama and French (1996) "size" factor (small minus big), the Fama and French (1996) "value growth" factor (high minus low), and the Carhart (1997) "momentum" factor (winners minus losers). Their 12th location index is a "default" premium index (the yield on Moody's US BAA rated corporate bond index minus the return on US Treasuries).

5. These are one month put and call options with three strike prices on five of the location indices. The strike prices are at the money, $\frac{1}{2}$ standard deviation out of the money and 1 standard deviation out of the money. The underlying indices are the Russell 3000 index, the MSCI Emerging Markets index, the Salomon Brothers World Government Bond index, the Lehman High Yield index, and the Federal Reserve Bank Trade Weighted Dollar index.

6. A stepwise regression adds explanatory variables (factors) in the regression model one by one, based on the increase of R^2 that their inclusion would generate. The process stops when the increase in R^2 is below some specified amount.

7. Comprising the Secretary of the US Department of the Treasury and the chairs of the Board of Governors of the Federal Reserve System, the Securities and Exchange Commission and the Commodity Futures Trading Commission.

8. The answering group included representatives of the largest hedge funds in the industry: Caxton Corporation, Kingdon Capital Management LLC, Moore Capital Management Inc., Soros Fund Management LLC and Tudor Investment Corporation.

9. A VaR with a confidence level of 99% implies that the loss should not exceed the VaR in 99 cases out of 100. See for instance Jorion (1997) for relevant background material.

19

Conclusion

Since the original concept created by Alfred W. Jones, hedge funds have indeed come a long shaky and shady way. Operating in almost complete secrecy for several decades, they only acquired public prominence in 1992 with George Soros's successful assault on the British pound. They created serious diplomatic incidents, as in 1997 when Asian governments talked of outlawing them. But the major event in their history was the shocking bankruptcy of Long Term Capital Management in 1998. It threatened financial markets worldwide. It sparked talk of stricter regulation. It reinforced the view that all hedge funds take on risks that are far above average. Last, but not least, it put many investors off hedge funds for good. At the end of 1998, in the opinion of most market participants, the days of hedge funds were clearly counted.

Three years later, the situation has dramatically changed. Aggressive pioneers such as George Soros or Julian Robertson have left their seats, but hedge funds are on their way to becoming the next big thing in investment management. New hedge funds are born every day. Experienced portfolio managers quit their jobs to work for hedge funds. Hedge fund experts have sprung up like mushrooms. And every one is talking about hedge funds and their vaunted benefits. Here is what they say:

- Hedge funds increase returns
- Hedge funds are noncorrelated
- Hedge funds reduce risk
- Hedge funds profit in both bull and bear markets
- Hedge fund managers are tomorrow's stars
- Invest today before we close access

And so it goes. As hedge fund marketing intensifies, many private and institutional investors are showing interest. Some will invest for better or for worse. Others will flee, still convinced that hedge funds are high rollers whose true place is in the casino. But the immense majority of investors will remain undecided. They realize that equity returns over the last 10 years were significantly above trend, and that they may not be so exciting in the future. Consequently, they are looking for true alternative investment opportunities. But are hedge funds the answer? It is difficult to say, given their diversity and short track records. Moreover, since hedge funds' investment strategies are often quite complex, it is difficult to understand what these people are really doing.

The lack of understanding of hedge funds is above all due to the lack of good information sources and the plethora of bad. Investors should therefore not blindly swallow the typical marketing pitch or consider the performance achieved in the past as a guarantee of future success. They should not trust financial intermediaries who recommend hedge funds to investors while simultaneously pocketing a commission for servicing the same hedge funds. Rather, investors should separate the wheat from the chaff. They should ask the right questions, roll up their sleeves, do their homework and take time to think things through. Then they should repeat the whole process until they feel completely confident with the final decision and its implications.

There is no doubt that there are traps for the unwary and that many will be put off either by the complexity or the jargon of the alternative world. Throughout this book, I have attempted to clarify several of the underlying concepts and methodologies. This will make the road safer for most readers. A lot still needs to be put in place, however, such as greater disclosure, proper benchmarks and an improved regulatory regime. This may come in the near future under the pressure of institutional investors. Indeed, hedge funds are today where mutual funds were in the 1980s—just at the beginning of the consolidation period necessary to sustain and secure future growth.

Could hedge funds become the mutual funds of tomorrow, a standard part of every investor's portfolio? They are likely to be. Many institutions—including large pension, endowment, and foundation funds—are increasing their exposure to hedge funds. Demography is also on their side as wealth passes from the conservative postwar generation to more risk-friendly baby boomers. According to a recent Merrill Lynch survey, at the end of 2000 there were 7.2 million millionaires (in US dollars) worldwide, including 57 000 people owning more than 30 million dollars each. All are potential targets. In addition, electronic offshore exchanges are taking off and hedge fund database sites are now aiding the investment process. Standard and Poor's and Fitch are developing criteria for rating debt secured by the market value of funds of hedge funds, and this should open the door to hedge fund securitization.

You may not be comfortable investing in hedge funds, but your children probably will be. At least in the surviving funds, if any.

Appendix

The statistics of hedge funds

We like to think of statistics as being the science of learning from data. But is it really a science or should it be considered an art? Naive observers are often surprised by the fact that different statistics concerning the same issue can produce very dissimilar or even contradictory results. To resolve this paradox, they simply conclude that statistics are not reliable indicators of reality. Consequently, there seems to be a pervasive notion that one can prove anything with statistics.

Reality is quite different. Inferences drawn from statistics rely on assumptions, methodologies, samples and substantive interpretation. Those versed in statistics clearly understand that each of these affects the validity of the final conclusions. Unfortunately, many snags lie in wait for unwary users. Among the most typical, we have proceeding from different assumptions, claiming assumptions that do not apply to the situation, using unrepresentative samples, applying incorrect methodologies, erroneously interpreting the results, forgetting to check for statistical significance and missing the difference between correlation and causation.

These snags are particularly perverse in the world of alternative investments, for three reasons. First, the traditional secrecy surrounding hedge fund activities precludes the use of intuition to confirm statistical results, although a safer way to play the game would be for statistics to confirm the intuition. Second, the extreme lack of data on hedge funds often results in very small samples, a situation in which traditional statistical methods fail to provide valid results. Finally, several actors bend the rules of statistics to support their viewpoint and hide their products' deficiencies behind pseudostatistical arguments.

Unfortunately, there is little hope that an appendix at the end of a book will change the situation in any way. Once again, my aim is simply to provide readers with a better understanding of the numbers and figures that populate hedge fund performance reports, and the ability to detect weak contents disguised behind carefully selected statistical facts. I have deliberately simplified the exposition and limited the mathematical content to a minimum, although I have included references to more advanced sources. However, there are still a few formulas around. This is the price to pay for entry into the quantitative world. As Derek Bok, a former Harvard president, once said, "If you think education is expensive, try ignorance."

RETURNS STATISTICS

In the world of hedge funds, the starting point of returns statistics is usually a time series of the fund's net asset value. Throughout this section, we will consider a hedge fund with the following series of 1-month holding period returns: 5%, 10%, −5%, 8% and 7%. This time series is admittedly far too short to compute any meaningful statistic, but we just use it for illustration purposes.

Single-period calculations

Comparisons of hedge fund performance are frequently based on holding period returns over 1-year, 3-year and 5-year periods, as well as from the fund's inception and from the beginning of the current year (year-to-date or YTD). The *holding period return* measures the relative change in a fund's net asset value over a given time period. For a holding period from time $t = 0$ to T, it is computed as

$$R_{0,T} = \frac{\text{NAV}_T - \text{NAV}_0}{\text{NAV}_0} \tag{A.1}$$

where NAV_t denotes the net asset value at time t. Note that the final net asset value should be adjusted to take into account all realized and nonrealized capital gains, accrued dividends and interest income, capital distributions (if any) and splits.

An important question with holding period returns is whether they are calculated before the deduction of management fees and other expenses (gross returns) or after (net returns). Both figures are useful, since gross returns reflect a manager's raw investment performance, while net returns reflect actual investor results. Similarly, it is important to know the net asset value calculation methodology, and in particular:

- The valuation methodology for infrequently traded or nonmarketable assets, such as nonlisted stocks, real estate, and private placements. Those who believe valuation does not matter should remember that the hedge fund Granite Partners collapsed when investors evaluated its holdings at market value rather than face value.
- The use of cash versus accrual accounting. In cash accounting, income is recorded only when received and expenses are recorded only when paid. Accrual accounting is based on the fundamental rule that all income earned for a period must be matched with the expenses that are assignable to that period. The industry recommended standard is accrual accounting, as required under Generally Accepted Accounting Principles (GAAP), but some hedge funds prefer the simplicity of cash accounting.
- The use of trade date versus settlement date. Trade date is the day on which an order is executed, whereas settlement date is the date on which an executed order must be settled (for purchases, the cash for the purchase must be paid; for sales, the proceeds of the sell will be placed in a cash account). The industry recommended standard is trade date. The current settlement period is usually three business days after the trade date for stocks and mutual funds and one business day after the trade date for options trades. It can be considerably longer in emerging markets.
- The manager's choice of adjustment methodology for intermediate withdrawals and contributions, if any.

Frequently, investors want to transform a holding period return into an annual figure, particularly for comparison purposes. This is called *annualizing*. When the holding period is less than a year, annualizing means taking the return made over a short period and calculating what the annual return would have been if the investment had continued to gain at the same rate for a full year. When the holding period is more than a year, annualizing means figuring out the constant annual return necessary to achieve the observed holding period return once compounding effects are taken into account.

A quick estimate of the annualized return is obtained by simply comparing the length of the holding period with one year, and linearly adjusting the holding period return. For instance, a 6-month return of 5% would give a 10% annual return (12/6 of the original value), while an 18-month return of 15% would also result in a 10% annual return (12/18 of the original value). Although useful, this approach is flawed because it does not take into account the compounding of interest.

The correct way of annualizing the holding period return (HPR) is as follows:

$$\text{Annualized return} = (1 + \text{HPR})^{\text{number of periods in year}} - 1 \tag{A.2}$$

where HPR is measured over a given period, and the power is adjusted accordingly. For instance, if the 6-month holding period return is 5%, the equivalent annual return would be $(1 + 5\%)^2 - 1 = (1.05)^2 - 1 \approx 10.25\%$. The power of 2 comes from the fact that we have two 6-month periods in a year. Similarly, an 18-month return of 15% would result in an annual return of $(1 + 15\%)^{(12/18)} - 1 = (1.15)^{(12/18)} - 1 \approx 9.77\%$.

Multiple-period calculations

The measurement of investment returns is more complicated in the case of returns over several periods. For instance, if we follow a hedge fund over 10 years on a monthly basis, we end up with a time series of 120 holding period returns. If we want to compare this fund with one of its peers, we now have 240 numbers to deal with. Since the average human brain fails miserably when dealing with more than 10 or 20 numbers, we need statistical tools to summarize and compare information. We first consider central tendency information, such as the mean (or average), the median and the mode. They provide information about the observations in the middle of a data set.

The *arithmetic average return* is computed simply by summing the return in each subperiod $(R_{0,1}, R_{1,2}, \ldots, R_{T-1,T})$ and dividing the total by the number of subperiods (T). Each subperiod should have the same length (e.g. 1 day, 1 month). Mathematically,

$$R_A = \frac{1}{T} \sum_{t=1}^{T} R_{t-1,t} \tag{A.3}$$

Using our initial data series of 1-month holding period returns, one would obtain an arithmetic average return equal to

$$R_A = \tfrac{1}{5}(5\% + 10\% - 5\% + 8\% + 7\%) = 5\%$$

Some managers also compute the *average gain*, which is a simple average (arithmetic mean) of the periods with a gain. Its calculation consists of summing all observed positive returns and then dividing the total by the number of gain periods. Similarly, the *average loss* is a simple average (arithmetic mean) of the periods with a loss. Its calculation consists of summing all observed negative returns and then dividing the total by the number of loss periods. In our example the average gain would be $\tfrac{1}{4}(5\% + 10\% + 8\% + 7\%) = 7.5\%$, and the average loss -5%.

The *gain to loss ratio* is a simple ratio of the average gain divided by the average loss (in absolute value) over a given period. Fund managers often use it to compare winning period returns with losing period returns. Although it is a rather intuitive measure, its interpretation is subject to caution because it hides the relative number of winning and losing periods, and because it does not account for compounding. In our example the gain to loss ratio would be $7.5\%/5\% = 1.5$. On average, the manager wins 1.5 times more than he loses. However, when one looks at the time series, it is obvious that the manager has been essentially winning. Whether this is luck or skill remains to be determined, but for sure, it is not displayed in the gain to loss ratio.

The *geometric average return* represents the return that, once compounded, would produce the same holding period return for a given investment. Its formula is more compli-cated than the arithmetic average, because it accounts for the effect of compounding. It multiplies all the subperiod returns, expressed as $(1 + R_{t,t+1})$, where $R_{t,t+1}$ is the percentage return between t and $t + 1$, and takes the root corresponding to the number of subperiods (T). Mathematically,

$$R_G = \left[(1 + R_{0,1})(1 + R_{1,2}) \cdots (1 + R_{T-1,T})\right]^{1/T} - 1 \qquad (A.4)$$

Note that the result would be the same regardless of the order of the returns. In our example, the geometric monthly mean return would be equal to

$$R_G = (1.05 \times 1.10 \times 0.95 \times 1.08 \times 1.07)^{1/5} - 1 = 4.86\%$$

If an investor started with \$100, and the investment experienced the series of returns shown, at the end of the five periods the investment would be worth \$104.86. As this example shows, the geometric mean and the arithmetic mean are different, with the geometric mean providing a more meaningful description of how an investment would fare over multiple periods. Note that the market convention is usually to express average returns on an *annualized basis*.

Which average should be preferred? Most hedge fund managers prefer the arithmetic figures, because they always result in a higher value than the geometric ones. The only situation where they would be equal is if all returns were identical. The key point is that it is improper to interpret the arithmetic average rate of return as a measure of the average return over an evaluation period, because it does not account for compounding effects. The proper interpretation of the arithmetic average rate of return is as follows: it is the average value of withdrawals, expressed as a fraction of the initial net asset value, that can be made at the end of each subperiod while keeping the initial net asset value intact.

The average return is usually the best indicator of the common behavior in a data set. For a symmetric distribution, the mean, the median and the mode are equal to each other. However, not all distributions are symmetrical. The presence of outliers—very high or very low returns—can significantly affect the average. In this case the *median return* is a better measure of central tendency. The median is simply calculated as the middle value in the data set. Simply stated, 50% of the observations are above it and 50% are below it. If there is an even number of data points, the median is calculated by taking the average (mean) of the two middle points. If we go back to our example time series, the median return would be 7%, with two values below it (-5% and $+5\%$) and two values above it (8% and 10%).

Unlike the average, the median is not affected by the presence of outliers; if we made the smallest value even smaller or the largest value even larger, it would not change the value of the median. A median value very different from the arithmetic mean therefore signals asymmetrical returns distributions.

Finally, the *mode* is the value that occurs most frequently in a data set. It is almost never used for returns, but is useful when the set of possible values is discrete and easily identified.

Multiple hedge fund aggregation

Another common aggregation in performance analysis is the case of several hedge funds over a single time period. This type of aggregation occurs for instance when calculating a performance index for a group of hedge funds. Let us say that we want to calculate a monthly performance index for a group of N hedge funds. How should we proceed? First we need to compute the holding period return for each hedge fund over the month. We denote these returns $R_i (i = 1, \ldots, N)$. Ideally they should be measured exactly over the same period and according to the same calculation rules. In practice they are often based on the monthly variation of the net asset value.

Next we need to assign a weight w_i to each fund. Two major weighting schemes are used in the industry, the equal weighting approach and the asset weighting approach:

- *Equal-weighted average*: each hedge fund return has an equal weight in the average. If there are N funds in a sample, each of these has a weight $w_i = 1/N$. The corresponding average can then be perceived as the average fund behavior, irrespective of the assets under management. If each fund in the sample has its dedicated manager, the equal-weighted average will also capture the average manager behavior.
- *Asset-weighted average*: each hedge fund return receives a specific weight in the average. This weight is based on the fund's assets under management in proportion to the total assets managed by all hedge funds covered by the average. If each fund has assets $A_i (i = 1, \ldots, N)$, the weight of each fund is $w_i = A_i / \sum A_i$. The resulting average figure can therefore be perceived as the average dollar invested behavior.

Finally, once we have the return (R_i) and the weight (w_i) for each hedge fund, the performance index is simply computed as a weighted average:

$$R_{\text{index}} = \sum_{i=1}^{N} w_i R_i \qquad (A.5)$$

In the case of multiple fund aggregation, some consultants prefer to report the median return rather than the average return. The *median fund return* is the return such that half of the funds have a higher return and half of the funds have a lower return. When the data set contains an odd number of returns, the middle value is the median value and corresponds to the median fund for the period considered. When the data set contains an even number of returns, the middle two numbers are added, the sum is divided by two and the resulting value is the median.

RISK STATISTICS

Central tendency statistics provide a good indicator of the average behavior of a sample of returns. However, two funds with the same average may have very different behaviors, depending on how representative is the average with respect to each observation. Consider Figure A.1. It represents the monthly returns over the period July 1996 to August 2001 of the hedge funds AG&J Power2 Ltd and P.A.W. Offshore Fund. The former is a market neutral fund active on utility stocks. The latter is a long/short fund that focuses on the technology, healthcare and retail sectors.

These two funds have the same average annualized return over the period (about 19%). However, their behavior differs greatly. In the case of AG&J Power2 Ltd, the average

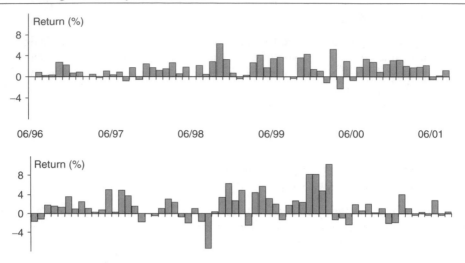

Figure A.1   Same mean but different risks

is quite representative of the individual monthly returns, while P.A.W. Offshore Fund's returns fluctuate widely around their average. Most investors would probably agree that risk is essential and qualify P.A.W. Offshore Fund as more risky than AG&J Power2 Ltd over the considered period. But what do they mean exactly by "risk"?

It is difficult to reach a consensus on how to define risk. Indeed, different investors will have different concerns, depending on the nature of their portfolio and/or the nature of the institution that employs them. They will therefore perceive risk differently. A pension fund may see risk as the failure to face his liabilities. An asset manager may perceive risk as a deviation from its benchmark. A statistician may define risk as potential deviations from the average. And a private investor may consider the probability of missing a target return and by how much.

Nevertheless, all these definitions share common characteristics. They combine uncertainty and the possibility of a loss, disappointing or unsatisfactory outcomes. Clearly, risk measures attempt to estimate the potential for loss of control and/or value. But the proliferation of risk measures is rather confusing for investors, essentially for two reasons. First, different risk measures will provide different orderings for the same set of funds. The reason is that they basically answer different questions. Indeed, there is no a priori reason for the answers to What is the fund that has the lowest probability of loss? being the same as the answer to What is the fund that has the smallest average deviation from its benchmark? Second, there is little or no conceptual cohesion between the different approaches to measure risk. Moreover, the absence of a single dominant approach to risk is also reflected in influential actuarial textbooks, where various different approaches to risk are shown as being appropriate in different application areas (e.g. Daykin *et al.* 1994; Booth *et al.* 1999).

In the following, we attempt to clarify the issue by reviewing the major risk measures that are applied in the hedge fund universe. We discuss their goals and essential properties, compare their advantages and deficiencies, and illustrate their application. Once again, I attempt to favor intuition over mathematical developments, but I do provide the formula for calculating each risk measure.

Volatility (standard deviation)

The most common statistical risk indicator in finance is certainly *volatility*. Volatility is a number that attempts to capture the dispersion of returns around the average return. The greater the volatility, the less informative the average. The formula for volatility is not simple. Intuitively, if one wants to measure the dispersion of returns around the average return, an appealing measure would be the average deviation, calculated as

$$- \bar{R}) \tag{A.6}$$

h this definition is that, whatever the ero value. The reason is simply that rvations, so that negative deviations lem, we may use the *mean absolute*

$$_t - \bar{R}| \tag{A.7}$$

mathematically. Finance practitioners deviation, to measure volatility. It is root of the *variance* (itself designated

calculating deviations from the mean ending up with a zero value and to ones. Finally, the squared deviations tions minus one. Mathematically, the

$$_{1,t} - \bar{R})^2 \tag{A.8}$$

s its mean return, and T is the number e volatility restores the dimensions and

$$_{-1,t} - \bar{R})^2 \tag{A.9}$$

difficulty when using equation (A.9) is , the window of data used. If volatility and one should choose a T as large as process (since more information will , a compromise has to be found between ing a biased quantity) or only the most al value). Note that some systems (e.g.

Riskmetrics) solve this problem by using an exponential smoothing model, which weights the most recent returns more heavily than older values.

Box Appendix.1   QUANT'S CORNER

Why $T - 1$ rather than T?

Dividing by $T - 1$ rather than T when computing the variance is usually of little practical importance, particularly when T is large. Technically, we most often want to estimate the variability of the population from which the current sample was drawn (e.g. we would like to generalize our results to all returns of a fund, given our random sample of returns). In this case we should always use $N - 1$ as the divisor in the computations; using N as the divisor results in purely descriptive statistics for the current sample.

Using log-returns

Because of the compounding property of simple returns, it is actually more correct to compute the volatility using continuously compounded returns. The procedure can be implemented as follows: (i) compute simple returns (R_{Pt}) from the fund's net asset value; (ii) convert these simple returns (R_{Pt}) into continuously compounded returns (r_{Pt}) by using the log function ($r_{Pt} = \ln(1 + R_{Pt})$); (iii) compute the arithmetic average of these log-returns; (iv) compute the standard deviation of these log-returns; (v) go back to the simple return universe by taking the exponential of the log-return standard deviation. This is the correct return volatility. However, for practical purposes, we neglect the corresponding bias and continue to use simple returns in this appendix.

Like returns, volatility figures are generally annualized. To annualize, one needs to multiply the volatility estimated using equation (A.9) by the square root of the observation frequency (12 for monthly, 360 for daily, etc.). For example, if five years of monthly data give an estimation of volatility equal to 10%, the corresponding annualized volatility would be 34.64% (10% times the square root of 12).

The shortcomings of volatility

Intuitively, volatility seems an appealing measure of risk. It is easily calculated, based on well-known statistical concepts and is easily interpretable—it measures how consistently a series of returns was delivered in the past. Naturally, the implicit argument is that the more consistently returns occurred in the past, the more likely it is that the investor will receive that return in the future. However, volatility also has some drawbacks as a measure of risk.

First, volatility only measures the dispersion of returns around their historical average. Since positive and negative deviations from the average are penalized equally in the calculation process, the concept only makes sense for symmetrical distributions. Most investors will feel comfortable with this symmetry assumption, because they recall the normal distribution from their introduction to statistics. However, in practice, most returns distributions are not normal or even symmetrically distributed. This creates problems, because even though they may have the same mean and volatility, two investments may significantly differ in terms of their higher moments such as skewness and kurtosis (see later). This is particularly the case for dynamic trading strategies, such as portfolio insurance and stop-losses; strategies involving buying or selling options; and strategies that actively manage their leverage. All these strategies are likely to be used by hedge funds and they create asymmetries and "fat tails" in returns distributions that render the volatility less meaningful and require asymmetric risk considerations.

Second, one may wonder how relevant the dispersion of returns around an average is from an investor's standpoint. Indeed, this runs contrary to the way most investors feel about returns. Few investors fret about their portfolios doubling. Most only perceive risk as a failure to achieve a specific goal, such as the risk-free rate or a benchmark rate. The level of this rate may vary from one investor to another, but the failure carries certain consequences. For instance, a pension fund that fails to achieve a minimum return may have to raise contributions. It would only consider risk as the downside of the returns distribution, the upside being success, talent or just luck. Volatility clearly does not capture this distinction.

Finally, the third argument against volatility is that investors are often more averse to negative deviations than they are pleased with positive deviations of the same magnitude. This is called *prospect theory* and was originally conceptualized by Kahneman and Tversky (1979). It calls for a heavier weight on negative returns, whereas in calculating volatility, deviations above and below the mean return are given weights equal to their probability of occurring. Therefore, even when the distribution is symmetrical, volatility will not be in line with investors' perceptions.

As a result of these limitations, misleading conclusions may easily be drawn when analyzing an investment using standard deviation alone. Just as an illustration, consider a position combining a long stock protected by an at-the-money put option. Even though we assume a normally distributed stock returns distribution, the protected stock distribution is not normal any more, but is positively skewed. Its downside risk is limited, while its upside potential is still virtually unlimited. The problem when using the volatility of such a position is simply that it no longer measures the risk. Since the downside is limited, an increase in the volatility can simply arise from outliers on the right side of the distribution, that is, from an increased probability of higher returns. Uncertainty is therefore greater, but risk clearly remains the same.

These major drawbacks of volatility as a measure of risk explain why investors and researchers have developed several alternative risk measures.

Downside risk measures

Unlike standard deviation, which indicates the variability of returns around an average and penalizes volatility above and below this average equally, downside risk measures attempt to define risk more in accordance with the investor's perception. That is, they consider that returns above a prespecified target represent an opportunity rather than a financial risk, while variability of returns below this target does matter (Figure A.2).

The calculation of a downside risk measure parallels that of variance and standard deviation. Starting from a sample of T returns $(R_{0,1}, R_{1,2}, \ldots, R_{T-1,T})$, one computes

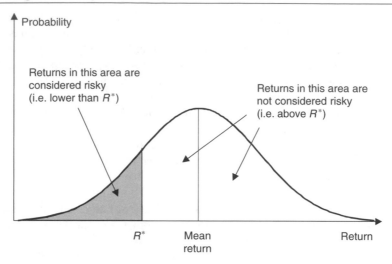

Figure A.2   Downside risk

the difference between each return $R_{t-1,t}$ and the prespecified target rate of return R^*. These differences are then squared and averaged. This gives a form of downside variance. Taking the square root yields the downside risk. Mathematically,

$$\text{Downside risk}_P = \frac{1}{T-1}\sqrt{\sum_{t=1}^{T} d_{t-1,t}^2} \qquad (A.10)$$

where

$$d_{t-1,t} = \begin{cases} R^* - R_{t-1,t} & \text{if } R_{t-1,t} < R^* \\ 0 & \text{otherwise} \end{cases}$$

Unlike standard deviation, downside risk accommodates different subjective views of risk by changing the target rate R^*. However, it is obvious that the choice of a specific target rate will have a large influence on the downside risk measure, and therefore on its accuracy and stability. Stability implies that, whatever the target rate chosen, the value of the downside risk will change by only an infinitesimal amount as we vary the target rate. Graphically, this means that the graph of the downside risk as a function of the target rate is approximately horizontal around the chosen point (or locally stable, as some would say). In practice, investors often set R^* equal to the average (historical) return, zero, or a given moving target such as the risk-free rate or any benchmark rate.

- When R^* is set equal to the average return, the corresponding downside risk measure is called the *semideviation*. Markowitz (1959) already considered it as a valuable alternative to volatility for those who are concerned about below average performance, but he did not apply it in his groundbreaking analysis. The reasons were essentially that computing power in the 1950s was insufficient to deal with the corresponding calculations; and with normally distributed returns, semideviation is proportional to volatility and provides no greater insight into the relative risk of different assets or portfolios.

Subsequently, the improvement in computing power and the gradual realization that returns were not normal led to the development of semideviation-based portfolio theories. However, semideviation has the major drawback that it is only observable ex post, i.e. once things have happened, because it requires the average return.

- When the target rate R^* is set at zero, the corresponding measure captures the variability of negative returns (i.e. losses). This measure is often used in the case of risk-averse private clients who are particularly concerned with the risk of losing money.
- When the target rate R^* is set equal to a moving target such as the risk-free rate or a market index, the corresponding measure captures the variability of returns below a benchmark. This is of particular concern for institutional investors, who typically have minimum returns requirements and are benchmarked against reference indices.

Other more intuitive downside risk statistics provide investors with more information than simply a downside deviation number. They also offer insight into the causes of the risk.

- *Downside frequency* tells investors how often returns fall below the minimum target return. It helps investors to assess accurately the likelihood of a bad outcome.
- *Gain standard deviation* is similar to standard deviation except that it calculates an average (mean) return only for the periods with a gain and then measures the variation of only the gain periods around this gain mean. In a sense, the gain standard deviation measures the volatility of upside performance.
- *Loss standard deviation* measures the volatility of downside performance. It calculates an average (mean) return only for the periods with a loss and then measures the variation of only the losing periods around this loss mean.

Although downside risk measures can provide additional insight into the risk profile of potential investments, downside risk is only slowly gaining acceptance in the financial community. There are essentially two reasons for this. First, in the context of normal distributions, downside risk measures are simply proportional to volatility and do not add much information. Most investors feel comfortable assuming normal distributions, even though this is not very realistic in practice. Second, many investors have just adopted standard deviation as a risk measure and they are reluctant to embrace another measurement tool that could yield conflicting results. This is accentuated by the fact that there are a number of ways to calculate downside risk, each of which can potentially yield different results. It is therefore essential that individuals interpreting downside risk statistics understand the calculation methodology because downside risk statistics calculated using different assumptions are not comparable.

The shortfall concept and value at risk

The concept of *shortfall probability* is indirectly linked to the idea of downside risk management. It measures the probability of a fund's returns dipping below a prespecified target R^*. Mathematically,

$$\text{Risk} = \text{Pr}(R_{t,t+1} < R^*) \tag{A.11}$$

The target rate R^* may be static (e.g. equal to zero) or stochastic (e.g. equal to an inflation rate, the risk-free rate or a market index return). The concept is therefore relative rather than absolute.

To assess how severe an undesirable event might be, shortfall probabilities are often accompanied by an indication of the maximum loss or the average shortfall (i.e. the expected value of the underperformance, conditional on being below the benchmark rate), or by value at risk figures.

Value at risk (VaR) is a relatively recent risk measure in finance, but it has been used for several years in statistics. The *value at risk* of a position is the maximum amount of capital that the position can expect to lose within a specified holding period (e.g. 10 days or 1 month) and with a specified confidence level (e.g. 95% or 99%). An example will make this clearer (Figure A.3). Say we want to compute the 1-month 99% value at risk of the Morgan Stanley Capital Index USA from December 1969 to October 2000, using monthly nonannualized data. All that needs to be done is to observe the series of 1-month returns for the stock, build up the corresponding returns distribution, and exclude 1% of the cases as being "abnormal" market conditions. The worst-case remaining return (−9.6%) is the value at risk of the index, expressed in percentage terms. It corresponds to the 1% percentile of the returns distribution, i.e. 1% of the observed values are lower than the VaR and 99% are higher than the VaR.

Other benchmark-related statistics

Although they are absolute performers, hedge funds also often produce ratios that compare their performance with that of a selected market index. These ratios do not rely on any

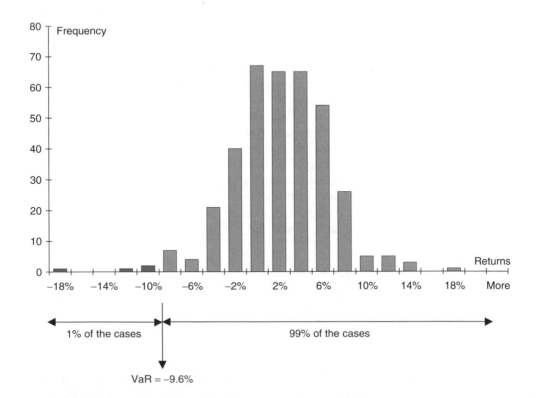

Figure A.3   Graphical interpretation of value at risk

statistical or financial theory, but just provide information on the relative performance of a fund with respect to a benchmark (usually a noncorrelated benchmark). Here are some of the most popular ratios on the investor side:

- *Capture indicator* is the average of the captured performance (i.e. the average ratio between the fund's returns and the benchmark's returns). It is somehow hard to interpret, because conclusions depend upon the sign of the benchmark's returns.
- *Up capture indicator* is calculated as the fund average return divided by the benchmark average return, considering only periods when the benchmark was up. The greater the value the better.
- *Down capture indicator* is calculated as the fund average return divided by the benchmark average return, considering only periods when the benchmark was down. The smaller the ratio the better.
- *Up number ratio* measures the number of periods in which a fund was up when the benchmark was up, divided by the number of periods in which the benchmark was up. The larger the ratio the better.
- *Down number ratio* measures the number of periods in which a fund was down when the benchmark was down, divided by the number of periods in which the benchmark was down. The smaller the ratio the better.
- *Up percentage ratio* measures the number of periods in which the fund outperformed the benchmark when the benchmark was up, divided by the number of periods when the benchmark was up. The larger the ratio the better.
- *Down percentage ratio* is a measure of the number of periods in which the fund outperformed the benchmark when the benchmark was down, divided by the number of periods when the benchmark was down. The larger the ratio the better.
- *Percentage gain ratio* is a measure of the number of periods in which the fund was up divided by the number of periods in which the benchmark was up. The larger the ratio the better.
- *Ratio of negative months over total months* is also a good indicator of the downside risk of a fund, although it neglects the absolute size of returns in positive and negative months.

Drawdowns

Drawdowns are another attempt to account only for downside risk. With drawdowns, the idea is to consider the loss (in percentage terms) incurred from a portfolio's highest value to the portfolio value at a specific date. It can be interpreted as the regret an investor would have for not selling at the highest price (Figure A.4).

A *drawdown* is basically any losing period during an investment record. The *maximum drawdown*, or *peak to valley*, is therefore the maximum loss (in percentage terms) that an investor could have experienced within a specific time period. The *uninterrupted drawdown* calculates the length and severity of an uninterrupted drop. Linked to the concept of drawdown is the *recovery time*, or *drawdown duration*, which is the time taken to recover from a drawdown and come back to the original level. By looking·at the size and duration of past drawdowns (expressed as a percentage of portfolio value), an investor can realistically assess the pain he would feel with that fund manager, were the situation to recur. He can then judge whether or not he can be comfortable with that manager, based on his history.

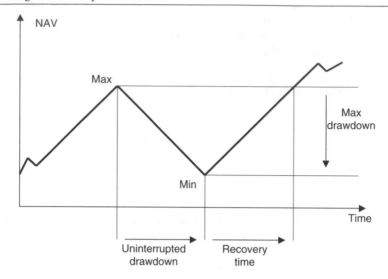

Figure A.4   The drawdown concept

SKEWNESS AND KURTOSIS

Skewness

Skewness is a measure of the symmetry of a returns distribution around its mean. If the returns distribution is skewed to the left (returns lower than the mean have higher probability) then skewness is negative; if the returns distribution is skewed to the right (returns higher than the mean have higher probability) then skewness is positive. As a reference, the standard normal distribution is perfectly symmetrical and has a skewness of zero.

Formally, skewness is related to the third moment of the distribution and is defined as

$$\text{Skewness} \;=\; \frac{T}{(T-1)(T-2)}\left(\frac{1}{\sigma^3}\right)\sum_{t=1}^{T}(R_{t-1,t}-\bar{R})^3 \qquad (A.12)$$

where T is the number of observations. When a distribution is skewed, the mean is "pulled" toward the extreme scores, and the mean is significantly different from the median. Therefore, positive skewness is desirable, since it implies more values on the right side and a mean typically greater than the median. In the case of a normal distribution, skewness should be zero.

Kurtosis

Kurtosis refers to the weight of the tails of a distribution, or "peakedness." Distributions where a large proportion of the observed values lie towards the extremes are said to be *platykurtic*. If, on the other hand, the observed values are bunched near the mean, the distribution is said to be *leptokurtic*. A normally distributed distribution of scores is said to be *mesokurtic*.

Kurtosis is also know as the fourth moment of the distribution; it is defined as follows:

$$\text{Kurtosis} = \frac{T(T+1)}{(T-1)(T-2)(T-3)} \left(\frac{1}{\sigma^4}\right) \sum_{t=1}^{T} (R_{t-1,t} - \bar{R})^4 - \frac{3(T-1)^2}{(T-2)(T-3)}$$

(A.13)

where T is the number of observations. Positive kurtosis indicates a relatively peaked distribution. Negative kurtosis indicates a relatively flat distribution. The normal distribution has zero kurtosis. Note that several managers do not subtract the second term from the kurtosis. As a result, when T is large, the threshold value for the normal distribution becomes 3 rather than 0.

Bibliography

Ackermann C. (1998) The impact of regulatory restrictions on fund performance. A comparative study of hedge funds and mutual funds. FMA presentation, October

Ackermann C., McEnally R. and Ravenscraft D. (1999) The performance of hedge funds: risk, return and incentives. *Journal of Finance*, **54**, 833–74

Ackermann C. and Ravenscraft D. (1998) The impact of regulatory restrictions on fund performance: a comparative study of hedge funds and mutual funds. Working paper, University of Notre Dame and University of North Carolina at Chapel Hill

Agarwal V. and Naik N.Y. (2000a) On taking the alternative route: risks, rewards, and performance persistence of hedge funds. *Journal of Alternative Investments*, **2**(4), 6–23

Agarwal V. and Naik N.Y. (2000b) Multi-period performance persistence analysis of hedge funds. *Journal of Financial and Quantitative Analysis*, **35**, 327–42

Agarwal V. and Naik N.Y. (2001) Performance evaluation of hedge funds with option-based and buy-and-hold strategies. Working paper, London Business School

Alessandrini F. (1999) Credit risk, interest rate risk, and the business cycle. *Journal of Fixed Income*, **9**(2), 42–53

Altman E.I. (1998) Market dynamics and investment performance of distressed and defaulted debt securities. Working paper, NYU Salomon Center, Leonard N. Stern School of Business

Altman E.I. (2000) The high yield bond market: a decade of assessment, comparing 1990 with 2000. Working paper, NYU Salomon Center at the Stern School of Business, August

Amin G.S. and Kat H.M. (2001) Hedge fund performance 1990–2000. Do the money machines really add value? ISMA Center, University of Reading

Balzer L. (1990) How to measure risk. AIC Conference on Investment Performance, Sydney, Australia

Bank of International Settlements (1999a) Banks' interactions with highly leveraged institutions. BIS, Basle

Bank of International Settlements (1999b) Sound practices for banks' interactions with highly leveraged institutions. BIS, Basle

Bank of International Settlements (2001) Review of issues relating to highly leveraged institutions. Basel Committee on Banking Supervision and the International Organization of Securities Commissions, Basle, March

Bekier M. (1998) Marketing of hedge funds: a key strategic variable in defining possible roles of an emerging investment force. Working Paper 1902, European University Studies, Series V

Bernstein P. (1996) Are stocks the best place to be in the long run? A contrary opinion. *Journal of Investing*, Summer, 6–11

Berset J., Hoebrechts P. and De Montauzon G. (2000) An introduction to statistical and risk performance analysis of hedge funds. Working paper, Union Bancaire Privée, February

Billingsley R. and Chance D. (1996) Benefits and limitations of diversification among commodity trading advisors. *Journal of Portfolio Management*, **23**, 65–80

Black F. and Jones R. (1987) Simplifying portfolio insurance. *Journal of Portfolio Management*, **14**(1), 48–51

Black F. and Perold A. (1992) Theory of constant proportion portfolio insurance. *Journal of Economic Dynamics and Control*, **16**, 403–26

Blake C.R., Elton E.J. and Gruber M.J. (1995) Fundamental economic variables, expected returns, and bond fund performance. *Journal of Finance*, **50**, 1229–56

Blake D., Lehman B. and Timmerman A (1999) Asset allocation dynamics and pension fund performance. *Journal of Business*, **72**, 429–62

Booth P., Chadburn R., Cooper D., Haberman S. and James D. (1999) *Modern Actuarial Theory*. London: Chapman & Hall/CRC

Brealey R.A. and Kaplanis E. (2000) Changes in the factor exposures of hedge funds. Working paper, Bank of England and Institute of Finance and Accounting, London Business School

Brennan M. and Schwartz E. (1977) Convertible bonds: valuation and optimal strategies for call and conversion. *Journal of Finance*, **32**(3), 1699–1715

Brennan M. and Schwartz E. (1980) Analyzing convertible bonds. *Journal of Financial and Quantitative Analysis*, **15**(4), 907–29

Brinson G.P., Hood L.R. and Beebower G.L. (1986) Determinants of portfolio performance II: an update. *Financial Analysts Journal*, July/August

Brinson G.P., Singer B.D. and Beebower G.L. (1991) Determinants of portfolio performance II: an update. *Financial Analysts Journal*, May/June

Brown S. (2001) Hedge funds: omniscient or just plain wrong. *Pacific-Basin Finance Journal*, **9**, 301–11

Brown S. and Goetzmann W. (2001) Hedge funds with style. Unpublished working paper, Yale University and NYU Stern School of Business

Brown S., Goetzmann W., Ibbotson R.G. and Ross S.A. (1992) Survivorship bias in performance studies. *Review of Financial Studies* **5**, 553–80

Brown S., Goetzmann W. and Park J.M. (1998) Hedge funds and the Asian currency crisis of 1997. NBER Working Paper 6427, February.

Brown S., Goetzmann W. and Ibbotson R. (1999a) Offshore hedge funds: survival and performance: 1989–1995. *Journal of Business*, **72**, 91–117

Brown S., Goetzmann W. and Park J.M. (1999b) Conditions for survival: Changing risk and the performance of hedge fund managers and CTAs. Working paper, New York University

Caldwell T. (1995) Introduction: the model for superior performance. In *Hedge Funds: Investment and Portfolio Strategies for the Institutional Investor*, Jess Lederman and Robert A. Klein (eds). New York: Irwin, pp. 1–17

Carhart M. (1997) On persistence in mutual fund performance. *Journal of Finance*, **52**, 57–82

Chan L.K.C., Jegadeesh N. and Lakonishok J. (1996) Momentum strategies. *Journal of Finance*, **51**, 1681–1713

Coldwell T. and Kirkpatrick T. (1995) A primer on hedge funds. Working paper, Lookout Mountain Capital

Cornelli F. and Li D.L. (2001) Risk arbitrage in takeovers. Working paper, London Business School and CEPR.

Cottier P. (1997) *Hedge Funds and Managed Futures*. University of St Gallen, Verlag Paul Haupt, Bern

Daykin C.D., Pentikainen T. and Personen M. (1994) *Practical Risk Theory for Actuaries*. London: Chapman & Hall

DiBartolomeo D. and Witkowski E. (1997) Mutual fund misclassification: evidence based on style analysis. *Financial Analysts Journal*, Sept/Oct, 32–43

Dowd K. (1998) *Beyond Value at Risk: The New Science of Risk Management*. New York: John Wiley

Dunbar N. (1998) Meriwether's meltdown. *Risk*, October, pp. 32–36

Edwards F.R. (1999) Hedge funds and the collapse of long-term capital management. *Journal of Economic Perspectives*, **13**(2), 189–210

Edwards F.R. and Liew J. (1999) Hedge funds and managed futures as asset classes. *Journal of Derivatives*, **6**(4), 45–64

Edwards F.R. and Liew J. (1999) Managed commodity funds. *Journal of Futures Markets*, **19**, 377–411

Edwards, F.R. and Ma C. (1988) Commodity pool performance: is the information contained in pool prospectuses useful? *Journal of Futures Markets*, **8**, 589–616

Eichengreen B., Mathieson D., Chadha B., Jansen A., Kodres L. and Sharma S. (1998) Hedge funds and financial market dynamics. Occasional Paper 166, International Monetary Fund, Washington DC

Fama E.F. and French K.R. (1992) The cross-section of expected stock returns. *Journal of Finance*, **47**, 427–65

Fama E.F. and French K.R. (1996) Multifactor explanations of asset pricing anomalies. *Journal of Finance*, **51**, 55–84.

Fama E. and McBeth J. (1973) Risk, return and equilibrium: empirical tests. *Journal of Political Economy*, **81**, 607–36

Favre L. and Galleano J.A. (2000) Portfolio allocation with hedge funds: the case study of a Swiss institutional investor. Working paper, HEC University of Lausanne

Fothergill M. and Coke C. (2000) Funds of hedge funds: an introduction to multi-manager funds. Working paper, Deutsche Bank, August

Freed S.F. (1999) An overview of long-short equity investing. Working paper, Willam Mercer Investment Consulting

Fung W. and Hsieh D.A. (1997a) Empirical characteristics of dynamic trading strategies: the case of hedge funds. *Review of Financial Studies*, **10**, 275–302

Fung W. and Hsieh D.A. (1997b) Survivorship bias and investment style in the returns of CTAs. *Journal of Portfolio Management*, **24**(1), 30–41

Fung W. and Hsieh D.A. (1998a) Price trend following trading strategies: theory and empirical evidence. Working paper, Foundation of Managed Derivatives Research, September

Fung W. and Hsieh D.A. (1998b) A risk neutral approach to valuing trend following trading strategies. Working paper, Duke University

Fung W. and Hsieh D.A. (1999a) A primer on hedge funds. *Journal of Empirical Finance*, **6**, 309–31

Fung W. and Hsieh D.A. (1999b) Is mean-variance analysis applicable to hedge funds? *Economic Letters*, **62**, 53–58

Fung W. and Hsieh D.A. (2000a) Measuring the market impact of hedge funds. *Journal of Empirical Finance*, **7**(1), 1–36

Fung W. and Hsieh D.A. (2000b) Performance characteristics of hedge funds and commodity funds: natural versus spurious biases. *Journal of Financial and Quantitative Analysis*, **35**, 291–307

Fung W. and Hsieh D.A. (2001a) The risk in hedge fund strategies: theory and evidence from trend followers. *Review of Financial Studies*, **41**, 313–341

Fung W. and Hsieh D.A. (2001b) Benchmarks of hedge fund performance: information content and measurement biases. Working paper, Duke University

Fung W., Hsieh D.A. and Tsatsaronis K. (1999) Do hedge funds disrupt emerging markets? Brookings–Wharton Papers on Financial Services

Gatev, E.G., Goetzmann W.N. and Rouwenhorst K.G. (1999) Pairs trading: performance of a relative value arbitrage rule. Working paper, Yale School of Management

Gilson S. (1995) Investing in distress situations: a market survey. *Financial Analysts Journal*, **5**, 8–27

Glosten L.R. and Jagannathan R. (1994) A contingent claim approach to performance evaluation. *Journal of Empirical Finance*, **1**(2), 133–60

Goldman Sachs & Co. and Financial Risk Management Ltd (1998) Hedge funds demystified: their potential role in institutional portfolios. *Pension & Endowment Forum*, July

Goldman Sachs & Co. and Financial Risk Management Ltd (2000) Hedge funds revisited. *Pension & Endowment Forum*, January

Goldman Sachs & Co. and Frank Russell Capital (1997) Report on alternative investing. December

Gouriéroux C., Holly A. and Montfort A. (1982) Likelihood ratio test, Wald test and Kuhn-Tucker test in linear models with inequality constraints on the regression parameters. *Econometrica*, **50**, 63–80

Grinblatt M. and Titman S. (1989) Mutual fund performance: an analysis of quarterly portfolio holdings. *Journal of Business*, **62**, 393–416

Henderson V. (1999) A probabilistic approach to passport options. PhD thesis, University of Bath, December

Henker T. (2000) Benefits of hedge funds for the German investor. Working paper, CISDM/ISOM University of Massachusetts

Henker T. and Martin G. (1998) Naive and optimal diversification for managed futures. *Journal of Alternative Investments*, Fall, 25–39

Henker T. and Martin G. (1998) Naive diversification for hedge funds. *Journal of Alternative Investments*, Winter, 33–38

Hull J. (1989) *Options, Futures, and Other Derivatives*, 3d ed. New York: Prentice Hall

Ineichen A.M. (2000) In search of alpha. Working paper, Warburg Dillon Read, October

Ineichen A.M. (2001) The search for alpha continues. Working paper, Warburg Dillon Read, September

Ingersoll J.E. (1977) A contingent-claims valuation of convertible securities. *Journal of Financial Economics*, **4**, 289–321

Jaffer S. (ed.) (1998) *Alternative Investment Strategies*. London: Euromoney

Jindra J. and Walkling R.A. (1997) Arbitrage spreads and the market pricing of proposed acquisitions. Working paper, Ohio State University

Jones A.W. (1949) Fashion in forecasting. *Fortune 88*, March, p. 186

Jorion P. (1997) *Value-at-Risk: The New Benchmark for Controlling Market Risk*. Burr Ridge IL: Irwin

Kahneman D. and Tversky A. (1979) Prospect theory: an analysis of decision under risk. *Econometrica*, **4**, 362–77

Kestin R. and Jaeger L. (2001) The benefits of alternative investment strategies in the institutional portfolio. Working paper, Swiss Alternative Investment Strategies Group, March

Kim M., Shukla R. and Tomas M. (1999) Mutual fund objective misclassification. *Journal of Economics and Business*, **52**, 309–23

Koski T., Lynch J. and Pontiff J. (1999) How are derivatives used? Evidence from the mutual fund industry. *Journal of Finance*, **54**(2), 791–816

Leland H.E. (1999) Beyond mean-variance: risk and performance measurement in a non-symmetrical world. *Financial Analysts Journal*, Jan/Feb, 27–36.

Lhabitant F.S. (1997) On the (ab)use of expected utility approximations for portfolio selection, portfolio performance and risk management. Working paper, presented to the 14th International Conference of the French Finance Association, Grenoble

Lhabitant F.S. (1998) Enhancing portfolio performance using options strategies. In *European Research Symposium Proceedings*, Chicago Board of Trade

Lhabitant F.S. (1999) On the performance of option strategies in Switzerland. *Finanzmarkt und Portfolio Management*, **3**, 318–38

Lhabitant F.S. (2000) Derivatives in portfolio management: why beating the market is easy. *Derivatives Quarterly*, **7**(2), 37–46

Lhabitant F.S. (2001a) Assessing market risk for hedge funds and hedge funds portfolios. *Journal of Risk Finance*, Spring, 1–17

Lhabitant F.S. (2001b) Hedge funds investing: a quantitative look inside the black box. *Journal of Financial Transformation*, **1**(1), 82–90

Liang B. (1999) On the performance of hedge funds. *Financial Analysts Journal* **55**, 72–85

Liang B. (2000) Hedge funds: the living and the dead. *Journal of Financial and Quantitative Analysis*, **35**, 309–36

Lintner J. (1983) The potential role of managed commodity-financial futures accounts (and/or funds) in portfolios of stocks and bonds. Presentation to the Financial Analysts Federation

Loomis C. (1966) The Jones nobody keeps up with. *Fortune*, April, p. 237–247

Ludgate Communications (2000) The future role of hedge funds in European institutional asset management. Research report, March

Malkiel B. (1995) Returns from investing in equity mutual funds 1971 to 1991. *Journal of Finance*, **50**, 549–72

Markowitz H. (1959) *Portfolio Selection: Efficient Diversification of Investments*. New York: John Wiley

Markowitz H.M. (1991) *Portfolio Selection: Efficient Diversification of Investments*. Oxford: Blackwell

Martino R.M. (1999) The due diligence process. In *Evaluating and Implementing Hedge Fund Strategies*, 2d ed., P. Lake, (ed.). London: Euromoney

Matos E. (2000) Distressed securities investing. White paper, Tremont Partners, November

McCarthy D., Schneeweis T. and Spurgin R. (1996) Investment in CTAs: an alternative managed futures investment. *Journal of Derivatives*, **3**(4) Summer, 36–47

McCarthy D., Schneeweis T. and Spurgin R. (1996) Survivor bias in commodity trading advisor performance. *Journal of Futures Markets*, October, 757–72

McCarthy D. and Spurgin R. (1998) A review of hedge fund performance benchmarks. *Journal of Alternative Investments*, Summer, 18–28

McFall L.R. (1999) Portfolios of alternative assets: why not 100% hedge funds? *Journal of Investing*, **8**(4), 87–97

Merton R.C. (1969) Lifetime portfolio selection under uncertainty: the continuous time case. *Review of Economics and Statistics*, **51**, 247–57

Merton R.C. (1971) Optimum consumption and portfolio rules in a continuous time model. *Journal of Economic Theory*, **3**, 373–413

Merton R.C. (1995) A functional perspective of financial intermediation. *Financial Management*, **24**(2), 23–41

Merton R.C. (1995) Financial innovation and the management and regulation of institutions. *Journal of Banking and Finance*, **19**, 461–81

Meyer L.H. (1999) Testimony before the Subcommittee on Financial Institutions and Consumer Credit, Committee on Banking and Financial Services. US House of Representatives, March 24, (www.federalreserve.gov/boarddocs/testimony).

Milken Institute (1998) Hedge funds and systematic risk demystified. December

Mitchell M. and Pulvino T. (2000) Characteristics of risk in risk arbitrage. Working paper, Harvard Business School and Kellogg Graduate School of Management

Moody's Investors Service (2001) Default and recovery rates of corporate bond issuers: 2000. Mimeo, February

Morgan Stanley Dean Witter (2000) Why hedge funds make sense. Working paper, November

Noe T.H. and Rebello M.J. (1996) Feasting on a corporate carcass: bluffing, bondmail, and reputation in the market for distressed-firm debt. Working paper, A.B. Freeman School of Business, Tulane University

Pagli J.M. (2000) Convertible securities hedging: a case study. *Journal of Alternative Investments*, Spring, 42–49

Park J. (1995) Managed futures as an investment set. Doctoral dissertation, Columbia University

Peltz L. (1996) 1996 Hedge fund profile. MAR/Hedge

Pendergast J.R. (2000) Predicting the ten-year LIBOR swap spread: the role and limitations of rich/cheap analysis. *Journal of Fixed Income*, **10**(3), 86–99

President's Working Group on Financial Markets (1999) Hedge funds, leverage and the lessons of long-term capital management, Report of the President's Working Group on Financial Markets, April 28, 1999

Purcell D. and Crawley P. (1998) The reality of hedge funds. Research note, Warburg Dillon Read

Rao R. and Szilagyi J.J. (1998) The coming evolution of the hedge fund industry: a case for growth and restructuring. Research monograph, RR Capital Management Corp. and KPMG Peat Marwick LLP

Richards A.J. (1999) Idiosyncratic risk: an empirical analysis with implications for the risk of relative-value trading strategies. Working paper, International Monetary Fund, November

Rohrer J. (1986) The red hot world of Julian Robertson. *Institutional Investor*, May, pp. 86–92

Saint-Denis N. (1998) The alternative investment sector and market efficiency. Masters thesis 9807, HEC University of Lausanne

Schifrin M. (1991) Sellers beware. *Forbes*, January 21

Schneeweis T. (1996) The benefits of managed futures. Working paper, CISDM/ISOM University of Massachusetts

Schneeweis T. (1998a) Dealing with myths of hedge funds. *Journal of Alternative Investments*, Winter, 11–5

Schneeweis T. (1998b) Dealing with myths of managed futures. *Journal of Alternative Investments*, Spring, 1–24

Schneeweis T. (1998c) Evidence of superior performance persistence in hedge funds: an empirical comment. *Journal of Alternative Investments*, Fall, 76–80

Schneeweis T. and Pescatore J. (1999) *The Handbook of Alternative Investment Strategies: An Investor's Guide*. New York: Institutional Investors

Schneeweis T. and Spurgin R. (1997) Comparisons of commodity and managed futures benchmark indices. *Journal of Derivatives*, Summer, 33–50

Schneeweis T. and Spurgin R. (1998a) Alternative Investments in the Institutional Portfolio. Working paper, AIMA

Schneeweis T. and Spurgin R. (1998b) Asset allocation: management style and performance measurement. *Journal of Portfolio Measurement*, **18**, 7–19

Schneeweis T. and Spurgin R. (1998c) Multifactor analysis of hedge funds, managed futures and mutual Funds. *Journal of Alternative Investments*, Winter, 1–24

Schneeweis T. and Spurgin R. (1998d) Sources of return to systematic CTA traders. Working paper, CISDM/SOM, University of Massachusetts

Schneeweis T. and Spurgin R. (1999) Quantitative analysis of hedge fund and managed futures returns and risks characteristics. In *Evaluating and Implementing Hedge Fund Strategies*, 2d ed., P. Lake, (ed.). London: Euromoney

Schneeweis T., Spurgin R. and Potter M. (1996) Managed futures and hedge fund investment for downside equity risk management. *Derivatives Quarterly*, Fall, 62–72

Securities and Exchange Commission (1998) Use of internet websites to offer securities, solicit securities transaction or advertise investment opportunities offshore. Working paper

Sharpe W.F. (1988) Determining a fund's effective asset mix. *Investment Management Review*, December, pp. 59–69

Sharpe W.F. (1992) Asset allocation: management style and performance measurement. *Journal of Portfolio Management*, **18**, 7–19

Silber W. (994) Technical trading: when it works and when it doesn't. *Journal of Derivatives*, Spring, 39–44

Sortino F. and Forsey H. (1996) On the use and misuse of downside risk. *Journal of Portfolio Management*, **22**(2), 35–44

Sortino F. and van der Meer R.A.H. (1991) Downside risk. *Journal of Portfolio Management*, **17**(4), 27–31

Spurgin R. (1998) How to game your Sharpe ratio. Working paper, Clark University

Spurgin R., Martin G. and Schneeweis T. (2000) A method of estimating changes of correlation between assets and its application to hedge fund investment. Working paper, CISDM

Tannenbaum M.G. (1999) US regulation of offers of investment advisory services and hedge fund marketing over the internet. Working paper, Tannenbaum Helpern Syracuse & Hirschtritt LLP, New York City

Tremont Partners Inc. and Tass Investment Research Ltd (1999) The case for hedge funds. Working paper

Various (2000) Sound practices for hedge fund managers. Working paper jointly published on the internet by a group of hedge fund managers.

Victoria-Feser M.P. (2000) Robust portfolio selection. Unpublished working paper, University of Geneva

Watson Wyatt/Indocam (2001a) Alternative investment review relating to the continental European marketplace. Mimeo, August

Watson Wyatt/Indocam (2001b) Alternative investment review relating to the United Kingdom marketplace. Mimeo, August

Zask E. (2000) Hedge fund industry research report. Working paper, Berkshire Capital Corporation, New York

Zweig J. (1998) Five investing lessons from America's top pension fund. *Money*, January, pp. 115–18

Websites

4 Hedge Funds.com	www.4hedgefunds.com
Allbourne Village	http://village.allbourne.com
Alternative Investment Management Assoc.	www.aima.org
Alvest	www.altvest.com
Barclays	www.barclaygrp.com
CreditSuisse First Boston/Tremont	www.hedgeindex.com
CTA Online	www.cta-online.com
Deutsche Bank	www.dbconvertibles.com
Eurohedge	www.eurohedge.co.uk
FRM	www.frmhedge.com
Fund of Funds.com	www.fundoffunds.com
Hedge Advisors Inc.	www.hedgeadvisors.com
Hedge-Bay	www.hedgebay.com
Hedge Fund 411	www.hedgefund411.com
Hedge Fund Association	www.thehfa.com
Hedge Fund Center	www.hedgefundcenter.com
Hedge Fund Consistency Index	www.hedgefund-index.com
Hedge Fund Net	www.hedgefund.net
Hedge Fund News	www.hedgefundnews.com
Hedge Fund Research	www.hfr.com
Hedge Fund Services (BVI) Ltd	www.hsftd.com
Hedge Manager Review	www.hedgemanager.com
Hedgebay	www.hedgebay.com
HedgeScan	www.hedgescan.com
HedgeWorld	www.hedgeworld.com
Hennessee Hedge Fund Advisory Group	www.hedgefnd.com
Laporte	www.laportesoft.com
LJH	www.ljh.com
Managed Account Reports	www.marhedge.com
Managed Funds Association	www.mfainfor.com
Plusfunds	www.plusfinds.com
RRCM.com	www.rrcm.com
TASS	www.tassman.com
Tremont Index	www.hedgeindex.com
Van Hedge Fund Advisors	www.vanhedge.com

Index